Indigenous Peoples as Subjects of International Law

For more than 500 years, Indigenous laws have been disregarded. Many appeals for their recognition under international law have been made, but have thus far failed – mainly because international law was itself shaped by colonialism. How, this volume asks, might international law be reconstructed, so that it is liberated from its colonial origins?

With contributions from critical legal theory, international law, politics, philosophy and Indigenous history, this volume pursues a cross-disciplinary analysis of the international legal exclusion of Indigenous Peoples, and of its relationship to global injustice. Beyond the issue of Indigenous Peoples' rights, however, this analysis is set within the broader context of sustainability; arguing that Indigenous laws, philosophy and knowledge are not only legally valid, but offer an essential approach to questions of ecological justice and the co-existence of all life on earth.

Irene Watson belongs to the Tanganekald, Meintangk and Boandik First Nations Peoples. She is a Professor of Law at the University of South Australia.

Indigenous Peoples and the Law

The colonial modalities that resulted in the pillaging of the 'New World' involved wholesale dispossession, genocidal violence and exploitation of their original inhabitants. It was not, however, until the latter part of the twentieth century that Indigenous peoples attained some degree of legal recognition. This book series focuses upon the manner in which Indigenous peoples' experiences of law have been transformed from an oppressive system of denying rights to a site of contestation, and the articulation of various forms of self-governance. Encouraging a range of theoretical, political and ethical perspectives on Indigenous peoples and the law, this book series aims to provide a comprehensive survey of the experience of Indigenous peoples and their changing relationship with national and international juridical frameworks.

Titles in this series:

Aboriginal Peoples, Colonialism and International Law: Raw Law
Irene Watson

Indigeneity – Before and Beyond the Law
Kathleen Birrell

The Literary and Legal Genealogy of Native American Dispossession: The Marshall Cases Trilogy
George Pappas

Indigenous Peoples as Subjects of International Law
Edited by Irene Watson

Forthcoming titles in this series:

Human Rights, the Rule of Law and Exploitation: Blood Minerals
Mark Harris

Scales of Governance and Indigenous Peoples: New Rights or Same Old Wrongs?
Edited by Irène Bellier and Jennifer Hays

Indigenous Peoples as Subjects of International Law

Edited by
Irene Watson

Routledge
Taylor & Francis Group
a GlassHouse Book

First published 2018
by Routledge

2 Park Square, Milton Park, Abingdon, Oxfordshire OX14 4RN
52 Vanderbilt Avenue, New York, NY 10017

a GlassHouse Book

Routledge is an imprint of the Taylor & Francis Group, an informa business

First issued in paperback 2018

British Library Cataloguing in Publication Data
A catalogue record for this book is available from the British Library

Library of Congress Cataloging in Publication Data
Names: Watson, Irene (Irene Margaret), editor.
Title: Indigenous peoples as subjects of international law / edited by Irene Watson.
Description: Abingdon, Oxon [UK] ; New York : Routledge, 2017. | Includes bibliographical references and index.
Identifiers: LCCN 2016055878 | ISBN 9781138645158 (hardback) | ISBN 9781315628318 (ebook)
Subjects: LCSH: Indigenous peoples (International law) | Indigenous peoples–Legal status, laws, etc. | Indigenous peoples–Civil rights. | Self-determination, National.
Classification: LCC K3247 .I5245 2017 | DDC 342.08/72–dc23
LC record available at https://lccn.loc.gov/2016055878

ISBN: 978-1-138-64515-8 (hbk)
ISBN: 978-0-367-18077-5 (pbk)

DOI: 10.4324/9781315628318

The Open Access version of this book was funded by Irene Watson.

Contents

Acknowledgements

I would like to thank all contributors for their collaboration and work on this project.

I am grateful to Greta Bird, Kathy Bowrey, Morgan Briggs, Margaret Davies, Michael Detmold, Peter Fitzpatrick, Natsu Taylor Saito, Isabelle Schulte-Tenckoff and Michael Watson for their generosity in reading and commenting on early draft chapters.

Research and editorial assistance provided by Jo Bird and Kate Leeson was also much appreciated.

In 2012, I was awarded an Australian Research Council Discovery Indigenous Award which enabled me to contribute to and edit this book.

I owe my thanks to Colin Perrin and the editors of this series for the opportunity to publish this body of work.

I acknowledge the work of Richard Bell and his permission to use the image from one of his wonderful paintings 'We Were Here First' as the book cover.

Contributors

Marcelle Burns is a Kamilaroi woman and a pre-doctoral fellow at the School of Law, University of New England, New South Wales, Australia. She has worked in First Peoples law and policy as an academic and solicitor for over twenty years. Her contribution to this book has been supported by an Australian Government Research Training Program Scholarship.

Ward Churchill is an independent activist/scholar of Cherokee descent. He is a former professor of American Indian studies at the University of Colorado/Boulder, and has published more than twenty books.

Ambellin Kwaymullina (LLB Hons) is an Aboriginal academic, writer and artist who comes from the Palyku people of the Pilbara region of Western Australia. She has worked in government and politics, and is presently a lecturer at the University of Western Australia Law School.

Roger Merino PhD is Professor of Public Policy and Legal Theory at the Universidad del Pacífico (Lima, Peru) and Visiting Scholar at the Harvard Law School's Institute for Global Law and Policy.

Steven Newcomb (Shawnee, Lenape) is co-founder/co-director of the Indigenous Law Institute and has advocated for Indigenous Nations/Peoples for over twenty years, including at the United Nations.

Tamara Starblanket is a Nehiyaw Iskwew (Cree Woman) from Ahtahkakoop Cree Nation in Treaty Six Territory on Great Turtle Island. Her research interests are studying the impacts that genocide has had on the land and Original Nations and Peoples. Understanding genocide and the collective historical and present-day trauma is necessary for a true movement towards self-determination.

Sharon Venne is an Indigenous Treaty person (Cree). She worked at the United Nations prior to the establishment of the Working Group on Indigenous Peoples in 1982. She has lectured internationally on the rights of Indigenous People, and worked to secure a UN Study on Treaties which reflects Indigenous laws and norms.

Irene Watson belongs to the Tanganekald, Meintangk and Boandik First Nations Peoples. She is a Professor of Law and the Pro Vice Chancellor Aboriginal Leadership and Strategy at the University of South Australia.

Introduction

Irene Watson

In 1981, Bart Willoughby recorded the lyrics to his song 'We Have Survived' on the album *Wrong Side of the Road* with Aboriginal band No Fixed Address. The opening line began 'We have survived the white man's world' and the chorus ended with 'And you know you can't change that'. Thirty-five years later, the lives of First Nations continue. Many of us have survived the trauma of colonialism and genocide, and the history cannot be changed, the fact of our survival cannot be altered.

This collection of writings is about First Nations' ongoing struggles to sustain our worlds and the nature which supports them. They acknowledge that we were here first and that we have survived the onslaught of colonialism and genocide, and that we are now living in two worlds, that of First Nations and that of the colonial. They are remembering that which has passed, but a past which is present and a present which is all the time becoming our future. Ambelin Kwaymullina's chapter does not explore the international legal order that exists, but the one that might exist, and asks the question: what may some of the norms be that might shape the international legal system were it based in Indigenous ways of knowing, being and doing, and what is the relevance of those norms to the international community today?

This volume is not about recycling old ideas because we have run out of new ones, but because nothing much has changed in the world of colonialism. Aboriginal resistance to assimilation is as relevant today as it has been since 1492. The events which have blighted our lives across the world for five hundred years – and continue to unfold – remain the unfinished business of de-colonisation. What has been said and written before needs to be said again and again until we all understand the truth, beyond the myths and lies of colonialism. It is an aim of this volume to build upon our knowledge and the meanings of being 'Indigenous' in the world today.

In 1977, Russell Means spoke before a United Nations forum and stated, 'I am an American Indian, not a Native American.' He went on to explain:

> I abhor the term Native American. It is a generic government term used to describe all the indigenous prisoners of the United States. These are

DOI: 10.4324/9781315628318-1

> the American Samoans, the Micronesians, the Aleutes, the original Hawaiians and the erroneously termed Eskimos, who are actually Upiks and Inupiats. And, of course, the American Indian.
>
> I prefer the term American Indian because I know its origins. The word Indian is an English bastardization of two Spanish words, En Dio, which correctly translated means in with God. As an added distinction the American Indian is the only ethnic group in the United States with the American before our ethnicity.
>
> At an international conference of Indians from the Americas held in Geneva, Switzerland at the United Nations in 1977 we unanimously decided we would go under the term American Indian. We were enslaved as American Indians, we were colonized as American Indians and we will gain our freedom as American Indians and then we will call ourselves any damn thing we choose.[1]

Naming and constructing who we are is essential to the colonial project and its long campaign to subjugate the 'natives' to colonial power. For centuries, an arsenal of euro-derived 'legal' tools has been applied towards those ends. For centuries, First Nations laws have been deemed non-existent; the idea that there is an absence of law in First Nations' territories supported the moral case for colonialism and was backed up by idealised notions such as the 'savage' and 'backward natives'.

Steven Newcomb describes international law as an organised system of domination, within which terms such as 'states', 'territories', 'jurisdiction', 'dominion', 'tribal peoples', 'native peoples' and 'indigenous peoples' constitute the context which relegates some peoples to a state of existence 'under' the 'dominance' of other peoples who are organised into 'states'. International law grew out of the distinctions constructed between civilised and non-civilised peoples, and those distinctions enabled and confirmed that international law favoured the 'civilised' 'family of nations'. Marcelle Burns' chapter maps how the concept of society is foundational to international law, and its purpose and use as a tool to exclude First Nations from 'recognition' within state regimes.

Many appeals for recognition under international law have been made by First Nations, and those moves have largely failed due to international law being viewed from a statist perspective. Ward Churchill maps the origins of state plenary power in the discovery doctrine and the consequential dispossession and genocide of First Nations as a product of that doctrine. Racism was deployed in the beginnings, as it still is, to normalise plenary colonial power, and that power has not only been normalised, but also masked as being beneficial and core to the 'civilising mission'. Churchill traces the relationship between state plenary power deployed by the nazis as being 'nothing

1 Russell Means, 'Opening Plenary Session' in The Geneva Conference, Official Report by International Indian Treaty Council, (1977) 1(77) *Treaty Council News*.

new or especially different' from what had already been done in the Americas. The colonisation of North America performed as a template for Hitler, as German troops were advised they had 'a duty to look upon natives as Redskins', and to conduct themselves as their US predecessors had during 'the struggle in North America against the Red Indians'.

In the twenty-first century, many First Nations remain confined to the 'domestic paradigm' of the occupying settler state. Our colonisation persists, but Indigenous philosophy, laws and knowledges remain foundational to our lives. Taking up this point, I further consider the language and philosophy of empire and how it is applied in the ongoing domination and subjugation of First Nations Peoples, knowing that at the same time the language and philosophies of our old people continue to centre our lives. I discuss how those languages and philosophies challenge those narratives which have worked to marginalise our ancient legal systems.

To date, little headway has been made in progressing a horizontal dialogue between colonialist interests and Indigenous-centred knowledges, laws and philosophy, while much literature and discussion concerning Indigenous rights is centred upon an anthropocentric, colonially constructed identity. Roger Merino argues that any inclusion of Indigenous Nations has meant adaptation to the new state, while exclusion means Indigenous Nations are eliminated in material and/or legal terms. Whether exclusion or inclusion, neither gives real credence to Aboriginal knowledges and laws.

This book challenges how colonial identities are constructed and represented in both colonial states and in international law, and its contributors respond with the aim of demythologising 'Indigenous recognition' and revealing the ontological realities of First Nations Peoples. Sharon Venne exposes how colonial states manufacture 'consent' through the use of organisations – either established or newly created – to imply that Indigenous Peoples and Nations have given consent, either through the introduction of legislation or other initiatives which provide the illusion of legitimacy, for state governments to act against the interests of Indigenous Peoples and Nations. Tamara Starblanket also exposes international law as a dominating, dehumanising and oppressive experience through an examination of the crime of genocide in international law and how states have excluded the Indigenous experiences of 'cultural genocide' or 'forced assimilation' from recognition as crimes of genocide.

To date, no major international research has attempted to evaluate how the exclusion of an Aboriginal knowledge-centred approach from international law has contributed to global injustices. Instead, the focus has been on models which have proposed the assimilation of First Nations Peoples by the respective states. In the past, assimilationist models were developed to accommodate claims for the 'recognition' and 'equality' of First Nations Peoples' 'rights', but whatever 'progress' was made, these efforts have proven largely of no benefit to our situation overall. Now it is timely to develop a new analysis of the exclusion of First Nations Peoples-centred approaches; indeed, it is now critical that international law and social policy developments stop ignoring the question and recognise the validity of Aboriginal laws, philosophy and knowledge as an essential approach to questions of justice.

The contributors write from the disciplines of critical legal theory, international law, politics, philosophy and First Nations histories. It is our ambition that this work will generate dialogue across the disciplines and advance conversations on international law and global justice. Lastly, this volume will fill a knowledge gap: how might we move beyond a rights discourse which is locked within a matrix of coloniality? In colonialism's shaping of international law, its refusal to recognise the laws and sovereignties of First Nations, and the concomitant disasters which entail, we are left to consider the question: how might we reconstruct international law so that it is liberated from its colonial origins?

Chapter 1

Aboriginal Nations, the Australian nation-state and Indigenous international legal traditions

Ambellin Kwaymullina

Australia is a continent, not a country.

This land is home to the hundreds of Aboriginal homelands that we name our Countries, each with a language, culture and people. It is home as well to the Torres Strait Islander People whose lands lie in the Torres Strait Islands off the Queensland coast (although, as an Aboriginal scholar, this chapter is founded in my understanding of Aboriginal systems). The term 'Aboriginal' as it is used throughout this chapter refers to the prior occupiers of mainland Australia, Tasmania and some offshore islands; when I intend to include Torres Strait Islander Peoples and Indigenous Peoples from elsewhere in the world, I will use the term 'Indigenous'. The many Aboriginal legal orders of our many different Countries are now often spoken of as if they form a single body of law. But the use of the singular to describe these legal systems, along with the grouping of our nations under the descriptor 'Aboriginal', hides a truth: that the Aboriginal legal tradition was always an international tradition. Aboriginal Nations formed complex networks of relationships, traded goods, entered into negotiations over shared law spaces, respected each other's boundaries and were subject to consequences if they did not. An international legal order did not begin with the writings of Grotius or Vattel or the rise of the Westphalian state; nor did an international human rights regime start with the *Universal Declaration of Human Rights* or with any of the human rights treaties and associated monitoring bodies that arose post-1945. These are newcomers all, systems in their infancy that imposed themselves onto ancient international legal orders arising from the interactions of the Indigenous Nations of this earth.

The purpose of this chapter is to reflect upon three of the norms that underlie the international legal tradition of Australian Aboriginal Nations. I am characterising these norms as 'narrative sovereignty', 'relationship-based citizenship' and the 'right to be human'. In so doing, I am applying an Indigenous perspective, which is to say, a perspective grounded in an Indigenous centre and which – consistently with Indigenous world views – is

DOI: 10.4324/9781315628318-2

holistic, non-linear and relationships-focused.[1] However, my analysis is only one Indigenous view among many. The Indigenous Peoples of the globe share commonalities in terms of earth-based world views, experiences of colonialism, and the present-day disadvantage which is colonialism's legacy.[2] But we are also highly diverse, and my own perspective is influenced by my own knowledge and experiences, as well as the culture and history of the Palyku People from whom I come.

The world(s), the Dreaming(s) and the apocalypse(s)

The legal systems of the Aboriginal Nations of Australia began in what is sometimes called the 'Dreaming'.[3] The Dreaming is the beginning from which all other beginnings emerge, for whatever existed before could not support life as we know it now. It should be noted, however, that in Aboriginal systems, terms such as 'begin' and 'end' do not carry linear implications. Time does not run from the past through the present and on into the future, but is simply part of larger cycles of existence.[4] Like all things, time exists in space

1 In this I am informed by the work of Indigenous thinkers in the area of Indigenous research methodologies including: Veronica Arbon, *Arlathirnda Ngurkarnda Ityirnda: Being – Knowing – Doing: De-colonising Indigenous Tertiary Education* (Post Pressed, 2008); Leroy Little Bear, 'Jagged Worldviews Colliding' in Marie Battiste (ed), *Reclaiming Indigenous Voice and Vision* (UBC Press, 2000) 77; Mary Graham, 'Some Thoughts about the Philosophical Underpinnings of Aboriginal Worldviews' (2008) 45 *Australian Humanities Review* 181; James (Sakej) Youngblood Henderson, '*Ayukpachi*: Empowering Indigenous Thought' in Marie Battiste (ed), *Reclaiming Indigenous Voice and Vision* (UBC Press, 2000) 248; Karen Martin, 'Ways of Knowing, Ways of Being and Ways of Doing: A Theoretical Framework and Methods for Indigenous Re-search and Indigenist Research' (2003) 76 *Journal of Australian Studies* 203; Karen Martin, *Please Knock Before You Enter: Aboriginal Regulation of Outsiders and the Implications for Researchers* (Post Pressed, 2008); Aileen Moreton-Robinson and Maggie Walter, 'Indigenous Methodologies in Social Research' in Maggie Walter (ed), *Social Research Methods: An Australian Perspective* (Oxford University Press, 2nd edn, 2009) 1; Martin Nakata, *Disciplining the Savages, Savaging the Disciplines* (Aboriginal Studies Press, 2007); Lester Irabinna Rigney, 'Internationalization of an Indigenous Anti-colonial Cultural Critique of Research Methodologies: A Guide to Indigenist Research Methodology and its Principles' (1999) 14(2) *Wicazo Sa Review* 109; Linda Smith, *Decolonizing Methodologies: Research and Indigenous Peoples* (Zed Books, 2nd edn, 2012).

2 For points of similarity between Indigenous Peoples worldwide, see United Nations Permanent Forum on Indigenous Issues, *State of the World's Indigenous Peoples*, UN Doc ST/ESA/328 (2009).

3 'Dreaming' is an inexact English approximation of an Aboriginal concept that has no English equivalent. For a critique of the term, see Vicki Grieves, *Aboriginal Spirituality, Aboriginal Philosophy: The Basis of Aboriginal Social and Emotional Wellbeing* (Cooperative Research Centre for Aboriginal Health, 2009) 8.

4 For an examination of the differences between linear and non-linear (Indigenous) time from a quantum physics perspective, see David Peat, *Blackfoot Physics* (Fourth Estate, 1995).

and is as susceptible to action and interaction as any other form of life. To say something 'begins' is to say that something new has entered the world, but it is perhaps never entirely correct to refer to anything as ending. Everything lives and everything moves through phases of creation; and while some transformations are so profound that it may not be possible to be sure what emerges on the other side of the transformative process, this is not the same as an end. Besides which, everything ultimately returns to Country, and since in holistic systems the whole is both more than its parts and in all its parts, every part of Country contains Country entire.[5]

Through their actions, the many Dreaming Ancestors embodied 'what is', along with the rules (the law) that would allow 'what is' to continue always. But just as there is not a single Aboriginal Country, there is not a single Dreaming. Rather, there are Dreamings who danced, sang, fought, stole, slept, and who – through these and a thousand other interactions – brought Aboriginal Countries into being. Among their stories are those of Old Man Karramala (Old Man Goose) who played a didjeridu and made a waterfall in Mak Mak Country;[6] the mouse Galu who found where Bangarra (blue-tongued lizard) had hidden all the water in the rainforest lands of the Jirrbal;[7] and the Nyungar tale of the little Djidi Djidi bird who outsmarted the eagle.[8] The journeys and actions of the Dreamings can be traced in the geography of individual Aboriginal Countries and in the patterns of behaviour of all life. The Dreamings are also the source of the law, which at its broadest is the ways of living in Country that sustain Country. For thousands of linear years, Aboriginal Nations moved through the cycles of creation laid down by the Dreamings and the world was constantly made anew. Then came the apocalypse.

As the West measures time, the apocalypse began on the east coast of Australia in 1788 and reached the lands of my people, the Palyku, in the 1860s. It was not a single apocalypse but a multitude; a cycle of destruction that repeated in every Aboriginal Nation. Each cataclysm varied in its details but its larger patterns of violence remained the same. Psychologist Judy Atkinson (Jiman and Bundjalung), drawing on the work of Donald Baker, has identified three cycles of violence: overt physical violence (invasion, disease, death and destruction); covert structural violence (enforced dependency,

5 I have previously written of this in Ambellin Kwaymullina, 'Seeing the Light: Aboriginal Law, Learning and Sustainable Living in Country' (2005) 6(11) *Indigenous Law Bulletin* 12.

6 See Deborah Bird Rose, Nancy Daiyi, Kathy Deveraux, Margaret Daiyi, Linda Ford and April Bright, *Country of the Heart: An Indigenous Australian Homeland* (Aboriginal Studies Press, 2002) 10.

7 See Maisie Yarrcali Barlow (author), Michael Boiyool Anning (illustrator), *Jirrbal: Rainforest Dreamtime Stories* (Magabala Books 2001) 35–45.

8 See Len Collard, 'Djidi Djidi, Wardong, Kulbardi, Walitj and Weitj: Nyungar Dream Time Messengers' (2009) 54(2) *Westerly* 7, 12–13.

legislation, reserves and removals); and psycho-social domination (cultural and spiritual genocide).[9]

Aboriginal people, like Indigenous Peoples elsewhere, lived through the end of the world but we did not end; nor did our culture or our Dreamings. But we are now nations existing within the nation-states that arose from, and inherited the benefits of, our dispossession. Further, the laws and legal institutions of these nation-states sprang from the lie of Indigenous inferiority that was required in order to assert the moral and legal authority required to claim our lands.[10] In 2007, the United Nations General Assembly made a limited acknowledgement of Indigenous rights in the form of the *Declaration on the Rights of Indigenous Peoples*. But, as has been pointed out by some Indigenous scholars, the reason those rights required elucidation and protection in the first place is because of their continued violation by the nation-states to whose dominion – and domination – we remain subject.[11]

Indigenous academic Leroy Little Bear (Blood Indian Tribe, Blackfoot Confederacy) once identified that one of the problems of colonialism is that it tries to maintain a singular order, suppressing the diversity of human world views and typically resulting in oppression and discrimination.[12] The Indigenous Peoples of the globe who are marginalised by this singular order often have our concerns framed as 'Indigenous problems', which overlooks three things. First, the degree to which the laws, institutions and policies of colonial nation-states created, promulgated and continue to benefit from the oppression of (and discrimination against) First Peoples. Second, justice is of its nature a universal value; to deny it to one erodes it for all. Third, diversity is necessary. There is a recognised link between cultural diversity and the biodiverse environments upon which the human species depends for survival, and Indigenous Peoples are the guardians of most of the world's cultural diversity.[13] Beyond this, a singular approach is unlikely to be sufficient to grapple with the increasing complexity of issues that face human societies.

9 Judy Atkinson, *Trauma Trails, Recreating Song Lines: The Transgenerational Effects of Trauma in Indigenous Australia* (Spinifex Press, 2002) 59–73.

10 See Irene Watson, *Aboriginal Peoples, Colonialism and International Law: Raw Law* (Routledge, 2014); Robert Williams, *The American Indian in Western Legal Thought: The Discourses of Conquest* (Oxford University Press, 1990); and for comment on the way in which the ideas embodied in notions such as the doctrine of discovery continue to affect Indigenous Peoples worldwide, see United Nations Permanent Forum on Indigenous Peoples, *Report on the Eleventh Session*, E/2012/43-E/C.19/2012/13 (7–18 May 2012).

11 See, eg, Steve Newcomb, 'The UN Declaration on the Rights of Indigenous Peoples and the Paradigm of Domination' (2011) 20(3) *Griffith Law Review* 578; Irene Watson, 'Aboriginal(ising) International Law and Other Centres of Power' (2011) 20(3) *Griffith Law Review* 619; Aileen Moreton-Robinson, 'Virtuous Racial States' (2011) 20(3) *Griffith Law Review* 641.

12 Little Bear, above n 1, 77.

13 United Nations Permanent Forum on Indigenous Issues, above n 2, ch 2.

Aboriginal Nations of 'Australia' and an international legal tradition

Narrative sovereignty

When Aboriginal people meet for the first time, it is common for us to introduce ourselves by reference to where we come from rather than who we are, or perhaps it is more accurate to say that in speaking of our Country we *do* speak of who we are. One of the reasons for the diversity of Aboriginal Peoples – and of Indigenous Peoples elsewhere in the world – is the biodiverse environments which form and inform all aspects of our existence. The Palyku are from inland, freshwater Country, a homeland that demands constant movement in order to avoid exhausting food and water sources and ensure that all life in Country survives. Homelands with more abundant resources require less movement but the same careful management, and the narratives of our Countries are the narratives of ourselves. The whole is more than its parts and the whole is in all its parts; every Country carries different strengths which are also the strengths of the people who belong to that land.

It flows from the above that to speak of 'sovereignty' is to speak of a concept very different from traditional Eurocentric notions of dominion over (non-living) territory. Country was given, not taken; to assert autonomy in regards to a Country is to assert a relationship to place comprised in equal part of rights over Country and responsibilities to it. A right cannot exist independent of a corresponding responsibility, for all Aboriginal relationships are reciprocal in nature, and in this sense are informed by the fundamental reciprocity that underlies all others: that you must care for Country if you expect Country to care for you.

The relationship between Aboriginal Peoples and their Countries is founded in story. It began with the narratives of the Dreaming whereby the many Aboriginal Countries were, and are, created. It continues through the daily participation in, and management of, the sets of relationships between all life that the Dreamings established. In the words of Whadjuck and Balardong Nyungar man Len Collard:

> As each generation of Nyungar passes through, it is our duty to listen to, or tell, and then remember the yarns. As the current and future generations of Nyungar, we take on these storytelling responsibilities, passing them on to future generations of Nyungar … so they are brought up to understand and take their responsibilities and place as active participants and custodians of such ancient *boodjar* [land] and *katitjin* [knowledge].[14]

14 Len Collard, '*Wangkiny Ngulluck Nyungar Nyittiny, Boodjar, Moort* and *Katitjin*: Talking About Creations, Country, Family and Knowledge of the Nyungar of South Western Australia' in Sally Morgan, Tjalaminu Mia and Blaze Kwaymullina (eds), *Speaking from the Heart* (Fremantle Press, 2008) 262, 263.

Narratives – whether in the form of song, dance, art or ceremony – also form evidence of sovereignty, although it is evidence that has often been poorly understood in the legal systems of the colonisers, which are accustomed to a different form of literacy. And from an Indigenous perspective, it is difficult to conceive of how it is possible to claim ownership of a land if you do not know its stories and hence cannot accurately place yourself within the network of relationships that is Country itself. The answer of the colonising states of Western Europe to this conundrum was twofold. First, an assertion of a claim of right over inhabited territories on the basis of the denigration of the existing inhabitants via the many iterations of the doctrine of discovery (the idea that land belonged not to its inhabitants but the first Christian European nation to 'discover' it) and like notions.[15] Second, the application of violence that cycled through the physical, structural and psycho-social stages identified by Atkinson, above. This twofold claim is inextricably interlinked, because the violence was itself made possible by the denigration of Indigenous Peoples that founded the legal claim of right.

Indigenous legal scholar Robert Williams has characterised the sustaining idea of colonialism as being that 'the West's religion, civilization, and knowledge are superior to the religions, civilizations, and knowledge of non-Western peoples'.[16] However, once Indigenous Peoples are recognised as fully realised human beings with ways of knowing, being and doing that are as valid as those of the West, this idea is shown for the lie it always was. But the courts of the colonisers have often proved adept at turning their gaze away from the question of whether the assertion of inherent European superiority could be sustained, and what consequences might flow if it could not. In 1823, Chief Justice Marshall of the US Supreme Court acknowledged that the discovery doctrine was an 'extravagant pretension', but concluded that it 'becomes the law of the land, and cannot be questioned' once a territory had been acquired and held under it.[17] In 1992, a majority of the Australian High Court was prepared to disavow the notion of *terra nullius*,[18] the idea that the Australian continent was a land uninhabited and hence open to be claimed because Indigenous Peoples were not sufficiently 'advanced' enough to be regarded as meaningfully occupying the soil (which was to say, our cultures and laws did not resemble those of Western Europe). But, like Chief Justice Marshall almost one hundred

15 For a discussion of the operation of the doctrine of discovery in English territories (including Australia), see Robert J Miller, Jacinta Ruru, Larissa Behrendt and Tracey Lindberg (eds), *Discovering Indigenous Lands: The Doctrine of Discovery in the English Colonies* (Oxford University Press, 2010).

16 Williams, above n 10, 6.

17 *Johnson v Macintosh* 8 Wheat 543, 591 (1823).

18 *Mabo v Queensland (No 2)* (1992) 175 CLR 1, 40–2 (Brennan J, Mason CJ and McHugh J agreeing), 109 (Deane and Gaudron JJ), 180–2 (Toohey J).

years before, the High Court has been quick to affirm the sovereignty of the coloniser.[19]

This means the conundrum of how others acquired sovereignty over Aboriginal Countries is still without a satisfactory answer. We always knew *terra nullius* for a lie, and this has now been recognised by the courts of the nation-state that arose from that fiction. But if this justification has been discarded, what remains? There has been talk of a treaty raised in the context of current discussions regarding the potential constitutional recognition of Australian Indigenous Peoples,[20] although the process by which this could be done so as to ensure proper representation of the multitude of Indigenous Nations of Australia is not clear. But even were a treaty to eventuate, it would address internal governance arrangements and would not alter the status of Indigenous Peoples in international law nor give international recognition to the hundreds of Australian Indigenous Nations. Like Indigenous Peoples elsewhere, we would remain non-state actors in a system controlled by states. This is not to diminish the achievements of Indigenous Peoples at an international level.[21] But nor is it to deny the role of the international legal order in facilitating and legitimising colonialism;[22] the way in which human rights violations against Indigenous and other marginalised peoples too often go unchecked;[23] or the degree to which Indigenous Peoples remain subject to the hegemony of the nation-states born of our dispossession.[24] Besides which, from an Indigenous perspective, there is a larger question to be addressed. If the singular social order established by colonialism continues and the diversity of the world is suppressed, how will this shape the future of the human species? In the absence of a shift in relationships that moves Indigenous Nations and the nation-states that claim ownership of our lands beyond the colonial paradigm, patterns repeat. My mother once wrote of this, in the context of a conversation with one of our Aboriginal grandfathers about travel to the stars:

> In 1992, they honoured James Cook by naming a space shuttle after the Endeavour and sending it winging its way to the stars with a woodchip

19 Ibid 31–2, 69 (Brennan J, Mason CJ and McHugh J agreeing), 78–9 (Deane and Gaudron JJ), 121 (Dawson J); *Walker v NSW* (1994) 182 CLR 45, 47–50 (Mason CJ); *Yorta Yorta Aboriginal Community v Victoria* (2002) 214 CLR 422, 443–4 (Gleeson CJ and Gummow and Hayne JJ).

20 Expert Panel on Constitutional Recognition of Aboriginal and Torres Strait Islander Peoples, *Recognising Aboriginal and Torres Strait Islander Peoples in the Constitution: Report of the Expert Panel* (2012) chs 8, 9.

21 For a history of Indigenous Peoples at an international level, see S James Anaya, *International Law and Indigenous Peoples* (Oxford University Press, 2nd edn, 2004) pts 1, 2; for a brief summary, see UN Permanent Forum on Indigenous Issues, above n 2, 1–4.

22 See Watson, above n 10; Anaya, ibid pt 1.

23 See UN Permanent Forum on Indigenous Issues, above n 2, 203–11.

24 See references above n 11.

> from the original ship on board. Coincidentally, that same year, the High Court of Australia finally recognised the rights of Indigenous peoples, leaving the door open to a form of native title over country. So one hot summer's night, when my grandfather and I were sitting outside looking up at the stars, I told him about Cook's spaceship and we talked about its significance and what it might mean to anyone living happily on another planet, unaware that the spirit of James Cook and his new spaceship was about to descend on them. [My grandfather] laughed and said, 'Those poor buggers in the stars, do you think they'll get stuck with Native title too?'[25]

Native title is something of a 'leftover' of a property right, a scrap from the colonial table that does not equate to freehold;[26] continues to exist only to the extent that it has not been extinguished by the property rights flowing from Anglo-Australian legal system;[27] and is further diminished by requirements of content and proof which are heavily influenced by essentialist Eurocentric notions of Indigenous culture.[28] Like the rights set out in the *Declaration on the Rights of Indigenous Peoples*, native title is important but fails to deal with the more fundamental resolution that is required. The questions a legal system founded in narrative sovereignty asks any system that would assert autonomy over the same territory are these: What are your stories? Where is the evidence of your understanding of the networks of living beings that comprise Country? How do you understand your place within these networks, which is to say, can you enumerate your relationships and in so doing explain both your rights and responsibilities? Australia, like other colonial nation-states, is recognised as a sovereign nation and in the Eurocentric international legal tradition this sovereignty is not affected by any failure in environmental stewardship; by the cycles of colonial violence required to seize, hold and work the land; or by human rights violations against Aboriginal and Torres Strait Islander Peoples. Such things may cause or contribute to legal disputes or adverse comments by international monitoring bodies but they do not, in and of themselves, affect title to the land. So within the Eurocentric international legal tradition there is no reason either to ask or answer the question *what are your stories?* But within the Aboriginal legal tradition, there is no nationhood – and hence no relations between nations – without the narratives that found the relationship between peoples and Country.

25 Sally Morgan, 'The Balance for the World' in Sally Morgan, Tjalaminu Mia and Blaze Kwaymullina (ed), *Heartsick for Country: Stories of Love, Spirit and Creation* (Fremantle Press, 2008) 254, 265.
26 See Richard Bartlett, *Native Title in Australia* (Lexis Nexis, 3rd edn, 2014) pt 2.
27 Ibid pt 3.
28 Ibid chs 7, 8, 9, 15; Simon Young, *The Trouble with Tradition* (Federation Press 2008); Australian Law Reform Commission, *Connection to Country: Review of the Native Title Act 1993 (Cth)*, Report No 126 (2015).

Relationship-based citizenship

In Aboriginal systems, to speak of belonging to a particular Aboriginal Nation or Nations is to speak of family. It is to say *this is my mother's Country, my grandmother's Country* – or *this is my father's Country, my grandfather's Country* – depending on whether the affiliation is matrilineal or patrilineal. All relationships ultimately trace back to the Dreaming Ancestors and are expressed through kinship systems that extend beyond human beings to plants and animals as well as sun, moon, rain, wind and other aspects (Ancestors) of a living world. The kinship system itself reflects the networks of relationships that is Country, and when Aboriginal people travel, they carry that network within themselves (as the whole is in all its parts). Country unfolds from a single point, and enfolds all that is – or to put this into linear terms, it enfolds all that was, is and will ever be.

It is now a relatively common practice in Australia for non-Indigenous people to acknowledge the Traditional Owners of Country,[29] particularly at an event or before the giving of a speech, although the larger point of such an acknowledgement is often overlooked. When an Aboriginal person acknowledges someone else's Country, it is not merely a sign of respect but a recognition that we are subject to the laws of that Country as interpreted and applied by the relevant legal experts (generally Elders).[30] It is also an act of self-protection, since it is well known to Aboriginal people that it is important to proceed with caution when you are a 'stranger to Country'; the land can react with hostility to unfamiliar people. An example of one of the ways in which Aboriginal people approach Country with respect is explained by Bardi and Indjarbandi woman Dawn Besserab:

> Growing up in my family and learning from my Elders, I was told that whenever I visited someone else's Country I should always yell out and tell them who I was, where I came from and what my business was. By showing respect for the spirits of Country, I would not come to any harm. But if I failed to do so, then something could happen to me and the people accompanying me.[31]

It is also a fundamental rule, common to all Aboriginal legal systems of Australia, that you cannot 'speak for someone else's Country', and in this sense you cannot tell someone else's story.

29 See, eg, Reconciliation Australia, *Welcome to and Acknowledgement of Country* <https://www.reconciliation.org.au/wp-content/uploads/2013/12/QA-welcome-to-country.pdf>.

30 For an examination of Aboriginal regulation of outsiders, see Martin, 'Ways of Knowing', above n 1, 208.

31 Dawn Besserab, 'Country is Lonely' in Sally Morgan, Tjalaminu Mia and Blaze Kwaymullina (eds), *Heartsick for Country: Stories of Love, Spirit and Creation* (Fremantle Press, 2008) 44, 51.

It follows from this that borders are of vital importance within and between Aboriginal Nations, although these borders were largely invisible to colonists who were accustomed to the edges of nation-states being marked by fences, walls or guards. The colonists were generally unable to perceive the places where one Country ended and another began, marked as these boundaries were and are by rivers, rocks, hollows, hills and forests and the many other physical expressions of the actions of the Ancestor spirits.[32] Further, there was little need for Aboriginal 'border patrols', given that the location of our boundaries was well known to Aboriginal people and that to trespass into someone else's Country was an act of stupidity that might well result in adverse consequences for the trespasser. In this way, Country is both the source of law and a legal actor that intervenes to enforce and protect its boundaries.

To be an Aboriginal citizen of an Aboriginal Nation is to exist within networks of relationships, the pattern – or story – of which was laid out by the Dreaming Ancestors, and which is upheld through the law. To enter a nation not your own is to carry the network of your own Country within you but also to exist within another network. There may be connections between your own Country and another's, for example through intermarriage or through songlines (the paths travelled by the Dreaming Ancestors as they moved across the land). If these connections cannot be determined, 'strangers' are often assigned a place within the kinship system of the nation they have entered. This brings them into the fabric of relationships that comprise that nation, and the right–responsibility duality encompassed by those relationships. Particular rights and responsibilities are dependent on the place occupied within the system, the overall objective of which is to sustain (balance) relationships and hence the world. In this sense, divisions are also connections. For example, the skin (kinship) system of the Palyku divides into four. These four points are sometimes called 'faces'; they are sections that stand face to face, and they balance by opposing each other. To belong to any category in a kin system is to be at once linked to all that is the same (in the sense of occupying the same side of the balance as you do) and to all that is different, in the sense of that which lies on other side of the balance point. In this way, boundaries divide but do not disconnect.

The internal manifestation of Anglo-Australian sovereignty is through a government divided into the three arms: legislative, judicial and executive. In very basic terms, the legislative (parliament) makes the laws, the judiciary (courts) interprets the laws, and the executive (vice-regal officials such as governors, as well as ministers and public servants) administers the laws. But in Aboriginal systems, the internal manifestation of narrative sovereignty is through the relationships laid out by the Dreaming Ancestors, rather than

32 For a discussion of boundaries and boundary protocols, see Watson, above n 10, 35–37.

through central institutions. This is why, writing with Blaze Kwaymullina, I have spoken of kinship as a relationship-based government, in that it is through kinship that laws are made, administered and enforced.[33] There are, of course, many kinship systems and the specific rules within each one are subject to interpretation by the relevant legal experts within that particular system; there is no universal homogenous model of Aboriginal kinship. But within each system, kin relations may well determine, for example, who can tell a certain law story; who cares for the sacred places inhabited by the ultimate law makers, the Dreaming Ancestors; who determines and administers punishment for a transgression; and who interprets or mediates change in specific rules (including by communication with the Ancestors) in order to apply those rules to new situations. To put this another way: relationship determines function rather than function determining relationship. In the Anglo-Australian legal system, it is the function of the judiciary to interpret the law and adjudicate legal disputes. But in Aboriginal legal systems, the person(s) in whom that function vests at any given moment depends on the relevant relationships. This may itself be subject to negotiation where different sets of relationships interact, and the network of relationships extends to non-human life and therefore to non-human legal actors.

When viewed in this light, the claim of the Anglo-Australian courts to possess the function of adjudicating the existence of Indigenous laws when determining native title claims is difficult to fathom. Anglo-Australian courts do not possess any of the relationships that would confer that function upon them. More broadly, the Anglo-Australian legislature, executive and judiciary collectively do not possess any of the relationships that would confer a right to exercise the functions of government over Indigenous Peoples or Indigenous Countries. Within the Anglo-Australian system itself, this does not affect the validity of governmental decision making. But in the context of resolving the broader issue with which all settler states must grapple – how to reconcile the rights of those who were here before with all those who came after – the need for the Anglo-Australian nation-state to develop respectful relationships with the many Indigenous Nations of Australia becomes a primary concern.

The right to be human

One of the points of distinction between Indigenous rights and human rights as framed by western legal institutions is that human rights belong to individuals, while Indigenous rights – as set out in the *Declaration on the Rights of Indigenous Peoples* – are collective. But this in itself points to a more fundamental difference: in Indigenous societies, to be a fully realised human being

33 Ambelin Kwaymullina and Blaze Kwaymullina, 'Learning to Read the Signs: Law in an Indigenous Reality' (2010) 34(2) *Journal of Australian Studies* 195, 204.

is to be part of a collective. It is also to be responsible to the collective, including by sustaining the relationships that constitute a lawful way of being. And amongst Aboriginal Nations this collective extends beyond human beings to all life in Country (and all of Country is alive).

What does it mean to conceive of humanity as part of a collective that encompasses non-human life? Kombumerri Elder Mary Graham once wrote:

> Western: what is the meaning of life?
> Aboriginal: what is it that wants to know?[34]

All life has meaning, and all life has a perspective, the nuances of which cannot necessarily be known to human beings. Everyone's view is confined by their place within the system; life does not exist in the abstract. To be a fully realised human being is therefore to exist in such a way so as to ensure that all life has the same opportunity for self-realisation. The Eurocentric international legal tradition makes a division between such areas as environmental law, human rights law and law relating to sovereignty of nation-states upon which the international system is built. Amongst Aboriginal Nations, these are all aspects of the same storied relationship. That relationship is made manifest through kin systems which place specific responsibilities on specific individuals in relation to family members, including those in non-human form. These connections can, in turn, give insight into the experience of life from perspectives not our own.

It is the continued existence of all life that makes any life possible. In such a context, it makes little sense to speak of 'human rights' as something that is separate from or superior to the network of connections that is Country. Nor, as ever, does it make sense to speak of rights as a concept shorn of responsibilities. The right to be human is a right to Country; a failure to fulfil the responsibility to care for Country is a failure of humanity. In this respect, the colonial apocalypse both was built on the denial of Indigenous humanity and continues to prevent Indigenous Peoples from exercising the right to be human by failing to resolve the sovereignty stories of those who were here before, and all those who came after.

Conclusion

Irene Watson (Tanganekald and Meintangk Peoples) concluded in her ground-breaking study of colonialism that Indigenous Peoples need to:

> find a new way of being, an old way of being, outside that of colonial power ... We have ancient models that pre-exist the colonisation of our

34 Graham, above n 1, 181.

> lands and lives. We don't really need to look anywhere else but at ourselves; we need simply to re-emerge as First Nations Peoples.[35]

In this emergence, Indigenous Peoples of Australia offer pathways into the future for all those who genuinely wish to engage with us in a way that respects that narrative sovereignty. To the extent that these conversations are between Anglo-Australian governments and Aboriginal Nations, it is an international dialogue. But if Anglo-Australian governments are unwilling to engage, there seems no reason why the dialogue cannot be explored by anyone with an interest in how Indigenous and non-Indigenous peoples can resolve colonial binaries and walk forward together.

35 Watson, above n 10, 164.

Chapter 2

Domination in relation to Indigenous ('dominated') Peoples in international law

Steven Newcomb

This chapter is an effort to make explicit an underlying feature of the language that scholars typically use when writing about the body of ideas known as international law and the relations between 'states' and peoples termed 'Indigenous'.[1] This feature of the language of international law[2] is a

1 Steven Newcomb, 'The UN Declaration on the Rights of Indigenous Peoples and the Paradigm of Domination' (2011) *Griffith University Law Review* 578, 588. The few working definitions of the term 'Indigenous Peoples' at the United Nations begin with the implicit image that distinct nations or peoples were existing free and independent of foreign domination in a particular place when a secondary and invading group invasively entered the scene and 'through conquest, settlement, or other means' established dominance over them. Those termed 'Indigenous' are then regarded as living *under* that state or condition of 'domination'. The use of the term 'dominance' by the United Nations in this context seems designed to create a euphemistic gloss so as to avoid using the word 'domination'. A process of colonisation creates the 'Indigenous' condition of existing *under domination* or *dominance*. Colonisation is accurately defined as a form of domination resulting from a nation or empire sending agents forth to a foreign geographical area to use violence to take over a distant territory by inserting its own people. This is done in an effort to dominate and control the original nations and peoples already existing in that place. Samuel Morison called this the process whereby 'Europeans began that amazing expansion of trade and settlement which resulted in world dominion'. Samuel Morison, *The Oxford History of the American People* (Oxford University Press, 1965) 34. This forms the context for the use of the term 'Indigenous' in international law. Indigenous Nations and Peoples are accurately re-expressed as distinct peoples that have been made to exist under the claimed dominion (domination) of a colonising or dominating power.

2 Antony Anghie, *Imperialism, Sovereignty and the Making of International Law* (Cambridge University Press, 2005) 310. Anghie points out that what is typically called international law is a product of colonisation and the colonial encounter. That encounter, which is a violent clash between the invading power and the original nations and peoples, results in a situation in which nations and peoples that were existing free from domination have been forced to exist under some form of foreign and colonising system of domination.

DOI: 10.4324/9781315628318-3

metaphorical pattern of domination[3] and subordination,[4] which generally remains below the level of conscious awareness in discussions about peoples called 'Indigenous' and their rights.[5] In this chapter, I will focus on some of the metaphorical patterns of domination that are typically found in scholarly writings about international law and 'Indigenous' Peoples in an effort to heighten awareness about a theme that has not been typically raised in international law scholarship.

As Glenn Morris has observed:

> The historical operation of a system of legal norms and standards, ordained by a handful of states, and imposed upon the overwhelming majority of the world's peoples without their consent or input, is considered perverse and unjust by most indigenous peoples.[6]

In that one succinct sentence, Professor Morris sums up the issue – which I identify as 'domination' – which is manifested as 'states' imposing standards, concepts and norms of their design and choosing on the original nations and peoples of a geographical area without their consent. This behaviour emerges from the origin of what is termed 'the state'. In *Our Enemy the State*, Albert J Nock quotes German scholar Franz Oppenheimer, who succinctly sums up the pattern of domination I will be drawing attention to in this chapter. This following pattern has resulted in certain nations and peoples being termed 'Indigenous'. As Nock puts it:

> [Franz] Oppenheimer defines the State, in respect to its origin, as an institution 'forced on a defeated group by a conquering group, with a view only to systematizing the domination of the conquered by the conquerors, and safeguarding itself against insurrection from within and attack from without. *This domination* had no other final purpose than the economic exploitation of the conquered group by the victorious group.'[7]

The patterns of domination made explicit in the above quotation are important for gaining insight into the nature of 'the state', and into the relations

3 Claus Mueller, *The Politics of Communication: A Study in the Political Sociology of Language, Socialization and Legitimation* (Oxford University Press, 1977). Domination is evident when one nation or people exercises daily control over another nation or people external to its will, or when one nation or people is made to live in subjection to the will of another nation or people.
4 Subordination is the corollary of domination.
5 *United Nations Declaration on the Rights of Indigenous Peoples*, GA Res 61/295, 61st sess, 107th plen mtg, UN Doc A/RES/61/295 (adopted 13 September 2007).
6 Glenn Morris, 'International Law and Politics: Toward a Right of Self-Determination for Indigenous Peoples' in Annette Jaimes (ed), *The State of Native America: Genocide, Colonization and Resistance* (South End Press, 1992) 55, 55.
7 Albert Nock, *Our Enemy the State* (Caxton Printers, 1946) 45 (emphasis added).

between 'the state' and 'Indigenous Peoples' in international law, which is a system of standards used by 'states' in their interactions with each other. Above, Oppenheimer characterises those termed 'the conquerors' (dominators) as having successfully created and 'systematised' the domination they have managed to achieve over those referred to as 'the conquered'. What Oppenheimer calls 'an institution that has been forced on a defeated group' is accurately phrased as 'a domination' that has been imposed on the group being dominated. Oppenheimer makes the pattern perfectly clear when he calls the pattern '[t]his domination'.

Metaphors of domination and international law

In *A Clearing in the Forest*, Steven L Winter points out that metaphors are 'our imaginative way of having a reality'.[8] It follows that metaphors of domination are the imaginative (cognitive) means by which a dominating society is able to constitute and maintain a reality of domination and subordination over nations and peoples being dominated.[9] C A Bowers says that metaphors carry forward and maintain the biases and misconceptions of the past.[10] International law serves as an excellent example of what Bowers calls 'the linguistic colonization of the present by the past'.[11] He points out that 'colonization involved taking for granted analogs [analogies] settled upon in the distant past which is part of how the metaphorical language of the dominant cultures represented the West as a civilization and the indigenous cultures as' inferior and subordinate 'tribes'.[12]

The above ideas provide an important insight: the systematic use of metaphors of domination, both mentally and linguistically, is a means by which polities called 'states' carry forward and maintain, from generation to generation, a reality of domination and dehumanisation, especially in relation to nations and peoples termed 'Indigenous'. By means of such a system of ideas and behaviours, one nation or people is able to *claim* to have 'conquered' another nation or people, and then additionally to claim on that basis *a right* to maintain a controlling will over that other nation or people, and over the lands, territories and vital resources (such as water) of the nation or people being dominated. The 'inter'

8 Steven Winter, *A Clearing in the Forest: Law, Life and Mind* (University of Chicago Press, 2001) 68.
9 Steven Newcomb, *Pagans in the Promised Land: Decoding the Doctrine of Christian Discovery* (Fulcrum Publishing, 2008).
10 Chet Bowers, 'Chet Bowers: Part 1: Linguistic Roots of the Ecological Crisis', *YouTube*, 14 September 2015, <https://www.youtube.com/watch?v=O0YSPtPnNio>; Chet Bowers, *The Way Forward: Educational Reforms that Focus on the Cultural Commons and the Linguistic Roots of the Ecological/Cultural Crisis* (Eco-Justice Press, 2012) 70–105.
11 Email from Chet Bowers to Steven Newcomb, 27 February 2016.
12 Ibid.

'relations' that *states of domination* have established between each other, and now maintain, are generally termed 'foreign relations' and 'international law'. Given this context, a shift to the viewpoint of those being dominated reveals a phenomenon that I call 'the domination of Indigenous Peoples by states'.

As the result of a process of reification,[13] a colonising nation or people will tend not to interpret or characterise its political system as one of domination. The descendants of those who managed to impose their political system forcibly on nations and peoples now termed 'Indigenous' will choose not to see the end result as a system of domination. Those who have inherited that system would no doubt defensively say that the system which their ancestors constructed on top of 'Indigenous' Peoples, and that is now being maintained by the current generation 'around' and 'on top of' those peoples, has nothing at all to do with 'domination'. There will be a tendency to engage in this denial because 'domination' suggests invalidity and illegitimacy. The successors of the system will undoubtedly prefer to frame that system in terms of 'democracy'[14] and 'civilisation'.[15] They are likely to say that their system was founded on the sanctity of 'property'.[16] Ironically, however, in keeping with the imperial Greco-Roman tradition, 'democracy', 'civilisation' and 'property' are all terms of domination.[17]

During the course of many centuries, systems of domination have been globalised under the terminology of the international system of 'states'.[18] From this perspective, 'states' is shorthand for 'states of domination'. A single state is shorthand for 'a state of domination'. In the context of the metaphors typically used in the United Nations, and in international law, the phrase 'Indigenous Peoples' is accurately re-expressed as 'dominated peoples'. Dominated ('Indigenous') nations and peoples are generally regarded as having been 'subjected' to 'conquest' by an invading and dominating nation at some time in the past.[19]

13 Peter Berger and Thomas Luckmann, *The Social Construction of Reality: A Treatise on the Sociology of Knowledge* (Anchor Books, 1967) 89–92.

14 US State Department, 'Announcement of U.S. Support for the United Nations Declaration on the Rights of Indigenous Peoples' (2011) <http://www.state.gov/documents/organization/184099.pdf>.

15 *Webster's Third New International Dictionary* (1993): 'The act of civilizing; *esp*: the forcing of a foreign cultural pattern on a population to which it is foreign.'

16 Gottfried Dietze, *In Defense of Property* (John Hopkins University Press, 1971). See also Charles Haar and Lance Liebman, *Property and Law* (Little, Brown, 1985) 1: 'If property starts with the first establishment of socially approved physical domination over some part of the natural world, then the nature of that domination – often called "occupancy" or "possession" – is important.'

17 Eli Sagan, *The Honey and the Hemlock: Democracy and Paranoia in Ancient Athens and Modern America* (Basic Books, 1991) 13–56.

18 Max Weber, *From Max Weber: Essays in Sociology* (Hans Gerth and C Wright Mills ed and trans, Oxford University Press, 1946) 78.

19 Karen Engle, *The Elusive Promise of Indigenous Development: Culture, Rights, Strategy* (Duke University Press, 2010) 73–99.

The metaphor and concept of 'conquest' is generally associated with the idea of some kind of military victory or triumph, as expressed above by Oppenheimer, by claiming to have 'won' or 'acquired' a foreign territory by force of arms or by other means.[20] However, when the perspective is switched from the viewpoint of those characterised as 'the conquering' nation or people, to the nations or peoples said to have been 'conquered', the words 'conquest' and 'conquered' are accurately re-expressed as *domination*.[21] As a mental exercise, think of the different understandings and associated inferences that would emerge if every time we were to see the word 'conquest' we were to reframe and re-express it as 'domination'. Use of that specific word by nations and peoples said to have been 'conquered' by the West is one means by which Indigenous Nations and Peoples can begin challenging this very idea by pointing out that 'conquest' serves as a cover word for domination.

Another approach can also be taken: make explicit the metaphors of domination and subordination, and refuse passively to accept and operate from the colonisers' perspective. For example, 'the conquest'[22] is a phrase accurately replaced with 'the domination'. As an exercise, reflect on the difference in connotation that would have arisen if Patricia Seed had chosen as a title for her book *Ceremonies of Possession in Europe's Domination of the New World 1492–1640*, instead of *Ceremonies of Possession in Europe's Conquest of the New World 1492–1640*.[23]

Dominated peoples and international law

The domination which states have constructed, maintained and used against colonised peoples for centuries has resulted in the phenomenon of 'dominated ("Indigenous") peoples'. Yet this specific issue generally remains out of focus when the word 'domination' is not used. The issue of domination has very long and very old roots indeed.[24] James Crawford, in his foreword to Antony Anghie's book *Imperialism, Sovereignty, and International Law*, has pinpointed the issue of domination that Anghie has identified in his research into the origins of international law. Crawford notes that Anghie 'examines a series of episodes in the legal history of the relations between the West and non-Western polities'.[25] Anghie, says Crawford, argues that these episodes have

20 The Compact Edition of the *Oxford English Dictionary* (1971) vol 1.
21 Richard Brown, *A Poetic for Sociology: Toward a Logic of Discovery for the Human Sciences* (Cambridge University Press, 1977) 47.
22 'Conquest' is often used by historians and scholars of international law, which suggests a victory or triumph rather than a form of domination.
23 Patricia Seed, *Ceremonies of Possession in Europe's Conquest of the New World 1492–1640* (Cambridge University Press, 1995).
24 Frances G Davenport, *European Treaties Bearing on the History of the United States and Its Dependencies to 1648* (Carnegie Institution of Washington, 1917).
25 James Crawford, 'Foreword' in Anghie, above n 2, xi.

been 'reproducing at different epochs and in different ways an underlying pattern of domination and subordination'.[26] From its beginning, international law was not 'exclusively concerned with the relations between states', Crawford notes, 'but, and more importantly, with the relations between civilizations and peoples'. 'Moreover', says Crawford, 'these were relations of *domination*'.[27]

Professor Anghie, in his chapter 'Francisco de Vitoria and the Colonial Origins of International Law', examines in detail Vitoria's discourse and arguments, and Vitoria's view that 'Indians were excluded from the realm of sovereignty'.[28] As Anghie concludes:

> ultimately, the one distinction which Vitoria insists upon and which he elaborates in considerable detail is the distinction between the sovereign Spanish and the non-sovereign Indians. Vitoria bases his conclusions that the Indians are not sovereign on the simple assertion that *they are pagans*.[29]

Given Jonathon Havercroft's acknowledgement that major critiques of sovereignty find it to be 'an unjust form of political domination that limits human freedom',[30] concluding that the Indians were not sovereign because they were not Christian left the 'Indians' wide open to a forcibly imposed unjust system of political domination by 'the sovereign Spanish', 'the all-powerful sovereign who administers this law' of *jus gentium*.[31] Anghie argues that the 'sovereignty doctrine was not developed in the West and then transferred to the non-European world'.[32] Rather, the 'sovereignty doctrine acquired its character through the colonial encounter'[33] because, Anghie contends, 'sovereignty [domination] was constituted through colonialism'.[34]

Then, as a more recent example, Anghie provides a detailed account of the positivist school of international law in the nineteenth century. He uses a wide number of synonyms for domination and dehumanisation, while explaining how 'Positivists developed an elaborate vocabulary for denigrating non-European people, presenting them as suitable objects for conquest, and legitimizing the most extreme violence against them, all in the furtherance of the civilizing mission discharging the white man's burden'.[35] Synonyms for domination and dehumanisation in that one sentence include 'denigrating', 'objects for conquest', 'extreme violence' and 'civilizing mission'. The average

26 Ibid.
27 Ibid (original emphasis).
28 Anghie, above n 2, 26.
29 Ibid 29 (emphasis added).
30 Jonathan Havercroft, *Captives of Sovereignty* (Cambridge University Press, 2011) 34.
31 Anghie, above n 2, 29.
32 Ibid 29.
33 Ibid.
34 Ibid 38.
35 Ibid.

reader may not recognise the phrase 'civilizing mission' as expressing the theme of domination. The connection is found in *Webster's Third New International Dictionary* (unabridged), which defines 'civilization' as 'the process of civilizing', for example '*the forcing* of a particular cultural pattern on a population to which it [the cultural pattern] is foreign' (emphasis added).

Forcing free and independent nations and peoples to undergo a politically coercive, dominating and multi-generational process of subjection to 'a foreign cultural pattern', purportedly in keeping with international law between 'states', has resulted in a trauma-inducing history for peoples now called 'Indigenous'. Thomas R Berger's book *A Long and Terrible Shadow* provides numerous example of the pattern of domination, subordination and dehumanisation that historically contextualises the relationship between nations and peoples termed 'Indigenous' and polities called 'states' in international law. In the following paragraph of 84 words, for instance, Berger provides at least ten examples of domination and dehumanisation, which I highlight using additions in brackets:

> The Spaniards came first to [invade] the West Indies; they waged a series of campaigns of extermination [domination] against the Indians of Hispaniola. On horseback, accompanied by infantry and bloodhounds [to hunt down the Indians] [domination], the *conquistadores* [dominators] destroyed almost at will [domination] the hunting and gathering tribes of the island. They raped [domination] and murdered [domination], sparing neither women nor children [domination]. Resistance [to Spanish domination] by the Indians was put down mercilessly [by means of domination]. By 1496, the Spaniards were in complete control of [had achieved complete domination over] the island of Hispaniola. Similar assaults [campaigns of domination] were made on Cuba and other islands of the Caribbean.[36]

Innumerable volumes of this sort of dark history illustrate the conceptual and behavioural roots of what Anghie calls 'the relationship between international law and the colonial confrontation', and the roots of what he terms 'sovereignty doctrine'.[37] Given that colonialism is simply another synonym for imperialism and domination,[38] Anghie's focus on 'the relationship between international law and the colonial confrontation' provides much-needed insight into what is seldom explicitly written about, namely, the domination of nations and peoples now commonly called Indigenous.[39]

36 Thomas Berger, *A Long and Terrible Shadow: White Values, Native Rights in the Americas since 1492* (University of Washington Press, 1967) 3.
37 Anghie, above n 2, 37.
38 Rene Maunier, *The Sociology of Colonies: An Introduction to the Study of Race Contact* (Routledge, 1949) 29–36.
39 Newcomb, 'UN Declaration', above n 1.

Some of the most basic vocabulary found in writings about Indigenous Peoples in the context of international law include 'state',[40] 'civilization',[41] 'Indigenous',[42] 'sovereignty',[43] 'symbolic acts of possession',[44] 'conquest'[45] and 'property'.[46] Each of these words, and all of them together when viewed as a single gestalt or paradigm, leads to the idea and pattern of domination. A deeper examination of these metaphors, their interpretation and the various contexts in which they are typically used provide us with an important insight: the idea system of international law has been used by the agents of polities called 'states' as a means of constituting and maintaining, on a seemingly permanent basis, a linguistic and behavioural reality of domination for nations and peoples called 'Indigenous'.[47] Yet scholars of international law tend to write as if there is no such thing as *the domination of Indigenous Peoples by states.*[48]

Indigenous Peoples are not part of an 'objective' physical reality

The idea of certain peoples being classified as 'Indigenous' is not part of an 'objective reality' *physically* existing in the world *independent of the human mind.* It is the human mind, and, more specifically, the western or occidental mind, that came up with the metaphorical idea of certain peoples being termed and categorised as 'Indigenous'. The category was developed based on particular characteristics or properties ascribed to 'Indigenous' Peoples in a dominating context of empire and colonialism, or in the contemporary context of a given 'state' of domination.[49] Peoples called 'Indigenous' in international law, for

40 Weber, above n 18. See Max Weber's definition of 'the state': 'Like the political institutions historically preceding it, the state is a relation of men dominating men, a relation supported by means of legitimate (i.e. considered to be legitimate) violence. If the state is to exist, *the dominated* must obey the authority claimed by the powers that be': ibid 78 (emphasis added).
41 See above n 15.
42 Newcomb, 'UN Declaration', above n 1, 588–9.
43 Havercroft, above n 30, 34. Eminent political philosophers such as Arendt, Foucault, Hardt and Negri, and Agamben agree in their assessment that 'sovereignty' constitutes 'an unjust form of political domination that limits human freedom'.
44 Seed, above n 23.
45 Ibid.
46 Dietze, above n 16.
47 Newcomb, *Pagans in the Promised Land*, above n 9.
48 The so-called 'conquest' has, from the perspective of those said to have been 'conquered', resulted in the imposition of an unjust form of political domination, which, ironically, is a definition of 'sovereignty' provided in Havercroft's *Captives of Sovereignty*, above n 30, based on his reading of a number of political philosophers.
49 United Nations Department of Economic and Social Affairs, *State of the World's Indigenous Peoples*, UN Doc ST/ESA/328 (2009) 6: 'The concept of indigenous peoples emerged from the colonial experience, whereby the aboriginal peoples of

example, are typically framed in terms of metaphors of hierarchy, and thus are characterised as 'occupying' a 'lower' order or 'subordinate' 'space' 'beneath' the political authority of 'polities' called 'states'.[50] The metaphorical imagery of Indigenous Peoples existing 'in' or 'within' the state, or being 'subject to' and 'under' the authority of 'the state', certainly serves this purpose.[51] The metaphor of a 'subordinate' position or status is sometimes stated in the United Nations as such peoples being 'non-dominant'.[52] This only makes sense in relation to the correlative of another people, society or state which is regarded as being dominant or dominating.

English philosopher Adam Smith mentioned this kind of pattern in his *Essay on Colonies* when he said that, during 'the course of many centuries among savage and barbarous nations', the colonisers carried with them 'the habit of subordination'.[53] This is accurately interpreted to mean that the colonisers (dominators) had a habit of using subordinating and dehumanising metaphors such as 'savage', 'barbarous' and 'uncivilised' (undominated) against the free nations and peoples living in the lands being colonised. Stated differently, the colonisers carried with them a mental habit of using metaphors of domination as part of the process of 'colonisation', which Samuel Eliot Morison defines as 'a form of conquest in which a nation takes over a distant territory, thrusts in its own people, and controls or eliminates the native inhabitants'.[54]

It would be difficult to devise a more perfect picture of domination than the one Morison provides in the above sentence, which goes well with Claus Mueller's definition of domination. In *The Politics of Communication*, Mueller defines domination as 'the control' by 'a limited number of individuals over the material resources of society', and 'over access to positions of political [decision-making] power'.[55] International law is one means by which such control has been achieved over nations and peoples termed 'Indigenous'. Through the centuries, a limited number of colonisers in leadership positions of power have mentally projected metaphors of domination and subordination

a given land were marginalized after being invaded by colonial powers, whose peoples *are now dominant* over the earlier occupants' (emphasis added). The phrase 'now dominant' is followed later in the same paragraph with an explicit mention of 'Domination and displacement of peoples'. The nations and peoples being dominated end up in 'a state of domination' by a given 'state' of domination.

50 Newcomb, *Pagans in the Promised Land*, above n 9.

51 Ibid.

52 Jose R Martinez Cobo, UN Special Rapporteur on the Problem of Discrimination Against Indigenous Populations, *Study of the Problem of Discrimination against Indigenous Populations*, UN Doc E/CN4/Sub2/1986/7/Add 4 (1986) para 379: 'They form at present non-dominant sectors of society …'

53 Adam Smith, *Essay on Colonies* (M Walter Dunne, 1901) 12.

54 Morison, above n 1, 34.

55 Mueller, above n 3, 129.

onto the nations and peoples that were originally living free of those mental projections, and of the dominating behaviours that follow from them.

Given this fact, peoples now called 'Indigenous' are the ones who have been both mentally and physically subjected, or dominated, by those engaged in the enterprise of colonialism and imperialism, or, in contemporary times, by those carrying out the role of 'the state'. Colonisation involves a given system of domination (for example, a 'state', 'kingdom' or 'monarchy') sending human beings forth as agents who are assigned the task of transporting a mental and physical system of domination into a 'newly located' ('discovered') geographical area where that system was not yet existing. They are expected to engage in the long and violent process of constituting that system over and on top of the original nations that were previously existing in that place free from a violently imposed and foreign domination. This forcible process of imposition is what has sometimes been 'the civilising mission',[56] as mentioned previously.

That the concept 'Indigenous Peoples' is metaphorically ensconced in an overall semantic context of domination generally goes unmentioned. This is somewhat remarkable given that the domination–subordination conceptual pattern is central to the working definition of what it means to be considered 'Indigenous' in both international law and the United Nations.[57] Metaphorically depicting such peoples as living a lower-order, dominated existence in relation to polities called 'states' seems to be a requisite of the idea system that elite humans of the West have developed and maintained as international law.[58] When Indigenous Nations and Peoples express the desire to free themselves from being dominated by a particular system ('state') of domination, some scholars typically frame this as 'talk of secession'.[59]

Such scholars frame the matter in this way even though it seems senseless for Indigenous Nations and Peoples to be characterised as attempting to 'secede' from a linguistic, metaphorical and behavioural system of domination imposed on them against their will, a system of domination to which they have not freely acceded. Scholars who engage in this inapt use of political terminology ought to be reminded that a desire by peoples who have been and are still being dominated to be freed from that ongoing and chronic predicament is not a desire for secession; it is a desire for liberation from an

56 Anghie, above n 2, 3–4.
57 United Nations Department of Economic and Social Affairs, *State of the World's Indigenous Peoples*, UN Doc ST/ESA/328 (2009).
58 Ibid.
59 Engle, above n 19, 73–99. See also Echo-Hawk, *In the Light of Justice: The Rise of Human Rights in Native America and the UN Declaration on the Rights of Indigenous Peoples* (Fulcrum, 2013) 44: 'Self-determination in the indigenous context does not include a right to succeed [sic] from states that recognize human rights, because the Declaration disclaims intent to dismember the territorial integrity or political unity of states.'

imposed system that constructs and maintains a mental, physical and trauma-inducing reality of domination on an ongoing and intergenerational basis.[60]

UN Declaration on the Rights of Indigenous ('dominated') Peoples

On 13 September 2007, the United Nations General Assembly adopted the UN *Declaration on the Rights of Indigenous Peoples*. In the years since the declaration's adoption, it has been typical to hear some Indigenous Peoples' advocates speak as if a sea change is on the horizon with regard to the treatment of the rights of Indigenous Peoples in international law. Indigenous Peoples' representatives who express this view seemed not to notice that the newly adopted UN declaration is not designed to end the relationship of domination between polities called 'states' and peoples termed 'Indigenous'. Nor does that document fundamentally change the manner in which that dominating relationship is written about in the idea system of international law. In the international arena and in the adopted text of the UN declaration, for example, the word 'States' is still spelled with the honorific capital 'S', and the word 'indigenous' is still spelled with a symbolically subordinate *lower* case 'i'.[61] This is both symbolic and constitutive of the domination system of 'the state' and of 'states'.[62]

Given the adoption of the UN *Declaration on the Rights of Indigenous Peoples* in 2007, it is common to hear the claim put forth that the idea system and

60 Eduardo Duran, Bonnie Duran, Maria Yellow Horse-Brave Heart and Susan Yellow Horse-Davis, 'Healing the American Indian Soul Wound' in Russell Thornton (ed), *Studying Native America: Problems and Prospects* (University of Wisconsin Press, 1998) 60.

61 US Statement to UN ECOSOC, E/CN4/Gr1987/7/Add12 (30 September 1987). The Office of Legal Affairs of the US Department of State's upper case/lower case stylistic technique resulted in the State Department violating the ordinary rule for capitalising the first letter of a proper noun, such as 'Indian'. In a response to complaints by the traditional Hopi Kikmongwis to the United Nations, the State Department wrote in an official US intervention about Felix Cohen 'considered by many to be the preeminent authority on federal indian [sic] law, in his Handbook of Federal Indian Law …'.

62 Ibid:

> It is clear that the concept of tribal sovereignty has been recognized by the United States Supreme Court as derived from international law subject to modification by the Congress of the United States … [T]reaties and statutes of Congress have been looked to by the [US] courts as limitations upon original tribal powers, or, at most evidence of recognition of such powers, rather than as the direct source of tribal powers. This is but an application of the general principle that 'it is only by positive enactments, even in the case of conquered [dominated] and subdued [dominated] nations, that their laws are changed by the conqueror [dominator]'.

standards of international law are developing new norms.[63] Evidence of this supposed development of international law standards pursuant to the UN *Declaration on the Rights of Indigenous Peoples* is said to be found in the fact that peoples called 'Indigenous' are deemed to have the right *to aspire towards* the attainment of certain rights *beneath* or 'under' state sovereignty (domination).[64] State governments seem to be saying to Indigenous Peoples, 'So long as you agree not to tamper with or contest the state's claim of sovereignty (domination) over your existence, you may aspire to one day, in some distant and indeterminate future, achieve certain rights *under* and *within* the system of state sovereignty (domination).'

How Indigenous Peoples' advocates will be able eventually to persuade state actors to recognise Indigenous Peoples as possessing such rights is not at all clear. However, Indigenous Peoples are considered by states to be more than welcome to make the effort *eventually* to achieve certain *'rights' under* state sovereignty (domination), just so long as they do not aspire to free themselves from the imposition of state sovereignty (domination).

Importantly, the UN *Declaration on the Rights of Indigenous Peoples* has resulted in no call for the United Nations' working definitions of the term 'Indigenous Peoples' to be refashioned. The idea of Indigenous Peoples is still being defined in the exact same manner after the adoption of the UN declaration as it had been before its adoption by the United Nations General Assembly. The relationship of domination between states and Indigenous Peoples is not explicitly addressed in the UN *Declaration on the Rights of Indigenous Peoples* let alone modified or ended by that document's adoption.

During the decades that Indigenous Peoples' advocates had been working towards reform in the international arena and in international law relative to Indigenous Peoples, the word 'domination' was only occasionally mentioned in relation to Indigenous Peoples' issues. On closer reflection, this seems odd given the specific working definition of peoples termed 'Indigenous' in international law. One definition was published in a 1986 report by the UN Special Rapporteur on the Problem of Discrimination Against Indigenous Populations. It includes tell-tale phrases that identify the pattern of domination: 'pre-invasion', 'pre-colonial', 'distinct from other sectors of the societies now prevailing' and 'non-dominant sectors of society'.[65] Oddly, the above phrases are not associated with the idea of domination in the mind of the average English language speaker. It is only upon reflection that the dominating nature of words such as 'invasion', 'colonial' and 'prevailing' become noticeable.

63 Echo-Hawk, above n 59, 39–40.

64 Ibid: 'indigenous self-determination runs parallel to state sovereignty [domination] and takes place within [ie "under"] the body of the state'.

65 Martinez Cobo, above n 52, para 379.

An aspiration to end the domination

As mentioned above, the UN *Declaration on the Rights of Indigenous Peoples* is designed to accord 'dominated' ('Indigenous') peoples the right *to aspire* to achieve certain rights *under, beneath, or within a state-run system of domination*. An important feature of that system is called 'the territorial integrity of the states'. Article 46 of the UN *Declaration on the Rights of Indigenous Peoples* specifically declares that peoples called 'Indigenous' may not question the existence of states, or their territorial integrity. This gives the impression that dominated peoples may not question or challenge the political existence and polity of their dominators. From the viewpoint of the international system of states, Article 46 seems to suggest that nations and peoples termed 'Indigenous' may not question the territorial domination that the states have claimed over the lands and territories of the original nations of the continent based on a claimed right of Christian discovery and domination.[66]

Most scholars of international law never focus on the domination of Indigenous Nations and Peoples by states, and thus never advocate ending such domination. They seem to suggest it is possible to maintain the domination system in relation to Indigenous Nations and Peoples, and at the same time eventually achieve a 'peaceful' coexistence between peoples called 'Indigenous' and states of domination.[67] Such scholars seem to envision a future in which the nations and peoples being dominated by states will have learned to 'reconcile' themselves to living *within* and *under* a given 'state of domination'.[68] At least one Indigenous scholar has said that the UN *Declaration on the Rights of Indigenous Peoples* is intended to 'incorporate Indigenous peoples into the body politic' of the state.[69] This view seems to coincide with the findings of the Truth and Reconciliation Commission of Canada.[70] From the viewpoint of states, efforts must be made to keep dominated peoples pacified and conciliated through a process of 'reconciliation' so they will not fundamentally question or challenge the state system of domination, or the violent basis upon which that system came into existence to begin with, as illustrated by the quotation from Oppenheimer above.[71]

The UN *Declaration on the Rights of Indigenous Peoples* is being treated by some scholars as a framework for achieving peaceful equilibrium between states of domination and peoples called 'Indigenous' without 'the domination

66 Echo-Hawk, above n 59, 45; Steven Newcomb, 'The Evidence of Christian Nationalism in Federal Indian Law: The Doctrine of Discovery, Johnson v M'Intosh and Plenary Power' (1993) 20 *New York University Review of Law and Social Change* 303.
67 Echo-Hawk, above n 59, 99–132.
68 Ibid.
69 Ibid 125–6.
70 Truth and Reconciliation Commission of Canada, *Honoring the Truth, Reconciling the Future* (2015) <http://www.trc.ca/websites/trcinstitution/index.php?p=890>.
71 Nock, above n 7.

of Indigenous Peoples by the state' ever becoming a focus of attention. The document itself is being characterised as 'aspirational' in keeping with the view that states are willing to take note of the fact that peoples called 'Indigenous' have certain aspirations for a more desirable future. No surprise there.

Neither state actors nor most representatives of Indigenous Peoples seem to be arguing that the UN declaration provides a means for liberating Indigenous Peoples from a given state of domination. Article 46 of the declaration, which refers to 'the territorial integrity of states', was apparently written from the statist viewpoint that the UN *Declaration on the Rights of Indigenous Peoples* may not be used by peoples called 'Indigenous' in an effort to challenge the state's system of domination exerted over and used against them.

Imperial states and original nations

The system of domination expressed through the language of international law makes it seem imprecise, from the viewpoint of states, to apply the term 'nation' to peoples termed 'Indigenous' in the international context, and in the general parlance of 'states'. A principle of international law which 'states' never apply to peoples termed 'Indigenous' was expressed by Chief Justice John Marshall in the US Supreme Court decision *Church v Hubbart* in 1804: 'The authority of a nation within its own territory is absolute and exclusive.'[72] Applying this principle of absolute and exclusive territorial authority to original Native Nations, as against the United States for example, would have very likely created a permanent barrier to the domination–subordination system of the United States in relation to original nations and in relation to the lands, territories and resources of original nations.

Article 46 of the UN *Declaration on the Rights of Indigenous Peoples* is predicated on this principle of exclusive 'state' territoriality. Article 46(1) of the UN declaration says that nothing is to be 'construed as authorizing or encouraging any action which would dismember or impair, totally or in part, the territorial integrity, or political unity of sovereign and independent States'. When we consider the point that 'sovereignty' is 'an unjust form of political domination that limits human freedom',[73] and Oppenheimer's point about 'the state' resulting from the systematising of domination by one nation or people over another,[74] as well as Weber's point that 'the state' is the result of 'the relation of men dominating men',[75] a question arises: will Article 46 of the UN declaration be interpreted by 'states' to mean that Indigenous Nations and Peoples may not focus on 'states', or on a particular state, as systems of domination? Will Article 46 be interpreted by states as meaning

72 *Church v Hubbart* 6 US 187, 234 (1804).
73 Havercroft, above n 30.
74 Nock, above n 7.
75 Weber, above n 18.

that Indigenous Nations and Peoples may not directly challenge the domination of Indigenous Peoples by states because such a challenge might threaten 'to impair the territorial integrity' and 'political unity' of 'states' of domination?

The fourth preambular paragraph of the UN *Declaration on the Rights of Indigenous Peoples* affirms 'that all doctrines, policies and practices based on or advocating superiority of peoples or individuals on the basis of national origin or racial, religious, ethnic or cultural differences are racist, scientifically false, legally invalid, morally condemnable and socially unjust'. US federal Indian law and policy are predicated on US claims of 'ascendancy'[76] (domination) and superiority on the basis of national origin, as well as on the basis of 'racial, religious, ethnic and cultural differences' between the society of the United States and the original nations of the continent. Justice Joseph Story demonstrated the religious argument the United States has used as a basis for claiming a right of domination over the original nations of the continent, and for refusing to apply the above-mentioned doctrine of territorial exclusivity to any original nation.[77]

Story said of the original nations: 'As infidels, heathens, and savages, they were not allowed to possess the prerogatives belonging to absolute, sovereign, and independent nations.'[78] This matches Francisco de Vitoria's conclusion mentioned above that Indians, as 'pagans', were not 'sovereign'.[79] Major thinkers of western Christendom regarded non-Christians as being disqualified from having a right to be deemed fully 'sovereign' and to remain independent of Christian European domination.

When Chief Justice John Marshall for a unanimous US Supreme Court said the United States had adopted the principle of 'Christian people' applying the 'right of discovery' to lands that were inhabited by 'heathens',[80] he, the Supreme Court as a whole and the United States government thereby applied a biblical context and form of reasoning against our nations and peoples. This biblical pattern of reasoning about non-Christian 'heathen' nations only having a right of 'occupancy' and a 'diminished' independence became an established precedent of the US Supreme Court as result of the *Johnson v M'Intosh* ruling,[81] which the United States first began imposing on our nations 194 years ago, as of 2017.

The conceptual system of US domination, and Native ('Indigenous') Nation subordination on the basis of Christian and biblical patterns of thought, is designed to prevent nations termed 'Indigenous' from being able effectively to exclude the United States from the territory of any original nation, while at

76 *Johnson & Graham's Lessee v M'Intosh* 21 US (8 Wheat) 543, 573 (1823).
77 Joseph Story, *Commentary on the Constitution of the United States Volume III* (Hilliard, Gray and Company, 1833) 5 § 1.
78 Ibid 135 § 152.
79 See Anghie, above n 2.
80 *Johnson v M'Intosh* 21 US (8 Wheat) 543, 576–7 (1823).
81 Ibid.

the same time making certain that every such 'Indigenous' Nation is regarded as 'subject to' the political and legal jurisdiction of the United States. The fact that religious categorisations serve as the starting point of this system of ideas has been well concealed for nearly two hundred years, in part because legal scholars replace 'Christian' with the word 'European'.[82] The United States claims to possess an absolute territorial exclusivity, based on international law, while arguing, based on international law, that Indian 'Nations' ('tribes') do not possess the prerogative of such territorial exclusivity.

On what basis does the United States assume, for example, that the original nations of the North American continent do not possess territorial integrity and territorial exclusivity? Because, centuries ago, the Christian nations of Europe claimed to have 'discovered' non-Christian Indian lands.[83] Polities called 'states', such as the United States and Canada, demand acknowledgement of what they presuppose to be their 'territorial integrity', but they reject out of hand the idea that territorial integrity and exclusivity are characteristics of original nations and peoples termed 'Indigenous'. Both the United States and Canada are to this day still using the metaphors of the ancient Christian law of nations against nations termed 'Indigenous'. They are doing so as a covert means of maintaining a 'state' system of domination over and against such nations, which the United States typically calls 'tribes'.

States such as the United States and Canada do, however, use the word 'nation' politically to communicate the sense of a 'domestic' and 'subordinate' nation, which is metaphorically characterised as existing 'within' or 'internal to' the territorial 'homeland' of a given state, such as the United States or Canada.[84] On that basis, Indigenous Nations that were originally existing free from domination are now deemed 'domesticated' 'nations' that are considered *subject to*[85] the domination system ('sovereignty') of a given 'state'. Because internationally recognised 'states' typically apply the term 'nation' to themselves, the term 'nation' is a cardinal feature of the lexicon of international law and of the lexicon used at the United Nations as applied to 'states'.[86] Indeed,

82 Robert Williams, *The American Indian in Western Legal Thought* (Oxford University Press, 1990) 317.

83 Edward Dumbauld, 'John Marshall and the Law of Nations' (1955) 104 *University of Pennsylvania Law Review* 38.

84 See, eg, Susana Mas, 'Trudeau Lays Out Plan for New Relationship with Indigenous People', *CBC News*, 8 December 2015 <http://www.cbc.ca/news/politics/justin-trudeau-afn-indigenous-aboriginal-people-1.3354747>. Notice that the Canadian Broadcasting Corporation editors declined to place an 's' on the word 'people', thereby avoiding the idea that Canada as a country is dealing with distinct nations termed 'peoples' with an 's'.

85 *The Compact Edition of the Oxford English Dictionary* (Oxford University Press, 1971): 'To make (persons, a nation or country) subject *to* a conquering or sovereign power; to bring into subjection *to* a superior; to subjugate [ie to dominate].'

86 Echo-Hawk, above n 59, 4–6, characterises 'Indigenous Peoples' as 'beyond the reach' of certain rights, and further says that 'Indigenous Peoples' have been not

'inter' and 'national' are obviously combined to indicate relations existing between nations, meaning between states. This terminology is considered to have nothing to do, however, with 'Indigenous' Nations which are regarded as falling into a domestic category of 'interior' or 'internal' affairs of the state. The UN *Declaration on the Rights of Indigenous Peoples* was drafted in keeping with this framework.

In typical writings about international law and the UN *Declaration on the Rights of Indigenous Peoples*, the words 'nation' and 'national' seem reserved solely as a synonym for polities called states.[87] In the official language of the United Nations, the terms 'nation' and 'national' are *never* used as an international law category for peoples called 'Indigenous'. Few if any non-Indigenous scholars who write about international law *ever* seem to express the view that peoples termed 'Indigenous' are rightfully distinct *nations* with a fundamental right to exist and live free and independent of some state's domination ('sovereignty'). Even the word 'peoples' (with an 's') is only applied grudgingly and cautiously,[88] if at all, to peoples called 'Indigenous' in the international arena. The reason is simple. Adding the letter 's' to 'people' denotes many entire peoples, which suggests that they are also *nations* and therefore potentially in competition with the dominationhood claimed by states in relation to a specific territory.

Does the domination of Indigenous Peoples by states violate their rights?

Question: Do Indigenous Nations and Peoples have the right to live free from the dominationhood of states? Dealing with this question requires that we focus on the category 'the rights of Indigenous Peoples'. If we think of that category as a list of rights which peoples called 'Indigenous' are considered to possess, another question arises: does that list of rights include 'the right to live free from domination by states'? If, on the basis of some rationale, one answers, 'yes it does', then it stands to reason that the current domination of the existence of 'Indigenous' Peoples by states is in violation of their right to

distinct nations in their own right, but 'vulnerable minorities captive to hostile or indifferent domestic forums in their own nations'. Thus, strangely, in a most colonising manner, Echo-Hawk has characterised the governments of 'states of domination' as being the Indigenous Peoples' 'own nations', rather than their own original nations being their own nations.

87 Asia-Pacific Forum of National Human Rights Institutions and UN Office of the High Commissioner for Human Rights, *The United Nations Declaration on the Rights of Indigenous Peoples: A Manual for National Human Rights Institutions* (2013) v. This extensive report uses the word 'national' only with regard to 'states', as in, eg, 'National Human Rights Institutions' and 'national implementation of the Declaration'. It only focuses on 'states' as 'nations', and *never* refers to 'Indigenous Peoples' as nations.

88 US State Department, above n 14.

live free from state domination. If, however, on the basis of some other rationale, one answers 'no, Indigenous Peoples do not have the right to live free from the domination of the state', then it follows that 'Indigenous' Peoples are presumed to be obligated, on the basis of some rationale, to continue living under the domination of a given state.[89] In this scenario, it is a sensible task to identify the rationale being used by states to presume that peoples termed 'Indigenous' are obligated to continue living under state domination.

Such a rationale for the domination of the original nations of the continent was expressed by US Supreme Court Justice Joseph Story in the early nineteenth century based on the *Johnson v M'Intosh* ruling: (1) the ancestors of the original nations were not Christians when the Christian nations of Europe invasively arrived, and (2) the Christians would not allow the original nations to possess the prerogatives belonging to absolute, sovereign and independent nations. Why is this? The answer is simple. The Christians used the power of the human mind to frame the original nations of the continent metaphorically as 'infidels, heathens and savages'. The Christians deemed the original nations to be disqualified from the category of 'absolute, sovereign and independent nations' based on Christian mental projections onto the original nations. Domination has a powerful mental dimension.

Story's rationale brings to mind another related point: The *domination of Indigenous Peoples by states* cannot be brought into focus without using the specific phrase 'the domination of Indigenous Peoples by states'. *Without that specific wording*, it is not possible for this issue to become a feature of our conscious awareness. Alternatively, *armed with that specific wording*, it then becomes possible to ask a question that heretofore has not yet been asked and addressed: 'Does the domination of Indigenous Peoples by states violate the rights of Indigenous Peoples?'[90] This leads to a related question: 'Does the list of rights for peoples termed "Indigenous" include the right to live free from domination by states, generally, or by any given state?' Again, whether we say 'yes, the rights of peoples termed "Indigenous" does include a right to live

89 Henry Wheaton, *Elements of International Law* (B Fellowes, 1836) 220: 'the constant and approved practice of nations shows that, by whatever name it be called, the uninterrupted possession of territory, or other property, for a certain length of time, by one State, excludes that claim of every other'. Logic would suggest that the long and uninterrupted possession of territory by the original *nations* of the North American continent and American hemisphere would exclude the claims of a right of domination asserted by all other invading and colonising nations. However, the principle of prescription expressed by Wheaton was deemed by the powers of Christendom only to apply to Christian nations, and was therefore deemed to be inapplicable to 'heathen', 'infidel' or 'barbarous' nations. See BA Hinsdale, 'Right of Discovery' (1888) 2(3) *Ohio Archæological and Historical Quarterly* 363.

90 This way of framing the matter presupposes that 'the domination of Indigenous Peoples by states' does indeed exist. Some might say that this presupposition is being presented here as a taken-for-granted truth without proof.

free from domination by states', or if we say that the list does not include such a right, it is necessary to identify the rationale being used to answer the question. Since the issue is never typically raised, the rationale for either answer is not readily identified.

Given the above ideas, another question arises that has not yet been posed in international law literature with regard to the UN *Declaration on the Rights of Indigenous Peoples*: is it possible for the 'right' of Indigenous Peoples to live free from domination to be realised or 'respected' while those peoples are still existing under the pattern and system of domination of a given state? Because international law scholars have not specifically focused on domination as a problem to be addressed with regard to Indigenous Peoples, there has been no call by those scholars to regard *the domination of Indigenous Peoples by states* as a violation of the right of Indigenous Peoples. It would seem that state actors have been silently making the assumption that states have an unquestionable right to maintain domination over 'Indigenous' Peoples. Then, again, it is possible that by pretending such domination does not even exist states have treated the domination of 'Indigenous' Peoples as something that does not need to be addressed.

Conclusion

Domination and dehumanisation are useful categories of analysis in the field of international law with regard to dominated nations and peoples termed 'Indigenous'. If our goal is the emancipation of original *nations* and peoples from systems of domination, then it seems certain that the UN *Declaration on the Rights of Indigenous Peoples* is *not* the document that will enable us to accomplish this aim. This is especially true given Article 46 of the declaration, and a statist interpretation of that document designed to maintain the reign of 'states of domination' over original nations.[91] What is worse is the number

91 Eg on 16 October 2006, the governments of Australia, New Zealand and the United States made a joint intervention at the United Nations opposing the UN declaration. Among other points made in the document, we find:

> There is no definition of 'indigenous peoples' in the text. The lack of definition or scope of application within the Chair's text means that separatist or minority groups, with traditional connection to the territory where they live – in all regions of the globe – could seek to exploit this declaration to claim the right to self-determination, including exclusive control of their territorial resources. And this text would allow them to wrongly claim international endorsement for exercising such rights.

'Statement by NZ Ambassador Rosemary Banks on Behalf of Australia, New Zealand and the United States on the Declaration on the Rights of the Indigenous Peoples' (USUN Press Release No 294(06), 16 October 2006) 2. (This document is on file with the author.)

of Indigenous Peoples' representatives who insist on interpreting the UN *Declaration on the Rights of Indigenous Peoples* in a manner that only serves to reinforce and maintain existing patterns of state domination, while altogether ignoring the need to call for an end to the domination of Indigenous Peoples by states.

Chapter 3

The 'natural' law of nations: society and the exclusion of First Nations as subjects of international law

Marcelle Burns

Introduction

'Society' has been identified as a foundational concept in the development of international law, defining both state sovereignty and membership of the family of nations.[1] Antony Anghie, for example, argues that society was a central concept shaping the emergent Eurocentric international legal order as it shifted from its foundations in natural law based on transcendental and universal values towards a scientific, positivist framework.[2] The Eurocentric construct of society, and the way it shaped the fundamental elements of (public) international law, had serious consequences for First Nations. As Anghie argues, nineteenth-century positivist international law devised a number of strategies to exclude non-Europeans from the emerging international legal order: first, by creating a distinction between so-called civilised and uncivilised peoples; and, second, by only admitting peoples who met European standards of civilisation as members of 'international society', and thereby linking international legal status to a 'cultural distinction'.[3] So, for Anghie, sovereignty and international law were constituted through colonialism, in ways that excluded non-European peoples as subjects of international law.[4] This characterisation does not, however, fully explain the significance of society, nor how it shaped sovereignty and sovereign power.

Anghie does not identify precisely *how* the positivists put the concept of society to such use, nor does he examine the crucial link between the nineteenth-century positivists' preoccupation with society and the work of their natural law predecessors. This chapter addresses these concerns to argue that the natural law origins of European international law, and in particular the work of Francisco de Vitoria (1483–1546) and Hugo Grotius (1583–1645), was grounded upon the concept of society in ways which constructed First Nations peoples, as

1 Antony Anghie, *Imperialism, Sovereignty and the Making of International Law* (Cambridge University Press, 2004) 59.
2 Ibid 48.
3 Ibid 57–8.
4 Ibid 38.

DOI: 10.4324/9781315628318-4

Irene Watson says, as 'special objects' within the emerging Eurocentric international legal order.[5]

Leading texts on Indigenous Peoples and international law tend to focus primarily on Vitoria, and pay little attention to how Grotius also shaped the position of Indigenous Peoples within the nasceant colonial regime.[6] First, they critique the Grotian theory of just wars for the support it provided to colonialism,[7] while giving very little attention to Grotius' vision of sovereignty and sovereign power, which operates to exclude Indigenous Peoples as fully fledged subjects of international law. Second, Grotius is also noted for his theory of property, which according to Robert Williams Jr is constructed in contrast to a mythical 'primitive hunter-gatherer state'.[8] While James (Sakej) Youngblood Henderson also credits Grotius with articulating the first comprehensive theory of international law,[9] he does not explore his work on society and the scope and nature of sovereign power.

In this chapter I aim to show that the concept of society was central to the formative natural law theories of international law, influencing who was deemed to hold sovereign power, the rights flowing from sovereignty, and as a consequence the way that Indigenous Peoples were positioned within the developing Eurocentric international legal order. I will do so by examining the work of Francisco de Vitoria, and also how Hugo Grotius extended Vitoria's work in important ways. I will show how society functions within their work to create a law of nations which was constructed to support European colonial expansion and the domination of Indigenous people, which informed the positivist tradition of international law that was to follow.

The natural law context of the 'law of nations'

Francisco de Vitoria and Hugo Grotius are widely acknowledged as two of the founding scholars of 'modern international law', as it is understood within the

5 Irene Watson, 'Aboriginal(ising) International Law and Other Centres of Power' (2011) 20(3) *Griffith Law Review* 619, 631.
6 See generally Robert A Williams Jr, *The American Indian in Western Legal Thought: The Discourses of Conquest* (Oxford University Press, 1990) 93–108; S James Anaya, *Indigenous Peoples in International Law* (Oxford University Press, 2nd edn, 2004) 19; Anghie, above n 1, 19–30; and critique by Yasuaki Onuma, 'Multi-civilizational International Law in the Multi-centric 21st Century World: Transformation of West-Centric to Global International Law as Seen From a Trans-civilizational Perspective' in Peter Haggenmacher, Pierre-Marie Dupay and Vincent Chetail (eds), *The Roots of International Law* (Martinus Nijhoff Publishers, 2014) 599, 629.
7 Williams, ibid; Anaya, ibid; Anghie, above n 1, 19–30.
8 Robert A Williams Jr, *Savage Anxieties: The Invention of Western Civilization* (Palgrave Macmillan, 2012) 203.
9 James (Sakej) Youngblood Henderson, 'The Context of the State of Nature' in Marie Battiste (ed), *Reclaiming Indigenous Voice and Vision* (University of British Colombia Press, 2000) 11, 15.

European context.[10] While the extent of their respective influence has been questioned, it is beyond the scope of this chapter to debate these issues.[11] I focus on these two scholars because they both shared concerns, albeit for very different reasons, about the morality and legality of the conduct of Christian European nations with respect to non-Christian peoples, and because they sought to address some disturbing questions arising from the European colonial project. Their works emerged at a time when medieval Europe was undergoing major transformation with the decline of religious authority, and a shift towards secular forms of power.[12] Ironically, this shift coincided with an intense period of European colonial expansion under the purported authority of a series of 'papal bulls' which granted Spain and Portugal rights to partition the world.[13] However, competition between aspiring European colonial powers, together with Protestant scepticism at the papal authority underpinning Spanish and Portuguese claims, created the need to develop a secularised rationale for colonisation that no longer relied upon religious justifications.[14]

Francisco de Vitoria (Vitoria), a Spanish Dominican theologian, wrote his major reflections 'On the American Indians' (1539) and 'On the Law of War' (1539) some forty years after Christopher Columbus' voyage of 'discovery' to the Americas, and in response to reports of 'bloody massacres and innocent individuals pillaged of their possessions and dominions' which raised 'grounds

10 On Grotius' significance as a founder of international law, see Arthur Nussbaum, *A Concise History of the Law of Nations* (Macmillan, 5th edn, 1964) 113; Yasuaki Onuma, *A Normative Approach to War: Peace, War and Justice in Hugo Grotius* (Clarendon Press, 1993) 1; Benedict Kingsbury and Adam Roberts, 'Introduction: Grotian Thought in International Relations' in Hedley Bull, Benedict Kingsbury and Adam Roberts (eds), *Hugo Grotius and International Relations* (Clarendon Press, 1992) 1, 3. Peter Haggenmacher argues that Grotius' primary concern was to articulate a theory of just war with respect to extra-national relations, rather than a theory of international law. Peter Haggenmacher, 'On Assessing the Grotian Heritage' in TMC Asser Instituut, *International Law and the Grotian Heritage* (TMC Asser Instituut, 1985) 150, 154. On Vitoria's primary influence, see Anghie, above n 1, 13–14; Williams, *American Indian*, above n 6, 98; Christopher R Rossi, *Broken Chain of Being: James Brown Scott and the Origins of Modern International Law* (Kluwer Law International, 1998) 5. See generally James Brown Scott, *The Spanish Origins of International Law: Francisco de Vitoria and His Law of Nations* (Clarendon Press, 1934).

11 See generally Yasuaki Onuma, 'When Was the Law of International Society Born? An Inquiry of the History of International Law from an Intercivilizational Perspective' (2000) 2 *Journal of the History of International Law* 1, 5; Rossi, ibid 5. Rossi notes that Scott was an ardent advocate of de Vitoria as the father of international law, a position which was strongly refuted by Nussbaum, ibid 296–306.

12 Onuma, *Normative Approach*, above n 10, 8.

13 Ibid 271–2.

14 Ibid 8.

for doubting the justice of what had been done'.[15] 'On the American Indians' questions the lawfulness of various claims to titles by the Spanish (including the Christian doctrine of discovery)[16] and also sets out what Vitoria regards as a number of 'just claims' to title over Indian lands. 'On the Law of War' articulates Vitoria's theory of 'just war' in which he argues that the 'possession and occupation of these [Indian] lands is *most* defensible in terms of the laws of war'.[17] However, it is Vitoria's lesser-known essay 'On Civil Power' (1528)[18] which establishes his vision of sovereignty that underpins his latter works and, importantly, defines sovereign power by invoking the concept of society. This essay has been described by Anthony Pagden as 'a defence of the Castilian monarchy, and of monarchies in general, as the most perfect form of political community'.[19]

In contrast, Hugo Grotius, a Dutch lawyer and jurist, started his treatise *The Law of War and Peace* (1625) as part of a defence of the actions of the Dutch East India Company, which captured a Portuguese vessel in the waters off the East Indies, and in doing so challenged Portugal's claim to exclusive trading rights in the area based on the authority of the papal bulls.[20] This work was animated by a concern that:

> Throughout the Christian world I have observed a lack of restraint in relation to war, such as even barbarous races should be ashamed of; I observed that men rush to arms for slight causes, or no cause at all, and that when arms have once been taken up there is no longer any respect for law, divine or human; it is as if, in accordance with a general decree, frenzy had openly been let loose for the committing of all crimes.[21]

While Vitoria and Grotius had very different motivations, there was substantial overlap in their work. First, they both emphatically rejected the Christian doctrine of discovery as legitimate grounds for colonial acquisition of Indigenous Peoples' lands.[22] Grotius makes the point (with reference to Vitoria) stating:

15 Francisco de Vitoria, 'On the American Indians' in Anthony Pagden and Jeremy Lawrance (eds), *Vitoria: Political Writings* (Cambridge University Press, 1991) 231, 238.
16 Ibid.
17 Francisco de Vitoria, 'On the Law of War' in Anthony Pagden and Jeremy Lawrance (eds), *Vitoria: Political Writings* (Cambridge University Press, 1991) 293, 295 (emphasis added).
18 Francisco de Vitoria, 'On Civil Power' in Anthony Pagden and Jeremy Lawrance (eds), *Vitoria: Political Writings* (Cambridge University Press, 1991) 1.
19 Anthony Pagden, 'Introduction' in Anthony Pagden and Jeremy Lawrance (eds), *Vitoria: Political Writings* (Cambridge University Press, 1991) xiii, xviii.
20 Hugo Grotius, *The Law of War and Peace* (Francis W Kelsey trans, Bobbs-Merrill, 1925) xiv–xv.
21 Ibid 20.
22 Vitoria, 'On the American Indians', above n 15, 265; Grotius, ibid bk 2, 22.9.

> [It is] Equally shameless ... to claim for oneself by right of discovery what is held by another, even though the occupant may be wicked, may hold wrong views about God, or may be dull of wit. For discovery applies to those things which belong to no one.[23]

For Vitoria, claims to title based on discovery were unjust because under his law of nations discovery could only apply to unoccupied lands, and as the lands in question clearly had an owner, such claims could not be allowed 'any more than it would if they had discovered us'.[24] Vitoria concedes, however, that titles based on discovery may have 'some validity' when considered in conjunction with another claim, leaving open the possibility of acquiring title over Indian lands on a different basis.[25]

Second, both Vitoria and Grotius also viewed as unjust wars or titles based on the grounds of refusing to accept Christianity, because 'unbelief' was not sufficient grounds to claim title or wage war.[26] As a consequence, they endeavoured to articulate a secularised law of nations, based on natural law, which for Grotius was determined from the precepts of divine or Christian law, as dictated by 'right reason', which was perceived as 'manifest and self-evident', and therefore immutable and universal.[27] Vitoria's natural law was (using Aquinas' definition) 'the participation in the eternal law by rational creatures', based on 'reason and enlightenment' as found in 'the general consensus of men'.[28] However, what constitutes 'right reason' and 'the general consensus of men' for Vitoria and Grotius is determined with reference to a particularly Eurocentric and Christian canon of philosophical thought.[29]

Third, both Vitoria and Grotius place great significance on 'rationality' as a precondition for recognition of sovereign power and consequent rights. Vitoria argued that 'barbarians' were rational beings, evidenced by the fact that 'they have some order in their affairs: they have properly organized cities, proper marriages, magistrates and overlords, laws, industries, and commerce, all of which require the use of reason'.[30] As rational beings they also possessed 'true dominion, both public and private',[31] and also could be regarded as 'legitimate' sovereigns.[32] Indeed, Vitoria's characterisation of Indigenous people as rational beings has been noted as one of his most significant

23 Grotius, ibid.
24 Vitoria, 'On the American Indians', above n 15, 264–5.
25 Ibid 265.
26 Ibid 270; Grotius, above n 20, bk 2, 40.8.
27 Grotius, above n 20, xl–xli.
28 Pagden, above n 19, xiv.
29 Williams, *American Indian*, above n 6, 101; Onuma, *Normative Approach*, above n 10, 377.
30 Vitoria, 'On the American Indians', above n 15, 250.
31 Ibid 251.
32 Vitoria, 'On Civil Power', above n 18, 17–18.

contributions to international legal discourse.[33] However, Vitoria also regarded barbarians as 'foolish and slow-witted', which he argued may provide grounds for 'subjecting the Indians' in other ways.[34] Grotius also observes (with reference to Vitoria) that 'the view seems defensible that, *if there exist any peoples wholly deprived of the use of reason, these cannot have ownership*, but merely for charity's sake there is due to them what is necessary to maintain life'.[35] As Williams and Anghie note, for Vitoria the natural law foundations and purported universality of this emerging law of nations made it binding on *all peoples*, with the attribution of reason to First Peoples also bringing them within its jurisdiction.[36] The purported universality of the law of nations also extended to Indigenous Peoples, who were included within its framework, yet also excluded and subjugated by it.[37] The consequences for First Peoples of being perceived as irrational will be explored further below.

Yet despite its apparent humanitarian and egalitarian foundations,[38] the naturalist law of nations developed by Vitoria and Grotius was also problematic because it privileged European forms of social, legal and political organisation, and presented them not only as 'exemplary', but as universal.[39] The consequence for Indigenous Peoples was that failure to conform to 'universal' standards based on European Christian norms was viewed as irrational, providing grounds for denying Indigenous Peoples 'rights' to property and sovereignty. The law of nations, as an emerging body of *legal disciplinary knowledge*, constructed a subjugated position for Indigenous Peoples within the Eurocentric international legal order. As I will argue, the concept of society was central to this construction, being fundamental to how the modern doctrine of sovereignty was conceived, and the scope and nature of sovereign power.

The Eurocentric concept of society

Underlying Vitoria and Grotius' vision of sovereignty and sovereign power was a concept of society. According to Vitoria, *societates*, meaning a partnership, is the natural form of human association, arising from the distinct human characteristics of speech and reason, and the need for humans to live together to fulfil their need for food, shelter, safety and security.[40] For Vitoria,

33 Williams, *American Indian*, above n 6, 99.
34 Vitoria, 'On the American Indians', above n 15, 251.
35 Grotius, above n 20, bk 2, 22.10.
36 Williams, *American Indian*, above n 6, 100; Anghie, above n 1, 23.
37 Peter Fitzpatrick, *Modernism and the Grounds of Law* (Cambridge University Press, 2001) 173.
38 Seth Gordon, 'Indigenous Rights in Modern International Law from a Critical Third World Perspective' (2006–07) 31(2) *American Indian Law Review* 401, 402.
39 Fitzpatrick, above n 37, 121.
40 Vitoria, 'On Civil Power', above n 18, 6–9.

people enter partnerships due to the necessity of helping to bear each other's burdens, and so according to this logic 'a civil partnership (*ciuillis societas*) is the one which most aptly fulfils men's needs'.[41] As a creature of necessity, society is not a human invention, but is founded in natural law, with the consequence that the very 'purpose and utility of public power are identical to those of *human society* itself'.[42] Indeed, Vitoria argues (with reference to Aristotle), that men are 'impelled by nature to *seek* society', and that those who do not 'should be counted as beasts'.[43]

For Grotius, the natural desire of society arises from the particular qualities of humans, being speech and the 'faculty of knowing and acting, according to some general principles'.[44] These qualities set humans apart from other living beings, and find their deepest expression in the concept of society:

> For Man is indeed an Animal, but one of a very high Order, and that excels all the other Species of Animals much more than they differ from one another; as the many Actions proper only to Mankind sufficiently demonstrate. Now amongst the Things peculiar to Man, is his Desire of Society, that is, a certain Inclination to live with those of his own kind, not in any manner whatever, but peaceably, and in a community regulated to the best of his understanding.[45]

According to Grotius, a person's natural inclination is to live in society, not merely out of self-interest, but because a person is 'more perfect' when their actions are 'designed for the service of another'.[46] Grotius also posits that municipal law stems from the need for people to form agreements and create obligations, this being the reason why 'bodies of municipal law have arisen'.[47] Grotius argues that the 'care of maintaining society, in a manner conformable to the light of human understanding, *is the fountain of right, properly so called*', and includes respecting private property; fulfilling obligations and promises; paying restitution for harm done; and an expectation of punishment if rights are transgressed.[48] Importantly, for Grotius 'rights' are constituted both in and through society, because *the mutual recognition and protection of rights is the very essence of society itself*. Rights are determined by the use of 'reason', with anything contrary to reason being inconsistent with natural law.[49] Society, according to Vitoria and Grotius, is synonymous with public or civil power,

41 Ibid 8–9.
42 Ibid 9–10 (emphasis added).
43 Ibid 8.
44 Grotius, above n 20, vii.
45 Grotius, above n 20, vi.
46 Ibid vi.
47 Ibid 15.
48 Ibid viii.
49 Ibid ix.

and is the conceptual vessel through which rights are asserted and defended, according to 'reason'. Public power is exercised in the interests of society which both constitutes and is constituted by law.[50] In this sense, 'society' represents a distinctly Eurocentric mode of legal and political practice which assumes the guise of universality under the rubric of an all-encompassing natural law. Moreover, the concept of society and the notion of rights are further refined to exclude non-European forms of political organisation, as unworthy of sovereign status in the emerging Eurocentric international law.

Society and the nature of sovereignty

Vitoria and Grotius also express distinct preferences for certain forms of society which they believe are most suitable for exercising sovereign power. For Vitoria, it logically follows from the necessity of civil societies that 'the city (*ciutias*) is … the *most natural community*, the one which is more conformable to nature'.[51] And for Vitoria, the *perfecta communitas* is not subject to the will of another, 'a perfect community or *commonwealth* [state] is therefore one which is complete in itself; that is one that is not part of another commonwealth, but has its own laws, its own independent policy, and its own magistrates'.[52] According to Vitoria, no society is self-sufficient without 'magistrates and authorities possessing executive power'.[53] In keeping with his role as advisor to the Castilian monarchs, Vitoria argues that, 'with all the most honoured and wise peoples of earth, the monarchy is not merely equitable and just, but also of all forms of government the most excellent and convenient to the commonwealth'.[54] Here Vitoria links society, community and commonwealth (state) as being the most perfect forms of human partnership, and the monarchy as eminently suited to possessing sovereign power.

Vitoria also maintains that non-Christian peoples may be legitimate sovereigns because 'there can be no doubt at all that the heathen have legitimate rulers and masters' (based on an analogy with pre-Christian secular forms of law which did not rely on divine law for their legitimacy).[55] And although Vitoria affirms that non-Christian sovereigns shall not be deprived of their kingship or power on the grounds of 'unbelief', they may be deprived of their power, where they have 'committed *some other injustice*',[56] such as preventing

50 Fitzpatrick, above n 37, 71.
51 Vitoria, 'On Civil Power', above n 18, 9 (emphasis added).
52 Vitoria, 'On the Law of War', above n 17, 301. Williams, *American Indian*, above n 6, 116, refers to the Nys translation of Vitoria in which 'state' is substituted for 'commonwealth'.
53 Pagden, above n 19, xxii.
54 Vitoria, 'On Civil Power', above n 18, 20.
55 Ibid 17–18.
56 Ibid 18 (emphasis added).

the spread of Christianity, or for 'practising any nefarious custom or right'.[57] Vitoria also identifies another possible ground for depriving Indigenous Peoples of their title and sovereignty: the perceived mental incapacity of 'barbarians':

> these barbarians, though not totally mad … are nevertheless so close to being mad, that they are unsuited for setting up or administering a commonwealth both legitimate and ordered in *human and civil terms*. Hence they have neither appropriate laws nor magistrates fitted to the task. Indeed they are unsuited to governing their own households (*res familiaris*); hence their lack of letters, of arts and crafts (not merely liberal, but even mechanical), or systematic agriculture, of manufacture, and of many other things useful, or rather indispensable, for human use. It might be therefore argued that for their own benefit the princes of Spain might take over their administration, and set up urban officers and governors on their behalf, or even given them new masters, *as long as this could be proved to be in their interest.*[58]

Indeed, Vitoria claims there are 'scant differences between the barbarians and madmen; they are little or no more capable of governing themselves than madman, or *indeed wild beasts*'.[59] Sovereign status is therefore conditional upon conforming to Christian norms which if transgressed provide the justification for depriving non-Christian peoples of sovereign power. The potential for non-recognition also exists where Indigenous Peoples are perceived as lacking the capacity to govern according to *human and civil terms*. Here the discursive production of an exemplary European society as the paragon of political and legal organisation operates to exclude other forms of law as simply unsuited to possessing or exercising sovereign power. While Vitoria attributes to First Nations rights to sovereignty and property, these 'rights' are effectively denied to Indigenous people when they are perceived as lacking the rationality either to realise or to sustain them. Here the positing of rights is deployed, as Peter Fitzpatrick observes, to create a system of domination.[60] A perceived lack of rationality points to a failure to administer a society in civil and human terms. Thus society functions to prescribe the conditions of sovereignty and sovereign power, and operates to exclude Indigenous Peoples as fully-fledged subjects within the Eurocentric international legal order.

For Grotius 'the common subject of supreme power is the State' which he regards as 'a *perfect society of men*'.[61] The state constitutes 'An association in

57 Vitoria, 'On the American Indians', above n 15, 284–8.
58 Ibid 290. Williams, *American Indian*, above n 6, 104 and 114 refers to the Nys translation which uses the term 'non-intelligence' rather than 'mad'.
59 Vitoria, ibid 290–1 (emphasis added).
60 Fitzpatrick, above n 37, 217.
61 Grotius, above n 20, bk 1, 3.7 (emphasis added).

which many fathers of families unite into a single person and the state gives the greatest right to the corporate body over its members. This in fact is the most *perfect society*.'[62] Sovereign power is indivisible, being 'not subject to the legal control of another'.[63] According to Grotius, sovereignty is also evidenced by certain types of legal institutions and processes, for example 'laws, courts, and public officials',[64] and the existence of 'tribunals and the other agencies' through which citizens and foreigners alike may *obtain their rights*.[65] While Grotius affirms that the 'common subject' of sovereignty is the state, sovereignty may be exercised in different ways: by a government of the people, a constitutional government, or by individuals with supreme power.[66]

Vitoria's qualified acceptance of Indigenous sovereignty is, however, radically subverted by Grotius whose vision of sovereignty explicitly privileges and sanctions imperialism. It excludes from sovereignty 'peoples who have *passed under the sway of another people*, such as the peoples of the Roman provinces'.[67] Thus Grotius regards colonised peoples as lesser subjects of the law of nations, stating: 'For such peoples are not in themselves a state, in the sense in which we are now using the term, but the inferior members of a great state, *just as slaves are members of a household*.'[68] And while Grotius recognises that sovereignty may be held by peoples under an 'unequal alliance' or treaty (for example, conquered peoples subject to treaties), he concedes that in the majority of cases the more powerful party 'gradually usurps the sovereignty properly so called'.[69] Here, Grotius departs from the natural law origins of his law of nations to articulate a notion of sovereignty which is more positivistic and 'factual' in the sense of explaining *just how things are*.[70] In doing so, Grotius provides tacit acceptance to forced invasion and colonial imposition as legitimate forms of territorial acquisition, which once asserted are accepted as *faits accomplis*. Hence, First Nations' sovereignty is not perceived as independent and self-sufficient in the same way that European sovereignty is: it is constructed as something lesser, and vulnerable to European intervention and colonial control.

Under the normative framework established by Vitoria and Grotius, only 'civil' societies constitute sovereign societies, and they are exemplified by European legal and political institutions such as courts and public officials exercising executive power. While Vitoria affords some recognition of First Nations as sovereign peoples, it is conditional upon adopting Christian values

62 Ibid bk 2, 5.22 (emphasis added).
63 Ibid bk 1, 3.7.
64 Ibid bk 1, 3.6.
65 Ibid bk 3, 2.2.
66 Ibid bk 2, 3.8.
67 Ibid bk 1, 3.7 (emphasis added).
68 Ibid (emphasis added).
69 Ibid bk 1, 2.21.
70 Fitzpatrick, above n 37, 169.

and having institutions to administer the 'human and civil needs' of the society thus constituted. Grotius further entrenches this division, denying sovereign status to peoples lacking European norms of political and legal organisation. Even worse, however, Grotius' law of nations legitimises colonial incursions onto the lands of First Nations peoples, condones the gradual usurpation of sovereign power and endorses it as a form of prescription. For European nations, sovereignty is marked by independence and indivisibility. In contrast, Indigenous sovereignty is vulnerable to colonial expansionary interests, with First Nations constructed as objects to be governed within the domestic sphere. The pattern of colonial entrapment thus ensured First Nation people's 'domestication and containment' within the municipal laws of colonial nation-states,[71] with the effect of nullifying First Nations' independent international legal status.[72]

International society and the 'law of nations'

Grotius and Vitoria also posit society and the natural sociability of people as evidence of the existence of a law of nations. For Vitoria, it is the binding nature of civil law upon the legislator in his ideal society, 'who should share the burdens of the commonwealth', that cements the authority of the law of nations.[73] He infers by corollary that there is a consensual law of nations, which has the force of 'positive enactment (lex)' because:

> The whole world, which is in a sense a commonwealth, has the power to enact laws which are just and convenient to all men; and these make up the law of nations. From this it follows that those who break the law of nations, whether in peace or in war, are committing mortal crimes ... No kingdom may choose to ignore this law of nations, because it has the sanction of the whole world.[74]

71 Watson, above n 5, 631.

72 The domestication and containment of First Nations within the state is exemplified in the notion of 'domestic dependent nations' as articulated by Chief Justice Marshall of the United States Supreme Court in *Cherokee Nation v State of Georgia* 30 US 1; 5 Pet 1 (1831). However, this limited status was denied to Aboriginal peoples in Australia in *R v Murrell* (1836) 1 Legge 72; and later in *Coe v Commonwealth* (1979) 53 ALJR 403, 409 in which Justice Gibbs stated that 'it is not possible to say, as was said by Marshall CJ ... that the Aboriginal people of Australia are organised as a "distinct political society separated from others", or that they have been uniformly treated as a state ... The contention that there is in Australia an Aboriginal nation exercising sovereignty, even of a limited kind, is quite impossible in law to maintain.' This position was affirmed in *Coe v Commonwealth (No 2)* (1993) 68 ALRJ 110, 115.

73 Vitoria, 'On Civil Power', above n 18, 40.

74 Ibid. A different translation of this passage also appears in Williams, *American Indian*, above n 6, 116, with 'state' begin substituted for 'commonwealth'.

Here, Vitoria invokes the notion of society as a civil partnership, to underpin a consensual law of nations binding upon international society which may enact laws for the *common good of all*. However, as I will argue below, what is viewed as 'just and convenient', or for the 'advantage' of the great society of states, is constructed from a particularly Eurocentric and Christian world view which excludes other modes of lawfulness which do not fit the civil society model.

For Grotius, the natural sociability of people inevitably leads to 'mutual relations of society' which underpin natural law, in contrast to municipal law which is based on mutual consent.[75] Natural law, however, is also shaped by 'expediency', so for people to obtain the things necessary to 'live properly', they must also 'cultivate the social life'.[76] Grotius argues by analogy that municipal laws should also cater for expediency and those prescribing laws for others must have some 'advantage in view'.[77] The common advantage of its members is also advanced as the rationale for a *consensual* law of nations:

> just as the laws of each state have in view the advantage of that state, so by mutual consent it has become possible that certain laws should originate as between all states, or *a great many states*; and it is apparent that the laws thus originating had in view the advantage, not of particular states, but of *the great society of states*. And this is what is called the law of nations, whenever we distinguish that term from the law of nature.[78]

So for Grotius, the law of nations, although based on natural law, is created from the consensus of a great many states which constitute the 'great society of states' with the purpose of promoting the mutual advantage of its members.[79] As we have seen, however, Indigenous Peoples are excluded from this 'great society' as non-sovereign actors.

For Grotius, the international context is also distinguished from municipal law because under the law of nations there are no 'higher authorities' so each state is free to judge its own actions.[80] And according to Vitoria, any prince who wages just war becomes, *ipso jure*, 'judge of the enemy and may punish them judicially'.[81] Therefore, within international society sovereign power takes on a special significance as it implicitly includes the prerogative to defend sovereign 'rights' through the waging of 'just war'.[82] According to Grotius, to 'violate another's right' within this mutually constituted system of

75 Grotius, above n 20, 15.
76 Ibid.
77 Ibid.
78 Ibid (emphasis added).
79 Ibid.
80 Grotius, above n 20, bk 2, 1.11.
81 Vitoria, 'On the American Indians', above n 15, 283.
82 Grotius, above n 20, xxvi.

society and rights is the very nature of injustice, so the preservation of 'human society' itself is equated with the 'proper business of justice'.[83]

With the historical emergence of the discipline of international law, civil society is extrapolated to the extra-national level to posit the existence of an international or 'human society'. States are the primary subjects of international society, and the pursuit of their mutual advantage is its central objective and purpose. For, as Fitzpatrick has observed, 'there is a complementary and constituent relation between international law and the nation, a relation not simply consequent on the existence of nation. That relation forms as an international society or community of nations.'[84]

While this emergent international law is ostensibly binding, having the consensus of the 'whole world', First Peoples are excluded from membership of international society because, by definition, they do not fulfil the prerequisite conditions for recognition. As Fitzpatrick has observed, this self-proclaimed international society is constituted to pursue a colonising project, bringing its determinate order and stability to an 'uncertain world'.[85] The law of nations therefore affords considerable power to states to pursue their mutual advantage in the interests of an international human society styled according to Eurocentric norms. This seemingly unlimited power is most clearly articulated in the theory of 'just wars' which, although not a central focus of this chapter, will be outlined briefly because it reveals the ultimate ends of this self-proclaimed Eurocentric international society, and the implications for the positioning of First Nations within the order it creates.

Just wars: in the interests of 'human society'

The power to wage public war was almost exclusively attributed to sovereign states, or those exercising sovereign power on behalf of the state,[86] with the clear implication that non-state actors or those viewed as lacking sovereign power could not lawfully wage a 'just war'.[87] This limitation had the effect of

83 Ibid xlv.
84 Fitzpatrick, above n 37, 147.
85 Ibid 182.
86 For Grotius, the right to wage public war can only be exercised by 'one who holds the sovereign power in the state', above n 20, bk 1, 3.4. According to Vitoria, the authority to declare war rests with the commonwealth, or a prince exercising commonwealth authority, 'On the Law of War', above n 17, 300–1.
87 Grotius also distinguishes between wars waged between different peoples being declared in the name of the state, as opposed to wars conducted by 'brigands and robbers'. He notes, however, that the latter may assume of a form of statehood '[i]f by the accessions of desperate men this evil grows to such proportions that it holds lands, established fixed settlements, seizes upon states and subjugates peoples, it assumes the name of a kingdom'. See Grotius, above n 22, bk 3, 2.2. Here, the law of nations also sanctions the creation of states by non-peaceful means.

rendering Indigenous resistance to colonial power not only unjust,[88] but contrary to the interests of international society itself.

For both Vitoria and Grotius, just wars may be waged to avenge injuries,[89] recover property and to inflict punishment.[90] For Grotius, the doctrine of just war is also constituted in and through international society, and includes actions necessary to secure a right. Grotius clarifies: 'By right I mean that which is strictly so called, denoting the *power of acting in respect to {international} society only*.'[91]

According to Grotius, such rights extend to, in the case of necessity, taking things belonging to others; and the right of 'innocent use' of the property of another, where there is no detriment to the owners.[92] Most significantly, 'innocent use' includes a right of passage over lands to engage in commerce, and a right of 'temporary sojourn'.[93] Indeed, Grotius regarded the right of passage for the purpose of trade so highly that 'No one, in fact, has the right to hinder any nation from carrying on commerce with any other nation at a distance. *That such permission be accorded is in the interests of human society*.'[94]

Vitoria also argues that there is a right to trade on the basis of 'natural partnership and communication' (or 'natural society and fellowship') which includes the right to 'lawfully trade amongst the barbarians'.[95] Vitoria concludes that, even if these rights were not supported by natural law, they are binding under the law of nations because 'the consent of the *greater part of the world* is enough to make it binding, especially when it is for the *common good of all men*'.[96] So, for Vitoria and Grotius, these rights are defendable in the interests of 'human society' and the 'common good of all men'. For Vitoria, if the barbarians resist the exercise of these rights, the Spanish may defend themselves with the use of force.[97] However, if all efforts to secure peace and safety fail, the Spanish may 'treat them no longer as innocent enemies, but as treacherous foes against whom all rights of war can be exercised, including plunder, enslavement, deposition of their former masters, and the institution of new ones'.[98]

88 Richard Tuck, 'Introduction' in Hugo Grotius, *The Rights of War and Peace* (Richard Tuck ed, Jean Barbeyrac trans, Liberty Fund, 2005) ix, xxix–xxx.
89 Grotius, above n 20, bk 2, 2.1; Vitoria, 'On the Law of War', above n 17, 298.
90 Grotius, ibid bk 2, 1.2.2.
91 Ibid bk 3, 1.2 (emphasis added).
92 Ibid bk 2, 2.8–11.
93 Ibid bk 2, 2.8–15.
94 Ibid bk 2, 2.13 (emphasis added).
95 Vitoria, 'On the American Indians', above n 15, 279. Williams, *American Indian*, above n 6, 101 cites the Nys translation which calls this 'natural society and fellowship'.
96 Vitoria, ibid 281.
97 Ibid 281–2.
98 Ibid 283.

For Grotius, to hinder the right to trade and commerce 'is at variance with the *nature of society*' itself.[99] Here, he posits the right to trade as the basis of wide-ranging rights in the interests of human society, with such interests constructed through a European, mercantile perspective.

As mentioned previously, Vitoria also viewed as just claims to title for the purpose of defending the innocent against tyranny, including 'practising any nefarious custom or rite', *even if consensual*.[100] In effect, this ground enabled the Spanish to claim just title based on a Christian world view of what was natural and right *against the voluntary will of Indigenous peoples* – a somewhat ironical position. Anghie identifies this as an 'extraordinary powerful right of intervention', which had the effect of universalising Spanish cultural norms.[101] For Grotius, it was permissible to wage a just war against those who offend against the law of nature because 'kings' have the right to punish those who injure not only their subjects but also those who 'excessively violate the law of nature or nation in regard to any persons whatsoever'.[102] This right is considered consistent with the '*liberty to serve the interests of human society*, through punishments' which lies in the hands of sovereigns, being 'themselves subject to no one'.[103] As Richard Tuck argues, on this view the practices of non-Europeans constitute breaches of the law of nature, highlighting the 'interventionary character' of Grotius' theory, which replicates the justifications for the Christian crusades of the past.[104] Here, Grotius defines acts which offend against the law of nature, including the rights of free trade and passage, as contrary to the interests of human society at large. Thus the preservation of human society itself, in terms dictated by a Eurocentric Christian world view, provides a powerful rationalisation for colonial intervention and claims to title. So despite the apparent rejection of religious rationales as the basis for war and colonial expansion, both Vitoria and Grotius reinscribe Christian values in their naturalist law of nations in ways that operate to subjugate First Nations to European colonial rule.

Conclusion

Society was a central concept in the historical formation of the Eurocentric law of nations based on natural law, being critical to how both sovereignty and international society were constructed in ways that excluded Indigenous Peoples as subjects of international law. Within natural law theories, society has a dual

99 Ibid (emphasis added).
100 Ibid 287–8.
101 Anghie, above n 1, 23.
102 Grotius, above n 20, bk 2, 20.40.
103 Ibid (emphasis added). Some examples of those who breach natural law cited by Grotius include those who 'act with impiety towards their parents', 'feed on human flesh', and 'those who practice piracy'.
104 Tuck, above n 88, xxviii.

aspect in that it is used to define both the entities that hold sovereign power, and the sum of its individual parts, which constitute 'human society'. At the national level, society is equated with civil society, and is entangled with the notion of rights which are constituted in and through society. It functions as a basic element of international law, with society being synonymous with the notions of state, statehood and sovereign power. In the international context, the concept of human or international society is constructed to serve the mutual advantage of its member states, which are also the arbiters of what is perceived as 'just', according to Christian Eurocentric norms.

Although the naturalist law of nations was constructed in universal and humanitarian terms which served to include First Nations within its jurisdiction, it privileged European-style political and legal arrangements, and in doing so excluded Indigenous Peoples from recognition within the emerging international legal order. The supreme sovereign power of states also entailed a monopoly over the right to wage 'just wars' and a meta-legal status in judging the justice of their own actions, determining what was rational, reasonable and necessary for the promotion of human society and for the *common good of all.* The construction of these 'rights' served to legitimise state power over Indigenous Peoples, bringing them within the colonial matrix of power. The Grotian law of nations also provided tacit approval of colonialism, and positioned First Nations people as objects to be governed within the domestic sphere, depriving First Nations of the status of free and independent peoples. In Foucauldian terms, the *episteme*[105] of colonialism created the conditions upon which to generate knowledge of a law of nations that operated to construct First Nations as 'special objects' of international law. The concept of society was central to the construction of this totalising discourse, which effectively excluded Indigenous Peoples as sovereign subjects of international law, and thus brought into being a new colonial world order.

105 Clare O'Farrell, *Key Concepts*, michel-foucault.com (30 October 2010) <http://www.michel-foucault.com/concepts/index.html>.

Chapter 4

Long before Munich: the American template for Hitlerian diplomacy

Ward Churchill

The lesson of Munich is that the signature of Hitler is worth nothing.
(French Premier Édouard Daladier, August 1939)

On 29 September 1938, Great Britain, France, Italy and the Third Reich entered into the Munich Agreement, allowing the latter to annex the 'Sudetenland', border areas of Czechoslovakia viewed by the nazis as being part of *Großdeutschland* (Greater Germany).[1] This, according to British Prime Minister Neville Chamberlain, would resolve territorial issues arising from the 1919 *Treaty of Versailles* without military conflict,[2] and thus guarantee 'peace for our time'.[3] This was a decidedly misguided view based upon German Chancellor Adolf Hitler's personal assurances as well as 'a signed statement that he had no further territorial ambitions' either in the Czechoslovakian

1 The term *Großdeutschland* refers to the areas of Europe encompassing all German-speaking peoples. Subsequently formulated as *Großdeutschland Lösung*, it called for their unification in a single state. As employed by the nazis during the 1930s, it referred to the area within the pre-1918 borders of Germany, plus Austria and areas such as the Sudetenland, substantially populated by *volksdeutsch* ('ethnic Germans'). On the agreement itself, see Keith Eubank, *Munich* (University of Oklahoma Press, 1963); David Faber, *Munich, 1938: Appeasement and World War II* (Simon & Schuster, 2008).

2 The *Treaty of Versailles* formally ended the First World War. It imposed terms upon the defeated Germany including admission of guilt, payment of reparations, demilitarisation, forfeiture of its overseas colonies and European 'protectorates', and cessions of territory. Although the terms were less harsh than those imposed by the *Kaiserreich* (Imperial Germany) on the new-born Soviet Union in the 1918 *Treaty of Brest-Litovsk*, Germans overwhelmingly resented the 'Crime of Versailles'. Hitler capitalised on these sentiments by pledging to repudiate the Treaty and, after coming to power, doing exactly that. See Alan Sharp, *The Versailles Settlement* (Palgrave Macmillan, 2nd edn, 2008). On relative leniency, see Correlli Barnett, *The Collapse of British Power* (Pan, 2002) 392, 316–9.

3 'Neville Chamberlain's "Peace for Our Time" Speech', 30 September 1938, <https://eudocs.lib.byu.edu/index.php/Neville_Chamberlain's_%22Peace_For_Our_Time%22_speech>.

DOI: 10.4324/9781315628318-5

rump state or elsewhere in Europe.[4] The Prime Minister's explanation was reinforced by Hitler's speech delivered at Berlin's Sportpalast on 26 September:

> This is the last territorial claim which I have to make in Europe ... I have assured [Chamberlain] further that, and this I repeat here before you, once this issue has been resolved, there will no longer be any further territorial problems for Germany in Europe![5]

Chamberlain should have known better. Hitler had already used the line about having 'no more territorial claims in Europe' shortly after he repudiated the 'Versailles *diktat*' by remilitarising the Rhineland on 7 March 1936.[6] Indeed, since 1920, he had openly announced his intention to recover *all* the territory stripped from the defeated Germany's pre-war expanse at Versailles.[7] Of the 25,000 square miles at issue, the Sudetenland comprised only one small portion; the lion's share had been allotted to the new-born Polish state.[8]

These stark realities led at least one British Foreign Ministry official to the accurate conclusion that the nazi leader's territorial ambitions would consist of 'lulling his opponents to sleep with fair words to gain time to arm his people, looking always to the day when he can throw off the mask and attack Poland'.[9] Hitler's invasion/annexation of Austria – the so-called *Anschluß*

4 Richard S Thompson, *Great Britain* (Infobase, 2014) 78.
5 'Adolf Hitler – Great Speech in Sportpalast', *Neues Europa*, 26 September 1938.
6 Quoted in A J P Taylor, *The Origins of the Second World War* (Hamish Hamilton, 1961) 133. Remilitarisation of the Rhineland was specifically forbidden under Arts 42–44. It was also a flagrant violation of the 1925 Treaty of Locarno, wherein international arbitration was required to alter territorial status along Germany's western border. See Gerhart Weinberg, *Hitler's Foreign Policy, 1933–1939* (Enigma Books, 2013) 188; William Shirer, *The Rise and Fall of the Third Reich* (Simon & Schuster, 1960) 294; Ian Kershaw, *Hitler, 1889–1936: Hubris* (W W Norton, 1998) 587.
7 Abrogation of the *Treaty of Versailles* was announced on 24 February 1920, along with 'unification of all Germans in the Greater Germany'. The translated platform appears as Doc 1708-PS in Office of United States Chief of Counsel for Prosecution of Axis Criminality, *Nazi Conspiracy and Aggression* (US Government Printing Office, 1946) vol 4, 208–11. On Hitler's intent to regain not only Germany's '1914 borders' but *much* more, see Adolf Hitler, *Mein Kampf* (Houghton-Mifflin Sentry Editions, 1962) esp 650–5.
8 Poland was established under Arts 34 and 87–93 of the *Treaty of Versailles*. Germany was required to cede part of East Prussia, Upper Silesia, and portions of Posen and Pomerania to the new state under Arts 34 and 88. See generally, T Hunt Tooley, *National Identity and Weimar Germany* (University of Nebraska Press, 1997).
9 'Notes by Sir Maurice Hankey on Hitler's External Policy in Theory and Practice, 24 October 1933' in *British Documents on Foreign Affairs* (University Publications of America, 1993) 339.

(unification) – in March 1938[10] revealed the sheer falsity of the 'fair words' with which Hitler larded his action in the Rhineland six months before he repeated them to Chamberlain in Munich.

The *Anschluß* placed Germany in the strategically advantageous position of being able to attack Czechoslovakia from three directions simultaneously. However, the Czechs, denied the right even to participate in the negotiation that resulted in the dismemberment of their country, desperately warned Britain and France – their supposed 'guarantors' – that ceding the Sudetenland to Germany would strip them of the extensive border defences they had constructed since 1933 and leave them wide open to invasion.[11] It took less than six months for their fears to be realised.[12] On 15 March 1939, in utter disregard of the terms he had agreed to in Munich, Hitler ordered his troops to occupy the remainder of Czechoslovakia, a task accomplished with virtually no opposition.[13] The only tangible response to this aggression by either Britain or France was their military alliance with Poland,[14] which, although

10 Articles 227–30 of the *Treaty of Versailles* precluded the unification of Germany and Austria, but, emboldened by the success of his earlier repudiations of its terms, Hitler unilaterally – and very publicly – 'annulled' any remaining German obligations thereunder in February 1937. Hitler ordered his troops to occupy the country, and then orchestrated a 'plebiscite' which claimed that 99.7 per cent of Austrians favoured the *Anschluß Österreichs* ('eastern unification'). See Faber, above n 1, 139–68; Jürgen Gehl, *Austria, Germany, and the Anschluss, 1931–1938* (Oxford University Press, 1963).

11 On Britain and France as 'guarantors of Czech interests', see Eubank, above n 1, 33; on Czech protests concerning border defences, 169, 216; on German intent to strip Czechs of fortifications, 162.

12 This would be no surprise to French premier Édouard Daladier who, in sharp contrast to Chamberlain, returned from Munich purporting that 'he did not believe a word' about Germany's territorially benign intentions and predicting that 'within six months France and England would be face to face with new German demands'. Nonetheless, he signed the agreement. See Paul N Hehn, *A Low, Dishonest Decade* (A&C Black, 2005) 25.

13 German military planning for the seizure of what remained of Czechoslovakia commenced less than two weeks after the Munich Agreement was signed. Once the rump state was occupied, it was partitioned, with the western (Czech) portion redesignated the *Protektorat Böhmen und Mähren* (Protectorate of Bohemia and Moravia) and incorporated directly into the Reich. The eastern portion, dubbed 'Slovakia', was administered by a collaborationist government as a puppet state. See US Chief of Counsel, above n 7, vol 1, 560–2, 577–80.

14 Polish–British Common Defense Pact, 25 August 1939. While both countries pledged to guarantee Poland's continuing independence on 31 March 1939, France left it to Britain to negotiate the details. This took until 25 August, only a week before the German invasion, which was far too late for its 'allies' to assist the Poles. See Stephen Schuker, 'End of Versailles' in Gordon Martel (ed), *Origins of the Second World War Reconsidered* (Routledge, 1999) 38. For the Polish view, see Anita J Prazmowska, *Britain, Poland and the Eastern Front, 1939* (Cambridge University Press, 2004).

it had entered into a mutual nonaggression pact with Germany in 1934,[15] was plainly next on Hitler's list of targets.

Having instructed German foreign minister Joachim von Ribbentrop in April to open covert negotiations with the Soviet Union for an altogether different sort of 'nonaggression' pact,[16] Hitler played for time, reiterating his boundless desire for peace and limited territorial demands. When the pact with the Soviets was finally signed on 23 August – in violation of Germany's Anti-Comintern Pact with Italy and Japan[17] – it contained a secret protocol defining the respective 'spheres of influence' to be enjoyed by Germany and the Soviet Union and dividing the whole of Poland between them.[18] Hitler was still trying to lure the western powers into something akin to a second Munich conference to 'resolve' the issue only a week before his troops crossed the Polish border on 1 September.[19]

Since Hitler's diplomatic subterfuge precluded his declaring war before the invasion was launched, Germany stood in violation of international customary law codified in the 1907 *Hague Convention on the Laws of War*,[20] and the 1928 *Pact of Paris* ('Kellogg–Briand Pact'), by which it renounced resort to military force as a means of resolving international disputes.[21] The same holds true with respect to the German invasions of neutral Denmark, Norway, Netherlands, Belgium and Luxembourg in April and May 1940, and of Yugoslavia a year later, although in each of these cases an additional violation of the *Hague Convention* was involved.[22] The onslaught against the Soviet Union on 22 June 1941[23] violated not only the *Hague Convention*'s

15 German–Polish Agreement, 26 January 1934. See Anna M Cienciala, 'The Foreign Policy of Józef Piłsudski and Józef Beck, 1926–1939: Misconceptions and Interpretations' (2011) 56 *Polish Review* 111.

16 Aleksandr Moiseyevich Nekrich, Adam Bruno Ulam and Gregory L Freeze, *Pariahs, Partners, Predators* (Columbia University Press, 1997) 107–11; Edward E Ericson, *Feeding the German Eagle* (Greenwood Press, 1999) 46–55.

17 The Anti-Comintern Pact, between Germany and Japan, was signed on 6 November 1936. Exactly one year later, Italy signed. See Weinberg, above n 6, 342–6.

18 Molotov–Ribbentrop Pact, 23 August 1939. See Geoffrey Roberts, 'The Soviet Decision for a Pact with Nazi Germany' (1992) 44 *Soviet Studies* 57; Roger Moorhouse, *The Devil's Alliance* (Bodley Head, 2014).

19 Office of US Chief of Counsel, above n 7, vol 1, 715.

20 Article 1 of the *Hague Convention (III) Relative to the Opening of Hostilities* requires that the initiation of combat operations be preceded by either a 'reasoned declaration of war' or an ultimatum attended by a 'conditional declaration'.

21 *General Treaty for Renunciation of War as an Instrument of National Policy*, 94 LNTS (entered into force 24 July 1929). See generally, Harold Josephson, 'Outlawing War: Internationalism and the Pact of Paris' (1979) 3 *Diplomatic History* 377.

22 Article 1 of the *Hague Convention (V) Respecting the Rights and Duties of Neutral Powers and Persons in Case of War on Land* provides that 'the territory of neutral Powers is inviolable'. Under Art 2 'belligerents are forbidden to move troops or convoys of either munitions of war or supplies across the territory of a neutral Power'.

23 See Stephen G Fritz, *Ostkrieg* (University Press of Kentucky, 2011) 42–4, 77–8.

prohibition of undeclared war, but the nonaggression pact into which Germany entered less than two years before.

In the aftermath of Germany's unconditional surrender in May 1945, with the self-styled 'Führer' dead by his own hand, his 'Thousand Year Reich' reduced to smouldering ruins, and the surviving nazi élite mostly in custody, the true depth of the duplicity embodied in Hitler's diplomacy was revealed. Since becoming head of state, *everything* he had said about his 'territorial ambitions' was not only false but deliberately misleading. As was known by his small circle of confidants, Hitler's ambitions were *never* limited even to a *de facto* repeal of the *Treaty of Versailles* and actualisation of *Großdeutschland* in its fullest geographic sense.[24]

Rather, he remained committed to the broader goal set forth in *Mein Kampf*: that of seizing additional *Lebensraum* ('living space') outside Germany,[25] defined during the meeting as including Czechoslovakia, Poland and Lithuania, but subsequently expanded in a 'general plan for the East' to encompass a vast and racially purified colonial dominion stretching to the Volga and beyond.[26] To this end, he routinely negotiated treaties with every intention of violating them, purely as a means of gaining tactical advantages, with attainment of each 'limited' territorial objective facilitating realisation of the next.[27] All told, as was shown during the 1945–46 prosecution of the surviving nazi leadership at Nuremberg, Germany had systematically violated no fewer than 69 separate treaties between 1933 and 1941, many of them repeatedly.[28]

24 There are a number of sources confirming this, not least the diaries kept by propaganda minister Joseph Goebbels, records of his 'dinner table conversations' with – more accurately, monologues inflicted upon – his confidants, and the testimonies of Göring, Rosenberg and others at Nuremberg. See, eg, Louis P Lochner (ed), *The Goebbels Diaries* (Charter, 1948); Hermann Rauschning, *The Voice of Destruction* (GP Putnam's Sons, 1940); H R Trevor-Roper (ed), *Hitler's Table Talk, 1941–1944* (Weidenfeld & Nicolson, 1953); G M Gilbert, *Nuremberg Diary* (Da Capo Press, 1995).

25 Hitler, above n 7, 650–5. See Klaus Hildebrand, *The Foreign Policy of the Third Reich* (B T Batsford, 1973) 15–21.

26 An initial draft of *Generalplan Ost* was prepared in 1940 and the final version submitted to Hitler in May 1942. While all copies were apparently destroyed prior to Germany's surrender, the recovery of collateral documents has allowed reconstruction of its contents. See Fritz, above n 23, 253–7; Alexander Dallin, *Germany Rule in Russia, 1941–1945* (Macmillan, 1957) 276–97.

27 Andreas Hillgruber, *Germany and the Two World Wars* (Harvard University Press, 1981) 52–3; Klaus Hildebrand, *The Nazi Dictatorship: Problems and Perspectives of Interpretation* (Arnold, 2000) 136–43. Both authors overstate the case by arguing that Hitler's 'ultimate goal' was literally 'world conquest' rather than establishing Germany as a world power. For a more balanced interpretation, see Mark Mazower, *Hitler's Empire* (Penguin Press, 2008) 2–5, 581–5.

28 See Office of US Chief of Counsel, above n 7, vol 1, 651–72, especially 652.

Hitlerian diplomacy was inherently violative of the hallowed principle of *pacta sunt servanda* ('treaties are to be obeyed') and thus *delicti juris gentium*, an offence – or, more accurately, a lengthy series of offences – against the law of nations.[29] Given the motives underlying the pattern of nazi treaty violations, moreover, it was held to be not merely unlawful but criminal, a 'Crime Against Peace'. This, as defined in the 1945 *London Charter of the International Military Tribunal* convened to sit in judgment at Nuremberg, consists of the 'planning, preparation, initiation or waging of a war of aggression, or a war *in violation of international treaties*, agreements or assurances, or participation in a common plan or conspiracy for the accomplishment of any of the foregoing'.[30]

To frame the charge in his opening statement to the tribunal, US Supreme Court Justice Robert H Jackson, who served as his country's chief prosecutor during the trial, first quoted Hitler's 23 November 1939 declaration to his military commanders: 'Agreements are to be kept only as long as they serve a certain purpose.'[31] He then rehearsed several Treaty violations knowingly committed by the defendants while planning and waging the German war of aggression, concluding that 'International Law, natural law, German law, any law at all was to these men simply a propaganda device to be invoked when it helped and ignored when[ever] it condemned what they wanted to do'.[32]

The case ended on 1 October 1946, with the convictions of several defendants for conspiring to wage aggressive war and crimes against peace, in significant part because of their conscious participation in Hitler's wholesale subversion of the treaty-centred legal regime of international order.[33] Despite the scale of the crimes against humanity at issue in the Nuremberg proceedings, and the tribunal's acceptance that the newly named crime of genocide had been perpetrated against several peoples,[34] it was adjudged that crimes against

29 On the force of the principle in customary international law, see Hans Wehberg, 'Pacta Sunt Servanda' (1959) 53 *American Journal of International Law* 775.

30 Office of US Chief of Counsel, above n 7, vol 1, 5 (emphasis added). See also 'War Crimes: IV. Violation of Treaties and Methods of Punishment' (1945) 22 *Bulletin of International News* 299.

31 Office of US Chief of Counsel, above n 7, vol 1, 161. Reichsmarschall Hermann Göring was far more blunt, responding to Jackson's opening statement with the off-record observation that he himself had 'considered your treaties ... so much toilet paper'. Quoted in Gilbert, *Nuremberg Diary*, above n 24, 67.

32 Ibid 161–2.

33 *Trial of the Major War Criminals before the International Military Tribunal* (International Military Tribunal, 1948) vol 22, 524–87.

34 It is generally contended that, since the word itself did appear therein, the crime of genocide was not at issue in the Nuremberg verdicts. It will be noted, however, that, in the indictment, commission of 'deliberate and systematic genocide' was subsumed under the broader heading of 'crimes against humanity'. The term was periodically employed during the trial to describe the nature of the offences perpetrated by given defendants, and British assistant prosecutor Hartley Shawcross devoted a considerable portion of his summation to detailing the 'horrible

peace – planning, preparing and initiating aggressive war in violation of treaties – constituted 'the supreme international crime'.[35] Although the reality was obviously far more complex, the term 'Munich' was cast as a convenient signifier, indicating the entire record of criminality embodied in Hitlerian diplomacy and the corresponding record of diplomatic 'appeasement' of France and especially Britain which arguably enabled the nazis' early successes and the catastrophe that followed.[36]

The US progenitor

> They made us many promises, more than I can remember. But they only kept one. They promised to take our land, and they took it.
>
> (Maȟpíya Lúta (Red Cloud), Oglala Lakota, 1882)

While it remains a mainstay of 'responsible' historiography that the nature and magnitude of nazi criminality was both unprecedented and unparalleled, such a view is not merely inaccurate but Eurocentric in the extreme.[37] As Aimé Césaire observed only five years after the collapse of the Third Reich, the nazis did nothing new or especially different apart from the fact that what they did was done in Europe, to Europeans.[38] Hitler's *real* crime, he

policy of genocide' implemented by the defendants. Hence, insofar as nothing to the contrary was said in the verdicts, and since facts recited by Shawcross in connection with his use of the term were frequently reiterated in the tribunal's findings of guilt, those convicted of crimes against humanity were concomitantly convicted of genocide as well. See *Trial of the Major War Criminals*, vol 2, 45–6; vol 17, 61; vol 19, 497–515.

35 *Trial of the Major War Criminals*, vol 22, 427.

36 Although Winston Churchill had much to say on the topic during the late 1930s, probably the strongest early articulation of the theme was in Victor Gollancz et al, *Guilty Men* (Faber & Faber, 1940), co-authored by Michael Foot, Peter Howard and Frank Owen under the collective pseudonym CATO. Churchill made the case more thoroughly in his *The Gathering Storm* (Cassell, 1948). A J P Taylor then advanced it as a historical 'truth' in his 1961 *Origins of the Second World War*, above n 6; a view fleshed out in Martin Gilbert, *The Roots of Appeasement* (Weidenfeld & Nicolson, 1966); Cameron Watt, *How War Came* (Pantheon, 1989); Frank McDonough, *Neville Chamberlain, Appeasement and the British Road to War* (Manchester University Press, 1998). For recent elaborations, see Faber, above n 1; R Gerald Hughes, 'The Ghosts of Appeasement: Britain and the Legacy of the Munich Agreement' (2013) 48 *Journal of Contemporary History* 688.

37 A cornerstone of this contention has long been the supposed 'phenomenological uniqueness' of the nazi judeocide. For firm rebuttals, see David E Stannard, 'Uniqueness as Denial: The Politics of Genocide Scholarship' in Alan S Rosenbaum (ed), *Is the Holocaust Unique?* (Westview Press, 1996) 163; Martin Shaw, *What Is Genocide?* (Polity Press, 2nd edn, 2015) esp 17, 55.

38 Aimé Césaire, *Discourse on Colonialism* (Joan Pinkham trans, Monthly Review Press, 2000) [trans of *Discours sur le colonialism* (first published 1950)].

argued, 'is the crime against the white man, the humiliation of the white man, and the fact that he applied to Europe colonialist procedures which until then had been reserved exclusively for the Arabs of Algeria, the "coolies" of India, and the "niggers" of Africa'.[39]

Césaire held that those engaged in reconstructing the West's imperial dominions were simultaneously fabricating an elaborate web of philosophical/scientific/scholarly 'interpretations' to conjure the illusion that nazism was an 'aberration', or at least 'anomalous'.[40] They were, he argued, seeking to 'absolve' the functional equivalents of the nazi scourge they themselves had 'cultivated' and for which 'they were responsible', aspiring to restore the comfort of a time when they could 'shut their eyes to [and] legitimize it' because it would be imposed only in the overseas colonies, upon 'non-European peoples' long viewed by Europeans as racial inferiors.[41] In this squalid endeavour, Césaire concluded, they were busily 'chew[ing] over Hitler's vomit'.[42]

The psycho-intellectual crux of the matter has always resided in denial.[43] As erstwhile nazi legal theorist Carl Schmitt correctly diagnosed the situation in 1953, one of the more significant outcomes of 'Hitler's War' was a shift in 'The West's' centre of gravity from Europe to its settler colonial offspring in North America, especially the United States.[44] Therefore, it is unsurprising

39 Ibid 36.

40 Thomas Mann pointed the way when he argued that the very idea of 'Nazi culture' was an oxymoron, a term that should be used 'only in quotation marks', and that nazism itself should be viewed as an 'isolated historical anomaly', 'no more than an unfortunate interlude', 'a period of night and winter'. As one observer has astutely framed the long-term result of such intellectual evasion, a 'common understanding of Nazism' is that it was 'a major anomaly of human history, a barbarous regression into pre-modern history ... a unique, sudden, incomprehensible, or "typical German" manifestation of demonic evil', the last being a 'very popular representation of Nazism ... [T]he "abnormalization" of Nazism as a demonical aberration can be [and is being] used today by scientists [and others] to establish a complete intellectual and social discontinuity between Nazi and contemporary science', politics, legality, historiography, art, philosophy and so on. Didier Pollefeyt, 'The Significance of Nazi Eugenics for Medical Ethics Today' in Michael Alan Signer (ed), *Humanity at the Limit* (Indiana University Press, 2000) 250, 250. Mann is quoted in Pamela M Potter, *Art of Suppression* (University of California Press, 2016) 70. The classic rebuttal of the notion of nazism's evil 'singularity' is, of course, Hannah Arendt, *Eichmann in Jerusalem* (Viking Press, 1963).

41 Césaire, above n 38, 36.

42 Ibid 63.

43 See Stanley Cohen, *States of Denial* (Polity Press, 2001) esp 1–18, 117–39, 278–95. Relatedly, see Joachim J Stavelsberg and Ryan D King, *American Memories* (Russell Sage Foundation, 2013); Alexander Laban Hinton (ed), *Hidden Genocides* (Rutgers University Press, 2014).

44 Indeed, 'America' – that is, the United States – has *always* 'claim[ed] to be the true Europe'. In the aftermath of the Second World War, it actually emerged as such, at least figuratively, since 'only the United States [was] capable' of

that denial in its most acute form has prevailed in the United States. *Every* uncomfortable reality has been expunged from the country's officially sanctioned historical narrative,[45] and, where that proves impossible, they are carefully sanitised, trivialised and otherwise 'contained'.[46] Those venturing analyses that transgress the closely drawn parameters of 'reputable scholarship' find their work, no matter how well argued and supported, perpetually branded 'controversial' while concerted efforts are mounted to discredit the material and/or its author(s).[47]

Constructing a plausible narrative through which to deny the 'Nazi connections' to US history has been problematic.[48] Hitler's explanation in *Mein Kampf* was that his intended conquest of *Lebensraum* in Eastern Europe would be based on that accomplished by the 'mostly Germanic' settlers of the 'upsurging American continent' in their westward drive 'from sea to shining sea'.[49] Nor was this the only time he had pointed out such linkages. He had informed his high command in October 1941 that 'Our Mississippi must be the Volga', and a bit later that 'in the east a similar process will repeat itself for the second time as in the conquest of America'.[50] German troops in the east, he declared, had 'a duty to look upon natives as Redskins', and to conduct themselves as their US predecessors had during 'the struggle in North America against the Red Indians',[51] wherein, he contended, 'millions of redskins [were] shot down to a few hundred thousand'.[52]

asserting 'England's former domination'. Carl Schmitt, *The Nomos of the Earth in the International Law of Jus Publicum Europaeum* (Telos Press, 2003) 291, 354–5.

45 The hub of official sanction resides in control over what children are – and are not – taught through the country's system of compulsory 'education' in both assigned textbooks and classroom instruction. See, eg, Gary B Nash, Charlotte Crabtree and Ross E Dunn, *History on Trial* (Alfred A Knopf, 1997).

46 See Edward T Linenthal and Tom Engelhardt (eds), *History Wars* (Henry Holt, 1996); Ellen Schrecker (ed), *Cold War Triumphalism* (New Press, 2004).

47 My personal experience in this regard is extensive, and I am by no means alone. See Don Eron, Suzanne Hudson and Myron Hulen, 'Colorado Conference of the Association of American University Professors Report on the Termination of Ward Churchill' (2012) 3 *Journal of Academic Freedom* <https://www.aaup.org/sites/default/files/ConferenceReport.pdf>. More broadly, see Valerie Scalamburio-D'Annibale, *Cold Breezes and Idiot Winds* (Sense, 2011); Henry Giroux, *Neoliberalism's War on Higher Education* (Haymarket Books, 2014).

48 The phrase in quotation marks is borrowed from the title of Stefan Kühl, *The Nazi Connection* (Oxford University Press, 2002).

49 Hitler's profession of admiration for the example set by the United States, and his intention to emulate it, are scattered throughout *Mein Kampf*, above n 7, but see esp 286, 641–55, 664. The passage 'from sea to shining sea' is from the iconic 1910 song 'America the Beautiful' and is used here for effect. It does not appear in *Mein Kampf*.

50 Quoted in Werner Jochmann (ed), *Adolf Hitler* (Knaus, 1980) 78; Ian Kershaw, *Hitler, 1936–1945: Nemesis* (W W Norton, 2000) 434–5.

51 Quoted in Trevor-Roper, above n 24, 55, 469.

52 Quoted in Ian Kershaw, *Fateful Choices* (Penguin Press, 2007) 387.

Reichsmarschall Hermann Göring not only asserted that Germany had merely followed the example set by the United States, but that it had been fully entitled to do so.[53] Foreign minister Ribbentrop argued that the methods employed by nazis to secure *Lebensraum* differed little from those of the United States, which, under the rationale that they were 'an inferior race', had routinely 'slaughtered the Indians' as a means of acquiring their lands.[54] By mid-1946, hints that the 'extinction of the Red Indians' might well be understood as genocide in the same sense as the nazi 'reduction' of Slavic *untermenschen* (subhumans) in Eastern Europe had begun to find their way into mainstream British coverage of the Nuremberg proceedings.[55] Comparisons between US and nazi policies were voiced in congressional testimony.[56]

In view of the extent to which such revelations might undermine the contrived and greatly 'exaggerated sense of innocence' with which the American self-concept has always been infused,[57] official abjuration at the highest level was deemed imperative. Hence, in mid-August 1946, before the first verdicts were read at Nuremberg, President Harry Truman publicly advanced an outright historical fabrication intended to make it 'perfectly clear' that the nazi and US approaches to territorial expansion had nothing in common:

> [While] many men and women, here and abroad, have failed to recognize [it,] in our transactions with the Indian tribes we have at least since the Northwest Ordinance of 1787 set for ourselves the standard of fair and honorable dealings, pledging respect for Indian property rights. Instead of confiscating Indian lands, we have purchased from the tribes that once

53 'After the US gobbled up California and half of Mexico, and we were stripped down to nothing, territorial expansion suddenly becomes a crime.' Quoted in Gilbert, *Nuremberg Diary*, above n 24, 66.

54 Ibid 152.

55 For the phrase quoted, see R W Cooper, *The Nuremberg Trial* (Faber & Faber, 1947) 109.

56 Attorney Ernest Wilkinson, for instance, referred to Hitler's having 'invoked the treatment of Western Indians during the period of "manifest destiny" ... as justification for the Nazi invasion[s] of Czechoslovakia and Poland to gain more *lebensraum*'. Roy L Brooks, *When Sorry Isn't Enough* (New York University Press, 1999) 262, citing US House of Representatives, *Creation of Indian Claims Commission: Hearings Before the Committee on Indian Affairs*, 108.

57 On American 'exaggerated innocence' as embraced by 'good Americans' in an entirely relevant context, see Stuart Creighton Miller, *'Benevolent Assimilation': The American Conquest of the Philippines, 1899–1903* (Yale University Press, 1982) esp 1, 253–67. A broader analysis is provided in Barry Spector, *Madness at the Gates of the City* (Regent Press, 2010). Also see Debra B Bergoffen, '9/11: America and the Politics of Innocence' in Dennis J Schmidt (ed), *Difficulties of an Ethical Life* (Fordham University Press, 2012) 72–87.

owned this continent more than 90 percent of our public domain, paying them approximately 800 million dollars in the process.[58]

Truman, of course, hedged his bets, acknowledging that in the process of acquiring its continent-spanning dominion the United States had no doubt 'made some mistakes and occasionally failed to live up to the precise terms of our treaties and agreements with some 200 tribes'.[59] That being so, he continued, the federal government had established a commission to effect 'the final settlement of all outstanding claims' by said 'tribes' against the United States for its wrongful taking of their lands.[60]

The claim that the United States had only 'occasionally' violated 'the precise terms' of its treaties with American Indians was a blatant falsehood. In fact, the country had effectively been in violation of *all* such treaties since 1903, when, in its *Lone Wolf* opinion, the Supreme Court assigned the federal government 'plenary power' over Indians, including the prerogative of retroactively – and unilaterally – altering their 'precise terms', or otherwise exempting itself from complying with them.[61] Similarly, far from having 'purchased' its 'public domain' from 'the tribes that once owned' them for the sum of '800 million dollars', it had been officially estimated as recently as 1943 that at least $3 billion would be required to settle the claims then known to be pending.[62]

In announcing formation of the Indian Claims Commission (ICC), Truman also neglected to mention that Congress had been adamantly refusing to establish any such entity since 1910,[63] abruptly reversing course only when comparisons to the

58 Statement by the President on Signing the Bill Creating the Indian Claims Commission, 13 August 1946, in *Public Papers of the Presidents of the United States* (US Government Printing Office, 1962) 414.

59 Ibid. Truman's reference to 'treaties and agreements with 200 tribes' is ambiguous at best. For the texts of the 369 ratified treaties compiled at the time his statement was made, see Charles J Kappler, *Indian Treaties, 1778–1883* (Interland, 1972, reprint of 1904 original). The texts of an additional 31 omitted by Kappler are included in Vine Deloria Jr and Raymond J DeMallie, *Documents of American Indian Diplomacy* (University of Oklahoma Press, 1999) vol 1, 181–232. This is quite apart from the scores of 'agreements' mentioned by Truman.

60 Statement by the President, 13 August 1946. He was referencing the *Indian Claims Commission Act*, 60 Stat 1049 (1946).

61 *Lone Wolf v Hitchcock* 187 US 553 (1903). For elaboration, see Blue Clark, *Lone Wolf v Hitchcock* (University of Nebraska Press, 1994); Walter R Echo-Hawk, *In the Courts of the Conqueror Decided* (Fulcrum Press, 2010) 161–86.

62 The estimate was submitted to Congress by Attorney General Francis Biddle, who was at the time of Truman's statement serving as US representative on the International Military Tribunal. As attorney general, Biddle argued against settling the American Indian land claims on grounds that paying even an amount equalling much less than a fair price would be far too expensive. See US House of Representatives, *Creation of Indian Claims Commission*, above n 56, 1466.

63 See Francis Leupp, *The Indian and His Problem* (Scribner's, 1910) 194–6; US House of Representatives, Subcommittee of the Committee on Indian Affairs, *Hearings on the Appropriations Bill of 1914* (64th Cong, 2nd sess, 1913) 99; Lewis

nazis' territorial seizures began to gain traction. Federal courts had been stonewalling efforts by Indians to be paid for confiscated lands since 1879;[64] and as recently as 1945, Supreme Court justice *cum* Nuremberg prosecutor Jackson ruled that Indian land claims were 'not compensable'.[65] Nor did Truman note that the ICC was explicitly precluded from returning land – no matter *how* it had been taken – to the Indigenous Nation(s) from which it was seized,[66] that any amounts paid as compensation would be determined by federal authorities subject to an endless variety of 'offsets' (deductions),[67] or that the Justice Department was charged with contesting each claim in every possible manner.[68]

It is clear that the ICC was neither 'the greatest submission ever made by a sovereign state to moral and legal claims' nor a 'pursuit of justice for its own sake', as one federal jurist was still insisting a quarter century after its creation.[69] Rather, it was conceived and structured to convey this (mis)impression while pursuing a diametrically opposing agenda. During the first twenty years of its operation the commission managed to 'retire' some $2 billion in claims, while awarding cash payouts of only $87 million.[70] The ICC nonetheless

Meriam, *The Problem of Indian Administration* (Johns Hopkins University Press, 1928) 805–11; John Collier, *From Every Zenith* (Sage Books, 1963) 294–9; *The Congressional Record* (21 June 1937) esp 6058, 6241, 6246, 6261.

64 It was not until 1879 that US courts formally acknowledged that American Indians were 'persons', and thus possessed with standing to bring legal actions. Doing so with regard to land claims, however, required an Act of Congress granting permission to proceed in each case. Given this hurdle, only 39 such claims were pressed between 1881 and 1923, none of them successfully. See *US ex rel Standing Bear v George Crook* 25 Fed Cas 695 (CCD, Nebraska, 1879); Stephen Dando-Collins, *Standing Bear is a Person* (Da Capo Press, 2005); E B Smith, *Indian Tribal Claims Decided in the US Court of Claims* (University Publications of America, 1976).

65 *Northwest Band of Shoshone Indians v US* 324 US 335 (1945). See Felix S Cohen, 'Indian Claims' in Lucy Kramer Cohen (ed), *The Legal Conscience: Selected Papers of Felix S Cohen* (Yale University Press, 1960) 264.

66 See Richard A Nielson, 'American Indian Land Claims: Land versus Money as a Remedy' (1972) 25 *University of Florida Law Review* 308.

67 See Howard Friedman, 'Interest on Indian Land Claims: Judicial Protection of the Fisc' (1970) 5 *Valparaiso University Law Review* 26; John R White, 'Barmecide Revisited: The Gratuitous Offset in Indian Land Claims Cases' (1978) 25 *Ethnohistory* 179; Russel Lawrence Barsh, 'Indian Land Claims Policy in the United States' (1982) 58 *North Dakota Law Review* 7, 13, 18–23; at 18, Barsh observes: 'Commission awards frequently represented less than one percent of the real value of the damages suffered by tribal claimants.'

68 Even those embracing the process acknowledged that the department was a relentlessly 'unsympathetic foe', a 'tough and clever opponent' dedicated to denying Indians *any* compensation wherever possible. See Harvey D Rosenthal, *Their Day in Court* (Garland, 1990) 23, 32, 87.

69 Quoted in John Kobler, 'These Indians Struck It Rich: The Utes' Treaty Land', *Saturday Evening Post*, 6 September 1972, 132.

70 US Senate, Subcommittee on Indian Affairs of the Committee on Interior and Insular Affairs, *Hearings on S 307, A Bill to Amend the Indian Claims Commission Act of 1946* (90th Cong, 1st sess, 1967) 74.

accomplished something of undeniable value: by the time of its dissolution in 1978, its efforts over a thirty-year period to document the legal basis of US title to every portion of 'the lower 48' states clarified the extent to which there was none:[71]

> From the close of the American Revolution to 1900, the United States took possession of more than two billon acres of land [belonging to] indigenous ... nations. Half of this area [*not* the '90 percent' touted by Truman] was purchased by treaty or agreement at an average price of less than seventy-five cents per acre. Another 325,000,000 acres, chiefly in the Great Basin area, was confiscated unilaterally by Act of Congress or Executive Order, without compensation. An estimated 350,000,000 acres in the contiguous forty-eight states ... were claimed by the United States without agreement or the pretense of a unilateral action extinguishing native title.[72]

The 675 million acres – more than a million square miles – that the United States had simply seized from Indigenous Nations,[73] using whatever force proved necessary, equals roughly one-third of the 48 contiguous states.[74] Moreover, the charade embodied in the ICC's effort to create an appearance of legitimate title acquisition through the imposition of *post hoc* cash 'settlements' did 'no more [to] put things right', in the words of American Indian Movement leader Russell Means, 'than if the Nazis had issued a check to the Vichy government after the fall of Paris'.[75] Legal scholar Vine Deloria Jr essentially concurred, observing that, rather than resolving territorial issues in favour of the United States, 'in an illegal taking by the government the land title of the tribe remains intact' unless *the Indians*

71 See generally, Jerome K Kuykendahl et al, *United States Indian Claims Commission, August 13, 1946–September 30, 1978: Final Report* (95th Cong, 1st sess, 1979). The commission's voluminous record – briefs, testimonies, findings and decisions – have been published in 200-odd volumes by Garland, and are available digitally through LexisNexis.

72 Barsh, above n 67, 7–8.

73 In comparison, when they reached the furthest limit of their eastward expansion in 1942, the nazis had seized about a three-quarters of a million square miles of Soviet territory. They held less than half a million square miles of the Soviet Union for more than a year, however, and adding Poland increases the total by only 120,000 square miles. See 'Operation Barbarossa', *New World Encyclopedia*, sec 6: 'Outcome'.

74 The Justice Department professed concern that the total might be even higher, warning Congress in 1956 that title to as much as half the continental United States was legally vulnerable. The area at issue is the equivalent of *all* federal landholdings in 1970. See Rosenthal, above n 68, 151; Public Lands Law Review Commission, *One-Third of the Nation's Land* (US Department of Interior, 1970).

75 Interview, April 1982.

voluntarily relinquish it.[76] Hence, the ICC's findings had merely 'clear[ed] out the underbrush' previously obscuring an accurate view of who actually owns which parts of the country.[77]

Now, as regards those treaties

Deloria's conclusion was correct with regard to the vast area to which the United States could point to no treaty or agreement as a basis for its assertion of legal title. However, it begged the question of whether the treaties by which Indigenous Nations had 'sold' their homelands to the federal government were themselves valid. Here, it is necessary to examine them through the lens of the international customary law codified in the 1969 *Vienna Convention on the Law of Treaties*.[78] Under Art 49 of that convention, treaties effected through fraud are deemed void, along with any benefits accruing to the perpetrator therefrom.[79] The same applies to treaties effected through coercion under Arts 51 and 52, and, under Art 50, treaties obtained by 'corrupting' signatories of the other party.

On 3 September 1783, Britain signed the *Treaty of Paris*, recognising the independence of the thirteen original US states and ceding to them, collectively, its 'discovery rights' to all territory between their western boundaries along the Allegheny/Appalachian mountain chain in the east and the Mississippi River in the west.[80] The rights conveyed included the monopolistic prerogative of acquiring land from Indigenous Nations located within the roughly 500,000 square miles involved, either by conquest or through treaty negotiations.[81] It

76 Vine Deloria Jr, *Behind the Trail of Broken Treaties* (Delacourt Press, 1974) 227.
77 Ibid 228.
78 Employing the *Vienna Convention on the Law of Treaties* is entirely appropriate because, according to the Swedish delegate to the drafting committee Hans Blix, 'It was generally agreed that most of the contents of the ... Convention were merely expressive of rules which existed under customary international law. Those rules obviously could be invoked as custom without reference to the present Convention.' Quoted in Ian Sinclair, *The Vienna Convention on the Law of Treaties* (Manchester University Press, 2nd edn, 1984) 8.
79 *Vienna Convention on the Law of Treaties*, UN Doc A/Con39/27 (1969) 289.
80 *Paris Peace Treaty* (3 September 1783). The boundaries of the area to which British rights were ceded are detailed in Art 2. The western boundaries of the thirteen colonies turned independent states were set by the Royal Proclamation of 7 October 1763, which designated everything west of the Allegheny/Appalachian mountain chain as unceded Indian territory. To a significant extent, the colonists' 'War of Independence' was fought to nullify the 'proclamation line', allowing Euroamerican expansion into Indian Country. See Thomas Perkins Abernathy, *Western Lands and the American Revolution* (Russell and Russell, 2nd edn, 1959).
81 Under the Eurocentric doctrine of discovery, the first European power to come upon an area previously unknown to/unclaimed by other European states held a monopoly in acquiring land in the area 'discovered' from its Indigenous owners.

is instructive that, as historian Allan Eckert observes, army commander in chief and future US President 'George Washington had *already* presented to Congress a paper, which he called a plan … by which the western lands belonging to the Indians could now most easily … and least expensively be wrested from them.'[82]

> He suggested … that the Indians be maneuvered into positions where they had little choice but to sell [by making] grants of land … to veterans of the Revolutionary War from such [strategically situated] parcels as the Virginia Military Lands and the Western Reserve Lands … Washington went on to make special mention of the fact that these settlers, being veterans [would] make an excellent militia to protect U.S. claims in the Ohio country … [By] heavily populating the Northwestern Territory, the settlers would soon kill off all the game and make the land so unattractive to the Indians that *they will be as eager to sell as we are to buy*.[83]

Only 'vacant land' (*vacuum domicilium*) could be claimed outright, although the principle was quickly extended to include 'ungoverned territory' (*terra nullius*). Acquisition of title by conquest was also recognised as legitimate under certain circumstances, but, for a number of reasons, the British found it more useful – and far less expensive – to negotiate treaties of cession/purchase with Indigenous Nations. The United States, deriving as it did from Britain, in a sense followed suit and eventually repudiated conquest rights altogether via the Stimson Doctrine. See Robert A Williams Jr, *The American Indian in Western Legal Thought* (Oxford University Press, 1990) esp 93–102; Sharon Korman, *The Right of Conquest* (Clarendon Press, 1996) esp 52–6, 238–9; Dorothy V Jones, *License for Empire* (University of Chicago Press, 1982) esp 21–35, 93–119.

82 Allan W Eckert, *That Dark and Bloody River* (Bantam Books, 1995) 440 (emphasis added). What Eckert refers to as a 'paper' is a pair of letters, the first from Washington to president of the Continental Congress Elias Boudinot on 17 June 1783, and the second to James Duane, chair of the Committee on Indian Affairs, on 7 September. Duane then incorporated the main elements of Washington's plan in a report to Congress dated 17 October 1783. For texts, see John C Fitzpatrick (ed), *The Writings of George Washington from the Original Manuscript Sources, 1745–1799* (US Government Printing Office, 1931–1944) vol 27, 16–18, 133–40; C Fred Worthington et al (eds), *Journals of the Continental Congress, 1774–1789* (US Government Printing Office, 1904) vol 25, 691–3.

83 Eckert, above n 82, 440 (original emphasis). Both the Virginia Military Lands and the Western Reserve Lands were large tracts in the 'Ohio country' allotted by the Continental Congress to Virginia and Connecticut, respectively, although Congress held no legal title. The 'Northwestern Territory', more usually called the Northwest Territory, encompassed all of the area west of Pennsylvania and north of the Ohio River, that is, the present states of Ohio, Indiana, Michigan, Illinois, Wisconsin and north-eastern Minnesota. See generally, Daniel P Barr, *Boundaries Between Us* (Kent State University Press, 2006). For the real reason why Washington felt an influx of militiamen might be useful in dealing with the Indians, see John Grenier, *The First Way of War* (Cambridge University Press, 2005) 10–13, 16–19, 148–69.

That, in Washington's estimation, was the point at which treaty negotiations should be initiated. He cautioned that it was important not to try to 'grasp too much' in any one transaction lest the Indians be provoked into mounting an armed resistance. Far better, he observed, to 'induce them to relinquish their territories and remove to the illimitable regions of the West' incrementally, area by area, treaty by treaty, taking care to consolidate gains and establish 'compact settlements' as 'forward posts' before taking the next bite, until the vast expanse east of the Mississippi was entirely free of its Indigenous owners:[84]

> He then very meticulously laid out for Congress a blueprint of negotiations ... First, government agents should [falsely inform] the Indians that as allies of the British, they had become conquered when the British surrendered, and had no land rights ... yet that the United States, in its generosity, would, if the Indians gave up their alleged claims, pay them a certain amount and provide them with new lands of their very own further west ... [T]reaty commissioners should [also] promise that the United States government *will endeavor to restrain our people from hunting and settling* on the new lands that had been so generously given to the tribes [in full knowledge] that the restrictions barring settlement would be very temporary [and that] when the Indians complained, as they obviously would, new negotiations could be undertaken [so that] with careful maneuvering, the tribes would again be ... pushed further west.[85]

Eckert rightly concludes that Washington's scheme, implemented in the 'dictated treaties' of *Fort Stanwix* (1784), *Fort McIntosh* (1785) and *Fort Finney* (1786), was 'immoral, unethical and actually criminal', while, with equal accuracy, Reginald Horsman depicts it as 'the prelude to the gradual extermination or expulsion of the Indians' east of the Mississippi.[86] Certainly, the

84 Fitzpatrick, above n 82, vol 27, 16–18.

85 Eckert, above n 82, 440–1 (original emphasis). Apart from the fact that not all of the peoples targeted for dispossession were British allies – the Oneidas, eg, fought alongside the insurgent colonists – the claim that those who *had* been British allies 'had become conquered', thereby forfeiting their land rights by virtue of the British surrender, had neither a legal basis nor a grounding in military custom. It was simply a bold-faced lie. As Washington well knew, there was nowhere 'further west' for the displaced Indians to go, other than into the territories of other Indigenous nations, which the federal government had no legal right to 'give' them.

86 Ibid 441; Reginald Horsman, 'American Indian Policy and the Old Northwest, 1783–1812' in Roger L Nichols (ed), *The American Indian* (Alfred A Knopf, 3rd edn, 1986) 137, 139. The *Fort Stanwix Treaty* was with the Six Nation Iroquois confederation (Haudenosaunee); the *Fort McIntosh Treaty* was with the Wyndots, Delawares (Lenapes) and Ottawas; the *Fort Finney Treaty*, also known as the *Treaty at the Mouth of the Great Miami*, was with the Shawnees. For texts, see Kappler, above n 59, 5–8, 6–8, 16–18.

pattern established at the very onset of US treaty making with American Indians corresponds with the criteria of fraudulence at issue in Art 49 of the *Vienna Convention*, that of making 'false statements, misrepresentations or other deceitful proceedings by which [the other party] is induced to give a consent to a treaty which it would not otherwise have given'.[87] This, in turn, casts in bold relief the hypocrisy infusing the lofty language of the 1787 *Northwest Ordinance*, proudly cited by Truman in 1946:

> The utmost good faith shall always be observed towards the Indians; their lands and property shall never be taken from them without their consent; and, in their property rights, and liberty, they shall never be disturbed, unless in just and lawful wars authorized by Congress.[88]

Cast not only as an articulation of principle but as a matter of law, the pledge may for obvious reasons be more accurately assessed as a lie. That US officials in every relevant capacity were perfectly aware that they were peddling false premises in their dealings with Indigenous Nations was amply demonstrated in August 1794, towards the end of Washington's first term as President. When his negotiators were finally confronted by Indians who had defeated military expeditions dispatched to 'chastise' them for attacking white settlers encroaching upon their territory,[89] they were undaunted by the prospect of the army being unleashed against them. This left the treaty commissioners little alternative but to concede the truth:

> For the first time they admitted that the American government had erred in its initial belief, following the Treaty of Paris, that because they had defeated the British, they had also defeated the tribes and thus rightly acquired the Indian lands by conquest. The … government now realized, they said, that the various Indian tribes were sovereign nations, undefeated and unsubdued, and that the lands north and west of the Ohio River were theirs.[90]

87 Drafting committee, quoted in Sinclair, above n 78, 16.
88 *An Ordinance for the Government of the Territory of the United States Northwest of the Ohio River* (13 July 1787) sect 14, art 3, in Worthington et al, above n 82, vol 32, 340–1.
89 The first of these was a mixed force of about 1,500 regulars and militiamen under Brigadier General Josiah Harmar, which was routed in October 1790. A larger force, commanded by Major General Arthur St Clair, was then dispatched. On 3 November 1791 it too was routed, incurring losses of over 630 dead – about a quarter of total US troop strength at the time and the most ever suffered by the army in a single battle with American Indians. See Eckert, above n 82, 526–9, 562–9, 738 n 744; Colin Galloway, *The Victory with No Name* (Oxford University Press, 2015) 66–7, 111–28.
90 Eckert, above n 82, 595. As one commissioner explained it, the government had 'put an erroneous construction on … our treaty with the King. As he had not

The Indians, an alliance of Shawnees, Miamis and several other peoples collectively referred to as the Wabash Confederation, then rejected the commissioners' attempt to purchase the area in which whites had settled in violation of the treaty signed at Fort Finney in 1786,[91] demanding that the United States instead remove the squatters, as it had obliged itself to do in the treaty, and quite reasonably suggesting that the amount offered for their land be divided among the evicted whites as compensation for *their* losses.[92] The result is illuminating. Washington, who had largely traded on his own reputation as an uncommonly vicious adversary – the result of a brutal scorched earth campaign he had launched against the Haudenosaunee (Iroquois Confederation) in 1779[93] – to cow Indians into accepting treaty terms, opted to refresh the lesson. Having enlisted Major General 'Mad Anthony' Wayne to double the size of the regular army in 1792, he ordered the general to use

purchased the country of [*sic*] you, of course he could not give it away; he only relinquished to the United States his claim to it' under the doctrine of discovery. Quoted in Randolph C Downes, *Council Fires on the Upper Ohio* (University of Pittsburgh Press, 1940) 323.

91 During the negotiations, the commissioners contended that the United States acquired title to a portion of the land at issue through the 1789 *Treaty of Fort Harmar*, although neither the Shawnees nor the Miamis were parties to it. For their part, the Six Nation Iroquois Confederation, with whom it *was* entered, flatly declared that 'the Fort Harmar cessions were a fraud'. The commissioners, concerned that a unified Indigenous resistance might otherwise be galvanised, thereupon 'announced [US] willingness to give up all lands ceded at Fort Harmer save that sold to [a pair of notorious groups of land speculators,] the Ohio Company and Symmes Associates'. The Shawnees and Miamis categorically rejected the 'compromise'. Downes, above n 90, 327, 323. For the *Fort Harmar Treaty* text, see Kappler, above n 59, 23–5.

92 The Indians enlisted a trusted British advisor, Alexander McKee, to prepare their response in written form and submit it to the commissioners on 15 August 1794. See Eckert, above n 82, 596.

93 Washington, still known as 'Town Destroyer' in many Indigenous traditions, ordered major general William Sullivan and his 5,000 seasoned troops to march through the heart of Seneca territory, in present-day western New York, laying waste to everything in their path, and 'not by any means, listen to any overtures of peace until the total ruin of their settlements is effected'. Forty-odd towns were burned, orchards levelled, crops ruined, fields salted and wells poisoned. The adjacent Mohawks were subjected to similar treatment, although the damage was less extensive. The number of Indians killed during the campaign was relatively small, since they consistently retreated in the face of Sullivan's much larger force, but, deprived of their food stores and shelter, many died of starvation and exposure over the winter. Neither peoples ever recovered from the onslaught and, while the goal of 'extirpating' them altogether was unmet, Washington's broader objective of 'inspir[ing] terror' in Indians more generally was by all accounts accomplished. For Washington's order to Sullivan, dated 31 May 1779, see Fitzpatrick, above n 82, vol 15, 189–93 (passages quoted at 192). For by far the best account of the 'Sullivan Campaign', see Barbara Alice Mann, *George Washington's War on Native America* (Praeger, 2005).

this 'Legion of the United States' to crush the Wabash 'recalcitrants' once and for all.

The general complied, leading an overwhelming force into the heart of Indian country and, after compelling the 'savages' to retreat at the battle of Fallen Timbers in August 1794, assigning his men to 'destroy every village, every trading post ... and every vestige of crops in a swath 10 miles wide and 50 miles in length'.[94] Rendered destitute, their economy obliterated, the Shawnees and Miamis sued for peace. The United States then imposed the 1795 *Treaty of Greenville* that deprived the Indians of virtually *all* their remaining territory, displacing them onto the lands of other peoples in the present-day state of Indiana.[95] Eventually, the Shawnee remnants, completely overrun by settlers even there, mostly agreed under the 1825 *Treaty of St Louis* to accept 'removal' *much* further west, onto a tract of what had been Osage land in south-eastern Kansas.[96]

Although Anthony Wayne's campaign was authorised by Congress, by no defensible interpretation can it be construed as the 'just war' described in the *Northwest Ordinance*. It was an 'aggressive' war in precisely the sense the term was employed at Nuremberg a century and a half later. The *Treaty of Greenville* was 'procured by the illegal threat [and] use of force' and was thus invalid under Art 52 of the *Vienna Convention*. Insofar as Wayne, who headed the commission that 'negotiated' it, ensured that his demoralised opponents were well plied with alcohol during the proceedings, and appears to have bribed some of them as well,[97] the treaty was also invalid under Art 50 of the convention, prohibiting the 'corruption' of signatories.

94 Eckert, above n 82, 619. Also see Grenier, above n 83, 200–1. For more detailed background, see Wiley Sword, *President Washington's Indian War* (University of Oklahoma Press, 1985).

95 *Treaty with the Wyandot, Etc* (3 August 1795), forcing the Indians to cede all of present-day Ohio other than a small remainder in the north-west corner of the state, as well as the southerly portion of what is now Indiana. For text, see Kappler, above n 59, 39–45. For further explication, and a map of the cession, see Eckert, above n 82, 624–5.

96 *Treaty with the Shawnee* (7 November 1825). Several additions and 'adjustments' were made under the *Treaty with the Shawnee, Etc* (29 October 1832), *Treaty with the Shawnee and Seneca* (29 December 1832), and *Treaty with the Shawnees* (10 May 1954). For texts, see Kappler, above n 59, 202–4, 370–2, 383–5, 618–26.

97 'As shown by the surviving quartermaster's receipts ... the army continued issuing large quantities of food [and] liquor to the Indians in attendance ... Wayne also had $25,000 worth of trade goods (not counting numerous kegs of Madeira and liquor) to facilitate the proceedings, [under stipulation that] the gifts be distributed only after his terms for the land cession were met.' While it was a time-honoured protocol of Indian diplomacy that gifts be dispensed by the hosts of any parlay, it was customary that they be given at the beginning, not the end, of the event. Moreover, the amount involved – an astronomical sum at the time – far exceeded the requirements of mere protocol. The United States was plainly 'cultivat[ing] clients among native leaders'. Robert M Owens, *Mr*

The mode of warfare waged by the United States against Indigenous Nations in the Southwest Territory was essentially identical to that in the Northwest.[98] So, too, was its approach to treaty making, a matter already apparent in the 1785–86 *Hopewell* treaties with the Cherokees, Choctaws and Chickasaws.[99] The Cherokees (Tsalagis), for example, ceded a considerable portion of their land in exchange for a guarantee that no whites be allowed to settle in the remainder, although, as the Cherokees pointed out during negotiations, some 3,000 families had *already* done so.[100] Rather than removing the squatters, or attempting to curb the influx, the United States simply convened a new treaty council in 1791 for purposes of convincing the Cherokees to cede the second illegally settled area as well.[101]

Again, the United States pledged that whites would be prevented from settling on the Cherokees' remaining territory – it was even provided that a passport would be necessary for any US citizen to enter it[102] – although, as always, thousands already had. The Cherokees were then informed in 1798 that they would have to cede this third area, with the United States guaranteeing the remainder of their homeland 'forever'.[103] The duration of eternity turned out in this instance to be barely more than six years, at which point they were compelled to cede still more land in the second *Tellico Treaty*,[104]

Jefferson's Hammer (University of Oklahoma Press, 2007) 28; Gregory Evans Dowd, *A Spirited Resistance* (Johns Hopkins University Press, 1992) 115.

98 'The Cherokees and Southern tribes were foolish enough to listen [to the British] and take the Hatchet Against us; Upon this our Warriors went into their Country, burnt their Houses, [and] destroyed their Corn.' George Washington, 24 December 1776, quoted in Grenier, above n 83, 146, 148–62.

99 *Treaty with the Cherokee* (26 November 1785); *Treaty with the Choctaw* (3 January 1786); *Treaty with the Chickasaw* (10 January 1786) in Kappler, above n 59, 8–16.

100 See Grenier, above n 83, 174–9.

101 *Treaty with the Cherokee* (2 July 1791), otherwise known as the *Treaty of Holston*, reaffirmed by the *Treaty with the Cherokee* (26 June 1794), in Kappler, above n 59, 29–34.

102 'Article IX: No citizen or inhabitant of the United States, shall … go into the Cherokee country, without a passport first obtained from the Governor of some one of the United States, or territorial districts, or such other person as the President of the United States may from time to time authorize to issue the same.'

103 *Treaty with the Cherokees* (2 October 1798), otherwise known as the first *Tellico Treaty*, wherein the United States claimed in the preamble that encroachments were due to its failure to properly mark the 1791 boundary, and that 'for purposes of … *remedying any inconveniences arising to citizens of the United States*' (emphasis added) as a result, it was necessary to 'adjust' the boundary. A further cession was required to maintain 'open and free [transit by] U.S. citizens' over a road already opened through Cherokee territory in complete disregard of the 1791 passport requirement. For text, see Kappler, above n 59, 51–5.

104 *Treaty with the Cherokees* (24 October 1804), in Kappler, above n 59, 73–4.

and so it went,[105] until, via the blatantly fraudulent 1835 *Treaty of New Echota*, they were forced to relinquish the balance of their territory east of the Mississippi.[106] Under the 1828 *Washington Treaty*,[107] they had also lost the supposed 'replacement lands' in Arkansas – *west* of the Mississippi – and pushed westward still further, into the 'Permanent Indian Territory' of Oklahoma (which was itself dissolved by the 1890 *Organic Act*).[108]

The Shawnee and Cherokee experiences with US treaty makers are emblematic. With only minor variations, they reflect those of every Indigenous Nation with which the United States entered into a treaty from its inception until the mid-1840s, when its initial goal of rendering the entire area in the *Treaty of Paris* 'Indian free' had been essentially attained. Thereafter, it expanded into a more immense domain stretching from the Mississippi to the Pacific, through a combination of the 1803 purchase from France of discovery rights in 'the Colony or Province of Louisiana',[109] the acquisition of Britain's discovery rights in Oregon Territory through the *London Convention* of 1818,[110] the annexation of Texas in 1846,[111] and the

105 The Cherokees were manoeuvred into three separate treaties ceding portions of their land in 1805, another in 1806, two more in 1816, and another in 1817. See Kappler, above n 59, 82–4, 90–2, 124–6, 133–4, 140–4.

106 *Treaty with the Cherokees* (29 December 1835), in Kappler, above n 59, 439–47. For background, see Theda Perdue and Michael Green, *The Cherokee Nation and the Trail of Tears* (Penguin Books, 2007); Russell Thornton, 'Cherokee Population Losses During the Trail of Tears: A New Perspective and a New Estimate' (1984) 31 *Ethnohistory* 289. More comprehensively – it covers the forced relocations not only of the Cherokees but of the Choctaws, Chickasaws, Creeks, Seminoles, Senecas, Shawnees, Lenapes and others to areas west of the Mississippi – see Gloria Jahoda, *The Trail of Tears* (Holt, Rinehart and Winston, 1975).

107 *Treaty with the Western Cherokee* (6 May 1828) in Kappler, above n 59, 288–91.

108 The *Oklahoma Organic Act*, 26 Stat 81 (1890), the *Curtis Act*, 30 Stat 495, 504 (1898), the *Burke Act*, 34 Stat 182 (1906) and the *Five Civilized Tribes Act*, 34 Stat 325 (1906) laid the groundwork for the proclamation of Oklahoma statehood on 17 November 1907. For background, see Angie Debo, *And Still the Waters Run* (Princeton University Press, 1940) 3–180.

109 As Britain had done in the *Treaty of Paris*, Spain ceded its right to acquire land within the 828,000 square mile Louisiana territory to France in the *San Ildefonso Treaty* of 1 October 1800. This right, *not* the land itself, is what the United States purchased by treaty from the French Republic in 1803. Not only did the United States agree in the treaty that 'the inhabitants of the ceded territory [would be] maintained and protected in the free enjoyment of their liberty [and] *property*' (emphasis added), but also, under Art 6 it was obliged to 'execute Such treaties and articles as may have been agreed between Spain and the tribes and nations of Indians until by mutual consent of the United States and the said tribes and nations other Suitable articles shall be agreed upon'. Treaty between the United States of America and the French Republic, 30 April 1803.

110 *London Convention*, 20 October 1818.

111 In a manner paralleling the procedure employed vis-à-vis Indigenous Nations east of the Mississippi, US settlers were already moving into Spanish Mexico's province of Texas by the time its border with the Americans' Louisiana Territory

forced cession of the northern half of Mexico under the 1848 *Treaty of Guadalupe Hidalgo*.[112] Its record vis-à-vis the 'western tribes' became, if anything, still worse.

With 'the west' foreclosed as a locale into which Indigenous Peoples could be 'removed', the US posture regarding American Indians became more openly exterminatory, as is attested in the example set by California after it became a state.[113] As both the constancy with which the United States pursued 'military solutions' to the 'Indian problem' and the methods used to attain them became more apparent to the peoples of the 'Great American Desert', coercion within the meaning of Art 51 of the *Vienna Convention*, and in many instances of Art 52 – intimidation of signatories – as well, became an inherent, if sometimes implicit, dimension of its negotiations even with peoples who had not directly experienced the army's aggression.[114]

was tentatively formalised in Art 3 of the 1819 *Adams-Onis Treaty* (about the same time that Mexico gained independence). The influx steadily increased, even after Mexico moved to halt it in 1829, and by March 1836 the settlers attained sufficient mass to declare Texas an independent republic. After repelling Mexico's attempt to restore control militarily the following month, the Republic of Texas functioned as such until it could arrange its annexation as a US state through the so-called *Tyler-Texas Treaty*. Since Mexico disputed the sovereignty of Texas, ratification of the latter Treaty in 1845 sparked the war between Mexico and the United States that was ended by the *Treaty of Guadalupe Hidalgo*. For background, see Gene M Brack, *Mexico Views Manifest Destiny, 1821–1846* (University of New Mexico Press, 1975) 18–80.

112 The *Treaty of Guadalupe Hidalgo* (2 February 1848), by which Mexico ceded 529,000 square miles of its territory to the United States, is usually misinterpreted as having left Indigenous land rights unsecured. Article 8, however, stipulates that 'Mexicans now established in territories previously belonging to Mexico, and which remain for the future within the limits of the United States, as defined by the present treaty, shall be free to continue where they presently reside … retaining the property which they possess in the said territories' and may also retain both 'the character of Mexicans [and] the title and rights of Mexican citizens'. Typically overlooked is the fact that, under its 1821 *Plan de Iguala*, Mexico conferred full citizenship upon all American Indians residing within its territorial boundaries. The 1848 Treaty secured their right to possess property within the ceded area in accordance with their own traditions (collectively), and obliged the United States to acquire title to Indian land by means of negotiation and purchase rather than seizure. This is apart from the issue of pre-existing grants of land made by Spain and Mexico, secured under Art 10 of the Treaty, deleted by the United States *post hoc* but reinstated by the *Protocol of Querétaro* (30 May 1848). Texts at 'Treaty of Guadalupe Hidalgo; February 2, 1848', *Avalon Project* <http://avalon.law. yale.edu/19th_century/guadhida.asp>. See Van Hastings Garner, 'The Treaty of Guadalupe Hidalgo and the California Indians' (1976) 9 *The Indian Historian* 10; Ernesto Chávez, *The US War with Mexico* (Bedford/St Martin's Press, 2007).

113 See Brendan C Lindsay, *Murder State* (University of Nebraska Press, 2012); Benjamin Madley, *An American Genocide* (Yale University Press, 2016).

114 As the matter is framed in a typically sterile academic analysis, a 'simple dynamic' was at work: '[T]he threat of defeat in war [was] sufficient to encourage

Instances of fraud became more blatant, as with the 1861 *Treaty of Fort Wise*, the result of a council called by the United States for purposes of supplanting the terms of the 1851 *Treaty of Laramie* with a new arrangement diminishing the land base of the Cheyennes and Arapahos by about 90 per cent.[115] When the Indians largely boycotted the proceedings,[116] US commissioners appear to have forged a few signatures and submitted the treaty to the Senate for ratification.[117] The latter body changed the provisions supposedly agreed to by the Indians, ratified its own version, then (re)presented it to them as a dictate.[118] Cheyennes and Arapahos refusing to abide

parties (specifically Indians) to settle for disadvantageous treaty terms.' Hence, as disparities between United States and Indigenous military capacities became ever more pronounced – and ever clearer to all concerned – the United States was increasingly able to 'drive harder and harsher bargains with the tribes'. Arthur Spirling, 'US Treaty-Making with American Indians: Institutional Change and Relative Power, 1784–1911' (2012) 56 *American Journal of Political Science* 84.

115 Under Art 5 of the *Treaty of Fort Laramie with the Sioux, Etc.* (17 September 1851), Cheyenne/Arapaho territory was recognised by the United States as encompassing all of eastern Colorado and a large portion of western Kansas. Based on the spurious assertion that the Indians were 'desirous of promoting settled habits of industry and enterprise among themselves, by abolishing the tenure in common by which they now hold their lands [and] assigning [it] in severalty to the individual members of the respective tribes', their domain was reduced to a barren tract in south-eastern Colorado under Art 1 of the *Treaty with the Arapaho and Cheyenne* (25 February 1861), known as the *Treaty of Fort Wise*. For texts, see Kappler, above n 59, 594–6, 807–11.

116 The Indians were quite aware of what was intended, at least in general terms. They had no desire to cede land, and most were fighting to staunch a mounting tide of whites pouring into their 1851 Treaty territory as the result of a gold discovery near the present-day city of Denver in 1858. When the treaty council occurred, 'only a few Cheyenne chiefs had come in [and] they represented only the peace faction', a distinct minority. 'The war faction stayed away, as did the Cheyenne Dog Soldiers [the *Hotamétaneo'o*, more literally translated as "Dog Men", an élite fighting force later called *Hotamémâsêhao'o*, or "Crazy Dogs"], who remained defiant in their camps on the Smoky Hill' River in western Kansas. David Fridtjof Halaas and Andrew E Masich, *Halfbreed* (Da Capo Press, 2004) 152.

117 While the handful of 'peace chiefs' attending the council are said to have been amenable to the treaty terms, 'they refused to bind their people until the question had been put to a vote' in which the war faction and, perhaps most especially, the Dog Soldiers were included. Yet, somehow, their signatures – or, more accurately, their marks – appeared on the document. It is possible that, rather than outright forgery, the chiefs were tricked by the local Indian agent into signing the treaty, without knowing that that is what it was, *after* the treaty commissioner had already left and the council presumably concluded. There is evidence that this was so, but, either way, the outcome was plainly fraudulent. See Stan Hoig, *The Sand Creek Massacre* (University of Oklahoma Press, 1961) 13; George Bird Grinnell, *The Fighting Cheyennes* (University of Oklahoma Press, 1955) 126 n 6.

118 Hoig, ibid 16–17.

by the 'treaty' were thereafter deemed 'hostile' and targeted for extermination in a military campaign that culminated in the 1864 Sand Creek Massacre.[119]

Once again, the example is merely representative. Even confirmed apologists for the colonial paradigm concede that the entire history of US treaty making with American Indians is replete with 'threats, coercion, bribery, and outright fraud by negotiators for the United States', and that the army was commonly employed to create conditions under which 'treaties were imposed upon them and they had no choice but to consent'.[120] It is thus virtually impossible to view Truman's 1946 assertion that the opposite was true as anything other than a 'Big Lie'.[121]

Ultimately, the challenge would be to find a single US treaty with American Indians that *did not* violate the *Vienna Convention*'s prohibitions of fraud, coercion and corruption. The same is true with regard to the 'land cession agreements', a semantic distinction employed after Congress prohibited further treaty making with Indians in 1871[122] to describe what were, in fact, treaties that continued to be made until 1911.[123] The question thus becomes whether

119 Ibid 129–62. Also see Ward Churchill, *A Little Matter of Genocide* (City Lights, 1997) 228–35.

120 Charles F Wilkinson and John M Volkman, 'Judicial Review of Indian Treaty Abrogation: As Long as the Water Flows, or Grass Grows Upon the Earth – How Long a Time is That?' (1975) 63 *California Law Review* 610, 611; in the second instance quoting the US Supreme Court's opinion in *Choctaw Nation v Oklahoma* 397 US 620, 630–1 (1970).

121 The term 'Big Lie' (*Große Lüge*) refers to a propaganda technique deriving from Hitler's observation in *Mein Kampf*, above n 7, 231, that 'the great masses of people ... will more easily fall victim to a big lie than a small one'. As nazi propaganda minister Goebbels explained in January 1941, 'when one lies, one should lie big, and stick to it'. Joseph Goebbels, *Die Zeit ohne Beispiel* (Zentralverlag der NSDAP, 1941) 367.

122 Further treaty making was prohibited in a rider attached to the *Indian Appropriations Act*, ch 120, 16 Stat 466 (1871). Although the term 'agreement' was formally employed from 1873 onwards, 'in instructions to federal negotiators in the field, and in the federal courts, both the process of negotiation and the documents were called treaties ... The major difference between treaties made before 1871 and those made afterward seems to have been that the later ones were ratified in statute form by both houses of Congress and that frequently the terms of the treaty were changed without any kind of hearing or consultation with the Indians', as the Senate had done with the *Treaty of Fort Wise* in 1861. Deloria and DeMallie, above n 59, vol 1, 249. See also George Rice, '25 USC § 71: The End of Indian Sovereignty or a Self-Limitation of Contractual Ability?' (1977) 5 *American Indian Law Review* 239.

123 Eg the Agreement with the Sioux, Arapaho, and Northern Cheyenne (23, 26 September, 11, 16, 21, 24, 27 October 1876) by which the Lakota supposedly ceded the Black Hills and contiguous portions of the 'Great Sioux Reservation' encompassing all of present-day South Dakota west of the Missouri River. Having reduced the Indians to a condition of absolute dependence upon the army for food, rations were cut off until the 'agreement' was signed. Although Art 12 of the still-binding *Fort Laramie Treaty* of 1868 specified that no instrument of cession would

the United States ever acquired legitimate title to *any* part of North America beyond the boundaries of the original thirteen states and perhaps a few enclaves such as New Orleans, St Louis and Detroit. To the extent that it did not, the land at issue is, to paraphrase President George H W Bush's 1990 description of Kuwait after the Iraqi invasion, illegally occupied territory, the legitimate governments of which have been usurped by a foreign aggressor.[124]

Before the court of history

> We must never forget that the record on which we judge these defendants today is the record on which history will judge us tomorrow.
>
> (US Chief Prosecutor Robert H Jackson, Nuremberg, 1945)

In some ways, Truman's attempt to deny the obvious had failed within three decades. By the early 1970s, not only radicals such as Sidney Lens,[125] but also popular historians such as John Toland[126] and mainstream academics such as Norman Rich were matter-of-factly acknowledging that:

> Neither Spain nor Britain {provided} the models for German expansion, but the Nordics of North America, who had ruthlessly pushed aside an inferior race to win for themselves soil and territory for the future. To undertake this essential task, sometimes difficult, always cruel – that was Hitler's version of the White Man's Burden.[127]

Since then, such observations have become quite common in serious historical analyses of the nazi expansion into Eastern Europe.[128] Recently, Carroll

be valid 'unless executed and signed by three-quarters of all adult male Indians', and fewer than 15 per cent of them did so even under the dire circumstances imposed upon them, Congress declared this to be sufficient and assumed title in the *Act of 28 February 1877* (19 Stat 254), also known as the 'Starve or Sign Act'. The Supreme Court confirmed these details in *United States v Sioux Nation of Indians* 448 US 371, 339–84 (1980).

124 George H W Bush, 'Address on the Invasion of Kuwait', 8 August 1990.

125 Lens contended that American triumphalist Homer Lea, who observed that the United States had 'been built up from the spoils of combat and conquest of the defenseless tribes' and extolled the virtues of 'military vigor' in bringing the country 'to the zenith of its physical greatness', was 'paid the dubious honor of having Adolf Hitler plagiarise a few paragraphs of his book for *Mein Kampf*'. Sidney Lens, *The Forging of the American Empire* (Thomas Y Crowell, 1971) 13.

126 John Toland, *Adolf Hitler* (Doubleday, 1976) vol 2, 802.

127 Norman Rich, *Hitler's War Aims* (W W Norton, 1973) 8.

128 'The vision that inspired the German colonial project in the East had {much} in common with the American ideology of the frontier', as Adam Tooze puts it. 'And the bloody conquest of the American West provided Germany with the historical warrant it needed to clear the Slavic population.' Stephen Fritz adds: 'If in execution the German plans for the occupied east resembled the last act in the

Kakel, a research historian at Johns Hopkins University, devoted an entire book to elaborating the connections between 'the American West and the Nazi East',[129] while another, by a professor of German studies at the University of Missouri is titled *Germany's Wild East*.[130]

The premise that the nature and objectives of nazi aggression in Eastern Europe was based upon the example set by the United States in its 'Indian wars' is no longer 'controversial', at least in its broad contours. The focus of denial has thus been increasingly narrowed, with particular weight placed on rejecting the idea that Indigenous Nations might be entitled to repossess at least *some* of the land taken from them,[131] and contending that the genocide perpetrated against them in the process was not 'really' genocide (with all the onus that would entail). The latter effort has centred in the first instance in a broader campaign to redefine the term 'genocide' by reducing it to a synonym for direct killing on a massive scale,[132] then attributing the Indigenous

bloody history of European colonialism, in inspiration Nazi ideas had more in common with American Manifest Destiny [with] Hitler … emphasizing that the bloody conquest of the American West provided both historical precedent and justification.' Mazower contends that after Carl Schmitt's 1939 lecture on why the United States presented 'a new model for Germany', Hitler 'started using what sounded very much like Schmittian language'. A number of similar examples might be cited. See Adam Tooze, *Wages of Destruction* (Viking Press, 2006) 469; Fritz, above n 23, 93; Mazower, above n 27, 577–8; Alan E Steinweis, 'Eastern Europe and the Notion of the "Frontier" in Germany to 1945' (1999) 13 *Yearbook of European Studies* 56, 57.

129 Carroll P Kakel III, *The American West and the Nazi East* (Palgrave, 2011).

130 Kristin Kopp, *Germany's Wild East* (University of Michigan Press, 2012).

131 This has devolved upon polemics to the effect that 'too much time has passed' for any form of restitution to be 'realistic', because of the 'fundamental unfairness' entailed in displacing the settlers now ensconced in areas from which Indigenous people were forcibly removed. In its more extreme form, the argument holds that Indigenous Nations have no rights because they never actually existed. Those subscribing to the first position have voiced no similar objections to the Zionist claim that a 2,000-year-old displacement of the Hebraic tribes (Jews) in Palestine imbued their descendants not only with a 'right of return', but a right to establish the state of Israel, expelling nearly a million Palestinians in the process. As concerns the second, it is noted that Hitler said the same with regard to Czechoslovakia, and Israeli Prime Minister Golda Meir with regard to Palestinians. An example of these polemics is provided in Paul Brodeur, *Restitution* (Northeastern University Press, 1985). For an archetypal articulation of the extreme position, see Allan van Gestel, 'When Fictions Take Hostages' in James A Clifton (ed), *The Invented Indian* (Transaction, 1990) 291. Hitler asserted that there was 'no such thing as a Czechoslovakian nation' in his 26 September 1938 speech at Berlin's Sportpalast. Meir's 1969 assertion that 'There is no such things as Palestinians … They do not exist' is quoted in Rashid Khalidi, *Palestinian Identity* (Columbia University Press, 1997) 147.

132 The literature devoted to advancing this argument is voluminous. For a representative sample, see the essays collected in George Andreopoulos (ed), *Genocide* (University of Pennsylvania Press, 1994). For rebuttal, see Raphaël Lemkin, *Axis*

population reduction in North America to 'natural causes',[133] and arguing in effect that each instance of mass murder was 'anomalous'.[134]

It has become fashionable to seize upon the term 'ethnic cleansing', popularised by journalists in 1992,[135] to conjure the desired illusion. A prime example is historian Gary Clayton Anderson's contention that the 'indiscriminate killing' of American Indians, 'while common' and motivated by 'extreme racial hatred', added up to 'the more moderate and well-understood process of ethnic cleansing ... not genocide'.[136] Anderson, in peddling this false distinction, ignores the fact that even the lone authority upon which he relies concedes that 'ethnic cleansing and genocide are distinguishable only by the ultimate intent' of the perpetrators,[137] and grossly misrepresents the 1948 *Convention on Prevention and Punishment of the Crime of Genocide* to bolster his argument.[138]

Rule in Occupied Europe (Carnegie Endowment for World Peace, 1944) 79–80, wherein the term is both coined and explained.

133 The linchpin of this perpetrator-free 'explanation' of Indigenous population loss is the 'virgin soil hypothesis' first advanced in Alfred W Crosby Jr, *The Columbian Exchange* (Greenwood Press, 1972) 36–8; further developed in Crosby's *Ecological Imperialism* (Cambridge University Press, 1986) 196–9, 215–16; popularised by Jared Diamond, *Guns, Germs, and Steel* (W W Norton, 1997) 211–12. Among the problems with the hypothesis – apart from the exculpatory use to which it has been put by deniers, who embraced it as 'fact' while neglecting to mention that Crosby himself described 'virgin soil epidemics' as a 'dismal genocidal process' – is that it omits the prospect that settlers and officials frequently and deliberately infected American Indians with pathogens to which they had no immunity. See Barbara Alice Mann, *The Tainted Gift* (Praeger, 2009); David S Jones, *Rationalizing Epidemics* (Harvard University Press, 2004).

134 Ward Churchill, *Perversions of Justice* (City Lights, 2003) 313–15.

135 See William Safire, 'On Language', *New York Times Magazine*, 14 March 1993, 23; Roy Gutman, *A Witness to Genocide* (Macmillan 1993); Norman Cigar, *Genocide in Bosnia* (Texas A&M University Press, 1995).

136 Gary Clayton Anderson, *The Conquest of Texas* (University of Oklahoma Press, 2005) 7, 15, 17.

137 While Anderson claims that the 'process of ethnic cleansing' is 'well-understood' as being 'more moderate' than genocide, the source he cites says precisely the opposite, ie that the term came into usage as a 'euphemism for genocide', and that it remains exceedingly 'imprecise'. Even when defined as the forced expulsion of undesired populations from particular areas – as opposed to genocide, falsely defined as 'the intentional killing of all or part of targeted groups' – 'both literally and figuratively, ethnic cleansing bleeds into genocide, as mass murder is [often, as in Texas] committed to rid the land of a people'. Norman M Naimark, *Fires of Hatred* (Harvard University Press, 2002) 3–4.

138 As Anderson has it, 'In Articles 2 and 3 of the 1948 UN Convention, genocide is defined as the intentional *killing* of people because of their "national, ethnical, racial or religious identity"' (emphasis added), later adding that such killing must be 'an act to destroy an *entire* ethnic group, as defined by the United Nations in 1948' (emphasis added). Article 3 has nothing to do with defining the crime. The relevant passage in Art 2 reads, 'In the present Convention, genocide means any of the following acts committed with intent to destroy, in

No less egregiously, although he repeatedly refers to Yugoslavia in his explication of how ethnic cleansing and genocide are supposedly demarcated under the 2000 *Rome Statute* establishing the International Criminal Court two years later,[139] he neglects to mention that the United Nations formally declared 'the abhorrent policy of "ethnic cleansing"' to be 'a form of genocide' in 1992,[140] or that, subsequently and repeatedly, it was judicially construed as such by the International Criminal Tribunal for the Former Yugoslavia.[141] Similarly, he offers not the least hint that acknowledged experts in the field routinely describe ethnic cleansing as 'implicit genocide',[142] a 'euphemism for genocide',[143] 'genocide's "territorial" and "spatial" dimension',[144] and a 'modality of genocidal violence.'[145]

There has been a mounting push-back against this sort of 'scholarly' dishonesty over the past thirty years, evidenced by a steadily lengthening roster

whole or *in part*, a national, ethnical, racial or ethnical group, as such' (emphasis added). 'Killing members of the group' is only one of the five 'acts' listed thereafter, and it is explicitly stated that intent to destroy the group 'in part' is no less genocidal than intent to 'destroy an entire ethnic group'. See Gary Clayton Anderson, *Ethnic Cleansing and the American Indian* (University of Oklahoma Press, 2014) 3, 9. For clarification of how the convention's 'in part' clause is *actually* interpreted vis-à-vis 'ethnic cleansing', see *Final Report of the Commission of Experts Established Pursuant to Security Council Resolution 780 (1992)*, UN Doc S/1994/674 (1994) esp [94].

139 Anderson, above n 138, 4, 6, 9, 12.

140 *The Situation in Bosnia and Herzegovina*, UN Doc A/RES/47/121 (18 December 1992). The point was reiterated in at least four subsequent United Nations General Assembly resolutions.

141 More than seventy individuals were charged with genocide in connection with 'ethnic cleansing' operations carried out in the former Yugoslavia during the early-to-mid 1990s. The cases in which verdicts had been reached before the publication of Anderson's book were *Prosecutor v Krstić* (Case No IT-98-33-T; judgment, 2 August 2001); *Prosecutor v Popović et al* (Case No IT-05-88-T; judgment, 10 June 2010); *Prosecutor v Tolimir* (Case No IT-05-88/2T; judgment, 12 December 2012). Radovan Karadzić has since been convicted of genocide.

142 Christopher R Browning, *Nazi Policy, Jewish Workers, German Killers* (Cambridge University Press, 2000) 25. As is observed elsewhere, 'by defining genocide as "deliberately inflicting on members of a group conditions intended to bring about its destruction in whole or in part [in Art 2c]," the 1948 UN Convention on Genocide in effect implicitly included ethnic cleansing. (The term itself was not in use in 1948).' Alfred A Cave, *Lethal Encounters* (Praeger, 2011) xi.

143 See Shaw, above n 37, 66–83. Also see the sharp framing offered by Rony Blum et al, '"Ethnic Cleansing" Bleaches the Atrocities of Genocide' (2007) 18 *European Journal of Public Health* 204, 204: '"[E]thnic cleansing" is … a euphemism for genocide … [Like] "racial hygiene" in Nazi medicine, it expropriates pseudo-medical terminology [in a way that] reifies a dehumanized view of the victims as sources of filth and disease, and propagates the reversed social ethics of the perpetrators.'

144 Kakel, above n 129, 243 n 1. Also see Shaw, above n 37, 81–2.

145 Carroll P Kakel III, *The Holocaust as Colonial Genocide* (Palgrave Macmillan, 2013) 188, 189–90, 201.

of historians and others detailing the reality that the US genocide(s) of American Indians was indeed genocide.[146] Should the trend continue, it will soon be no more controversial to employ the proper term in characterising the destruction of North America's Indigenous Peoples than it has long since become to acknowledge the conceptual linkages joining US and Hitlerian policies of expansion. It should be a short step to recognition that, notwithstanding the ICC's lengthy sham, much of the United States remains 'occupied America',[147] and that the country itself is a 'colonial settler state' of the sort the nazis sought to establish in Eastern Europe.[148]

In view of the extent to which the officially endorsed orthodoxies of denial have been eroded over the past seventy years, it is surprising that little attention has been paid to the relationship between 'Munich' and the pre-existing example set by the United States in its diplomatic relations with the Indigenous Nations of North America. Every one of the signature characteristics of Hitlerian diplomacy – the professions of a desire for peace while preparing for and regularly threatening war, repetitious assurances of entertaining 'no further territorial ambitions' while pursuing a step-by-step plan to acquire further vast expanses of *Lebensraum*, continuous violation of treaty guarantees and proposals 'to sanctify treaty-breaking by sealing a new treaty'[149] – was a technique integral to the US approach to treaty making with American Indians from the first moment of the Republic.

That Hitler was well aware of other aspects of the process through which 'the Nordics of North America' had successfully undertaken 'the winning of the west',[150] and that he set about adapting them to the markedly different circumstances in which he was operating, is beyond dispute. There is no logical reason to assume that he was not equally aware of the diplomatic/treaty-making dimension as well. On the contrary, since Hitler was instructed

146 See Churchill, *A Little Matter*, above n 119; Cave, above n 142; Kakel, *American West*, above n 129; Kakel, *Holocaust*, above n 145; Lindsay, above n 113; Mann, *George Washington's War*, above n 93; Madley, above n 113; David E Stannard, *American Holocaust* (Oxford University Press, 1992); Lilian Friedberg, 'Dare to Compare: Americanizing the Holocaust' (2000) 24 *American Indian Quarterly* 353; Andrew Woolford, Jeff Benvento and Alexander Laban Hinton (eds), *Colonial Genocide in Indigenous North America* (Duke University Press, 2014).

147 The quotation is from the title of Rodolfo Acuña, *Occupied America* (Canfield Press, 1972), but is obviously applicable to American Indians.

148 The term in quotation marks was first popularised by Maxine Rodinson's *Israel* (Pathfinder Press, 1973), and has since evolved into the descriptor of an entire analytic paradigm. See Lorenzo Veracini, *Settler Colonialism* (Palgrave Macmillan, 2010); Damien Short, *Redefining Genocide* (Zed Books, 2016).

149 Gollancz et al, above n 36, 42.

150 Among books Hitler is known to have admired is amateur historian *cum* US President Theodore Roosevelt's triumphalist – and deeply racist – *The Winning of the West* (G P Putnam's Sons, 1889–1896). See Klaus P Fischer, *Hitler and America* (University of Pennsylvania Press, 2011) 11–12.

in geopolitics by no less than Karl Haushofer[151] and read widely on matters bearing on the history of US–Indian relations,[152] it would be astonishing if he was not.

The United States has long employed a line of legal argumentation closely paralleling the above-discussed 'genocide was not *really* genocide if we committed it' mode of denial, to the effect that treaties with Indigenous Nations, unlike the treaties with European nations entered into and broken by the nazis, were never 'really' treaties in the first place. This dates from Chief Justice John Marshall's 1831 opinion in *Cherokee v Georgia*, holding that US relations with American Indians were *sui generis*, 'marked by peculiar and cardinal directions which nowhere else exist', and were uncontemplated in the law of nations.[153] While Marshall's assertion contradicted US legal doctrine until that point,[154] as emphasised in the dissenting views expressed by other justices in *Cherokee* itself,[155] it has underpinned the country's Indian policies ever since.

The utility of Marshall's fabrication in lending an aura of legitimation to the fulfilment of settler ambitions is demonstrated by the fact that, despite much bitterness accruing from the US wars to win and retain independence

151 See Kershaw, *Hitler, 1889–1936*, above n 6, 248–9.

152 It may be that 'Hitler had a magpie mind [and] speed-read books looking for material he counted as useful – meaning anything that fitted into his mosaic of misplaced historical analogy and pseudoscience', but that hardly diminishes the fact that he was influenced by what he read, or that he apparently read a *lot*. Among the 16,000-odd books comprising his personal trove were many 'well-thumbed volumes' – including translations of historical and theoretical works by Americans – replete with his marginalia and evidence that he was 'an inveterate underliner'. See 'Know a Man by His Books', *The Economist*, 2 October 2008; Timothy W Ryback, *Hitler's Private Library* (Alfred A Knopf, 2008).

153 *Cherokee v Georgia* 30 US (5 Pet) 1, 16 (1831). For further analysis, see Ward Churchill, *Acts of Rebellion: The Ward Churchill Reader* (Routledge, 2003) 8–11.

154 As Secretary of State Thomas Jefferson put it in 1793, '[T]he Indians [have] full, undivided and independent sovereignty as long as they choose to keep it, and that might be forever.' Or, to quote Attorney General William Wirt in 1828, insofar as 'Indians are independent to the purpose of treating, their independence is to that purpose as absolute as any other nation … Like all other nations, they have the power of war and peace. Like any other nation, their territories are inviolable by any other sovereignty … They are entirely self-governed – self-directed. They treat, or refuse to treat, at their pleasure; and there is no human power that can rightly control their discretion in this respect.' Andrew A Lipscomb (ed), *The Writings of Thomas Jefferson* (Thomas Jefferson Memorial Association, 1903–1904) vol 1, 341; 'Georgia and the Treaty of Indian Spring [July 28, 1828]' in *Official Opinions of the Attorneys General of the United States* (US Government Printing Office, 1869) vol 11, 110–66; quotations at 133–4.

155 Marshall's opinion was endorsed by only one justice. Four others lodged strong dissents on the grounds indicated, but not jointly. Hence, Marshall's view prevailed. See Jill Norgren, *The Cherokee Cases* (McGraw-Hill, 1996) 100–9; Echo-Hawk, above n 61, 87–120.

from Britain, his 'trilogy' of opinions ostensibly defining the legal relationship between the United States and Indigenous Nations – not only *Cherokee*, but the second of the so-called Cherokee Cases, *Worcester v Georgia* (1832), and the earlier *Johnson v McIntosh* (1823)[156] – were quickly cited as precedent by the courts of the three remaining Anglophone settler colonies/states of Canada,[157] Australia[158] and New Zealand (Aotearoa).[159] By the 1840s, they were being embraced in recommendations on colonial policy advanced by the British House of Commons.[160] The Privy Council was still invoking *McIntosh* in opinions pertaining to its African colonies well into the twentieth century.[161]

The most striking example is Canada, where the courts began to invoke Marshall's 'Indian opinions' almost before the ink was dry on the *British North America Act 1867* (UK) making it self-governing.[162] More than a century later, the Canadian Supreme Court was still extolling *McIntosh* as 'the *locus classicus* of the principles governing aboriginal title',[163] and thus consistently ruling that 'an Indian treaty is unique; it is an agreement *sui generis* which is neither created nor terminated according to the rule of international law'.[164] In 1990, and again in 1996, it went further, drawing upon the earlier-mentioned – and *Cherokee*-derivative – *Lone Wolf*

156 *Worcester v Georgia* 31 US (6 Pet) 515 (1832); *Johnson v McIntosh* 21 US (8 Wheat) 543 (1823).
157 See Bruce Clark, *Native Liberty, Crown Sovereignty* (McGill-Queens University Press, 1991) 12–28.
158 Since Australia did not engage in treaty making with Indigenous Peoples, the colony's early jurists were interested mainly in Marshall's treatise on discovery doctrine. See Blake A Watson, 'The Impact of the American Doctrine of Discovery on Native Land Rights in Australia, Canada, and New Zealand' (2011) 34 *Seattle University Law Review* 507, 512–18; Peter H Russell, *Recognizing Aboriginal Title* (University of Toronto Press, 2005).
159 Having entered into the Treaty of Waitangi with the islands' Indigenous Maoris in 1840, New Zealand's jurisprudence has from the outset hewed closely to Marshall's formulations. See *Queen v Symonds* (1847) NZPCC 387 [380], [390], [392]; Watson, 'Impact of the American Doctrine', ibid 526–9.
160 During 1840, legal authority Edward Gibbons Wakefield, testifying before a select committee formulating recommendations regarding colonial policy pertaining to New Zealand, explained the 'well-understood principle of law in America' in '*Johnstone v. Mackintosh*'. In its report, submitted a year later, the committee elevated Marshall's view to 'a principle of *international* law' (emphasis added) and recommended that it be adopted. See Select Committee on New Zealand, *Report* (House of Commons, 1841) vii, ix, 48, 55, quoted in Watson, 'Impact of the American Doctrine', above n 158, 523–4.
161 See, eg, *In Re Southern Rhodesia* (1919) AC 211; *Tijani v Sec, Southern Nigeria* (1921) 2 AC 399; *Oyekan v Adele* (1957) 2 All ER 788.
162 *Connelly v Woolrich* (1867) 11 LCJ 197.
163 *Calder v British Columbia (AG)* (1973) SCR 313 [120].
164 *Simon v Queen* (1985) 2 SCR 387 [404]. Canada cited both *McIntosh* and *Worcester* as well as the more recent *US v Santa Fe Railroad* 314 US 339 (1941) as precedents. The passage is repeated in *R v Sundown* (1999) 1 SCR 393 [24].

opinion to assert Canada's 'right' unilaterally to alter the terms of treaties with Indigenous Nations.[165]

The upshot is that, in both the United States and its Canadian appendage, treaties with Indigenous Nations are accorded the status of being, at most, 'analogies to … international law' imbedded within their respective domestic codes,[166] and both countries have taken 'a reductionist approach to interpreting their Treaty obligations, but an expansionist approach to interpreting the privileges they gained' therefrom.[167] The postures assumed by both countries are in obvious violation of Art 27 of the *Vienna Convention*, holding that 'a party may not invoke the provisions of its internal law as justification for its failure to perform a treaty', as well as Art 37 of the UN's *Declaration on the Rights of Indigenous Peoples*,[168] wherein states are obliged to observe and enforce '*sui generis*' treaties no less than others. Only Canada has as yet been called to account on that score by an international body.[169]

Despite the ubiquitous transgressions of Indigenous rights perpetrated by countries that internalised Marshall's fabrications to mask the criminality of their policies, only the US record served as the template for Hitlerian diplomacy. This, added to the doctrinal overlaps between manifest destiny and *Lebensraumpolitik* as rationales for expansionism, the racism infusing both nazism and Euroamerica's 'Aryanist' ideologies,[170] the mutual embrace of

165 *R v Sioui* (1990) 1 SCR 1025; *R v Badger* (1996) 1 SCR 771. See Ann Laquer Estin, '*Lone Wolf v. Hitchcock*: The Long Shadow' in Sandra L Cadwalader and Vine Deloria Jr (eds), *The Aggressions of Civilization* (Temple University Press, 1984) 215.

166 John Borrows, 'Wampum at Niagara: The Royal Proclamation, Canadian Legal History, and Self-Government' in Michael Asch (ed), *Aboriginal and Treaty Rights in Canada* (University of British Columbia Press, 2011) 169, 171. See also Grace Li Xiu Woo, *Ghost Dancing with Colonialism* (University of British Columbia Press, 2011) 182; Christine A Klein, 'Treaties of Conquest: Property Rights, Indian Treaties, and the Treaty of Guadalupe Hidalgo' (1996) 26 *University of New Mexico Law Review* 201, 211.

167 Indigenous Bar Association of Canada, 'Strengthening Partnerships between States and Indigenous Peoples: Treaties, Agreements, and Other Constructive Arrangements' (16–17 July 2012) 4.

168 United Nations, *Declaration on the Rights of Indigenous Peoples*, UN Doc A/RES/61/295 (13 September 2007).

169 *Hul'qumi'num Treaty Group v Canada*, Inter-American Commission on Human Rights Case No 12.374, accepted on 30 October 2009. See also Séanna Howard and Akilah Kinnison, 'Submission to the U.N. Committee on the Elimination of Racial Discrimination by Hul'qumi'num Treaty Group in Relation to Canada's 19th and 20th Periodic Reports' (20 January 2012) 3–4.

170 It is worth noting that Hitler proclaimed the then much-celebrated American zoologist – and staunch Aryanist – Madison Grant's 1916 book, *The Passing of the Great Race*, to be his 'bible'. See Kühl, above n 48, 85. For deeper background, see Reginald Horsman, *Race and Manifest Destiny* (Harvard University Press, 1981).

eugenics,[171] the massive conscription of racially defined 'inferiors' as slave labour,[172] genocide and aggressive war completes the picture of how the United States provided the model upon which Hitler's intended empire was to be constructed. Césaire's 'discourse on colonialism' has been validated to an extent that perhaps not even he could have imagined.

In any contest, including the struggle to effect constructive socioeconomic and political change, it is imperative, as the Chinese strategist/philosopher Sun Tzu famously observed more than 2,500 years ago, truly to 'know your enemy'.[173] Sun went on to say that the key to whatever success one's opponent might enjoy will be invariably be 'based on deception'.[174] Placing ever greater emphasis on and corresponding awareness of the US role as *the* prototype of 'Hitler's empire' will go far towards stripping away the liberal democratic veneer under which it has sought to conceal the ugly reality,[175] exposing it for what it is and has always been. Given the dominance of the United States in the contemporary world imperial system, this is a worthy objective, shedding light as it does on the nature of the system as a whole.[176]

171 Prior to the 1930s, the United States led the world not only in theorising and teaching eugenics, but in implementing eugenics policies. Both before and after the nazi assumption of power, the Rockefeller Foundation and other US funders underwrote the Kaiser Wilhelm Institutes and other centres of 'racial research' in Germany, and as late as 1935 American eugenicists were still accepting honours for their contributions to 'racial science' from German universities. Kühl, above n 48, 20–1; Edwin Black, *War Against the Weak* (Four Walls Eight Windows, 2003) 277–312.

172 This applies not only to the antebellum era of formal slavery in the United States, but to the *de facto* slavery embodied in the system of 'convict leasing' and penal 'chain gangs'. By comparison, the nazis' utilisation of slave labour was far less extensive and sustained. See Edward E Baptiste, *The Half Has Never Been Told* (Basic Books, 2014); Ned Sublette and Constance Sublette, *The American Slave Coast* (Lawrence Hill Books, 2016); Douglas A Blackmon, *Slavery by Another Name* (Doubleday, 2008). For comparison purposes, see Tooze, above n 128, 513–38; Mazower, above n 27, 307–18.

173 Sun Tzu, *The Art of War* (Filaquarian, 2007) 49.

174 Ibid 7.

175 The guise itself is deceptive. Despite its image as the preferable alternative to fascism, liberalism was the source of colonialism in its modern form, and the horrors described by Césaire. The vaunted 'liberty' it purports to enshrine was from the beginning a benefit accruing exclusively to the colonising population, racially defined, never to the colonised 'others'. These dynamics are explored in a number of sources. For a succinct and elegant handling, see Lisa Lowe, *The Intimacies of Four Continents* (Duke University Press, 2015) 101–33.

176 See especially Ellen Meiksins Wood, 'Democracy as Ideology of Empire' and Adam Hanieh, 'Praising Empire: Neoliberalism under Pax Americana', both in Colin Mooers (ed), *The New Imperialists* (Oneworld, 2006) 9, 167. For additional perspectives, see James H Mittleman (ed), *Globalization* (Lynne Rienner, 1997); Richard Falk, *Predatory Globalization: A Critique* (Polity, 1999); James Petras and Henry Veltmeyer, *Globalization Unmasked* (Zed Books, 2001).

It reveals that those countries seeking to justify their present settler colonial configurations by espousing legal doctrines arising from the Marshall trilogy, all of them important players in the system of globalised imperialism, are ultimately appealing to principles enunciated far more clearly by nazism's *kronjurist* ('crown jurist') Carl Schmitt.[177] This exposure of the dictatorial core of (neo)liberalism's vaunted 'democratic alternative' to the totalitarian impulse of modernity in ways previously unnoticed even by Schmittian scholars can only serve to further discredit the principle ruse through which the (neo)colonial order is stabilised and perpetuated.[178] Here, not only the domestic legal codes and triumphalist national discourses of the United States and its imitators are at issue,[179] but

177 In his 1922 essay, *Politische Theologie* (*Political Theology*), a term he employed to describe the concept of sovereignty, Schmitt defined 'the sovereign' as being 'he who decides upon the exception', ie who is empowered to step beyond the rule of law 'in the public interest'. This is precisely the circumstance Marshall sought to legitimise in *McIntosh* through the fabrication of new law. His innovation, refined in the *Cherokee* Cases, purported to include American Indians under the umbrella of the US legal system while simultaneously excluding them from it, a manoeuvre readily encompassed within Schmitt's concept of 'the state of exception'. Marshall argued from a position in which sovereignty was theoretically vested not in an individual, but in 'the people' by way of the state, while Schmitt argued the opposite. In a 1921 essay, Schmitt demonstrated that the supposedly unbridgeable distinction is illusory. For the passage quoted, see Carl Schmitt, *Political Theology* (MIT Press, 1988). For the implications of Schmitt's theory, and its applicability to liberal democratic contexts, see Giorgio Agamben, *State of Exception* (University of Chicago Press, 2005) esp 35, 54–5. Also see Georgio Agamben, *Homo Sacer* (Stanford University Press, 1998) esp 49–50.

178 In *Die Diktator* (translated as *Dictatorship*) (1921) he introduced the concept of 'the state of exception' crystallised a year later in *Political Theology* (ibid). Schmitt pointed out that, while 'the constitution of a state [may be] democratic', it will invariably provide for the declaration of a 'state of emergency' (*Ausnahmezustand*) by the head of state during which constitution procedures are suspended to one or another extent, and that 'every [such] exercise of state power independent of the approval of the majority can be called dictatorship'. This was the procedure used by the nazis to gain power in 1933 and to consolidate and sustain it. Agamben observes that exercise of what might be called 'the dictatorial option' has always been routine practice in liberal democracies, and that it has been uninterruptedly employed since 2001. See Carl Schmitt, *Dictatorship* (Polity, 2014) 148–79; Agamben, *State of Exception*, ibid 1–31. For an interesting, marginally successful, attempt to apply these concepts to Indigenous Nations, see Mark Rifkin, 'Indigenizing Agamben: Rethinking Sovereignty in Light of the "Peculiar" Status of Native Peoples' in Marcelo Svirsky and Simone Bignall (eds), *Agamben and Colonialism* (Edinburgh University Press, 2012) 77. On the '"peculiar" status' itself, see Natsu Taylor Saito, *From Chinese Exclusion to Guantánamo Bay* (University Press of Colorado, 2006) 19–22, 28–31.

179 For a broad analytical survey of such discourses in the United States, see Amy Kaplan and Donald L Pease (eds), *Cultures of United States Imperialism* (Duke University Press, 1993). As prime examples of similar swill being expounded on an even grander scale, see Niall Ferguson, *Empire* (Basic Books, 2003); Niall Ferguson, *Civilization* (Allen Lane, 2011).

entire vectors of international law concocted since 1945 as a means of universalising their self-serving juridical fables.[180]

Marking a path

> To know how to get to where you want to go, you have to know where you are right now. And in order to know *that*, it's necessary to know where it was you were the day before. Past, present, future. They're all parts of the same whole. Lose track of any one of them, you're lost.
>
> (Noble Red Man (Mathew King), Oglala Lakota, 1982)

The reality is that liberalism is simply the less honest face of nazism, and quite possibly the face nazism itself would have displayed a century or more after winning its war of extermination in the east.[181] This reality necessitates a fundamental change in the 'rules of engagement' observed by those purporting to oppose the status quo and seek its constructive transformation. From *that* perspective, placing reliance upon state-sanctioned methods in hopes of effecting liberal 'solutions' to problems at hand is no less patently absurd than arguing that such an approach might have led to fundamental alterations of nazism.[182]

The notion that anything of substance obtains from such purely cosmetic gestures as the official 'apologies' lately offered by the United States to the Kanaka Maoli (Indigenous Hawaiians) and American Indians for the devastation of their societies, usurpation of their governments, obliteration of their economies and expropriation of their homelands – absent *any* concrete form of restitution – is ludicrous.[183] So too, the idea that state/settler-sponsored 'truth

180 The issues are brilliantly distilled in Antony Anghie, *Imperialism, Sovereignty, and International Law* (Cambridge University Press, 2005) 211.

181 A solid case has been made that the basis of the massive popular support enjoyed by Hitler until the autumn of 1943 was not that Germans were more racist than other Europeans, but the petty benefits they gleaned from the nazis having established a remarkably generous welfare state. The fact that German living standards were being underwritten though the systematic plunder of non-Germanic 'others' was accepted or simply ignored. See Götz Aly, *Hitler's Beneficiaries* (Metropolitan Books, 2007).

182 Myriad contradictions exist in reliance upon state-sanctioned methods. One aspect is fruitfully examined in Peter Gelderloos, *How Nonviolence Protects the State* (South End Press, 2007).

183 Through a joint resolution effected on 23 November 1993 (PL 103–150), the 103rd Congress formally apologised to the Kanaka Maoli for the US role in illegally overthrowing their government a century earlier, annexing their homeland and leaving them destitute as a people. Nothing has been done to reinstate their government, restore their property or compensate them for the damages inflicted. In another joint resolution on 20 April 2009 (PL 111–118 § 8113), the 111th Congress apologised to American Indians 'on behalf of the United States' for the 'long history of depredations and ill-conceived policies of the

and reconciliation' processes promoted as 'healing' the psychic and other wounds inflicted on Indigenous individuals by the ongoing reality of genocidal colonisation might, unless attended by a bedrock change in power relations, be anything other than a means of instilling acquiescence among the subjugated.[184] Finally, the premise that legislative/juridical tweaks and policy adjustments designed to make the settler-state structure more 'inclusive' do anything other than *strengthen* the present order is delusional.

To locate genuinely liberatory alternatives to the continuation of business as usual, it is necessary to look outside the liberal paradigm altogether. Marxism, which exhibits much the same degree of overlap with liberalism as did nazism, offers nothing in that regard.[185] Anarchism, given its foundational rejection of the state – separating itself from the eurosupremacist stream of (neo-)Hegelian mystification as one of the more important common denominators linking the other three[186] – is in many respects far more promising. Its promise resides mainly in its capacity to intersect with the precolonial modes of non-authoritarian political organisation still maintained by many Indigenous societies around the world.[187] The latter, as explained by Indigenous legal

Federal Government', including 'forced removals [and] bloody ... massacres', to 'bring healing to this land' without 'authoriz[ing] or support[ing] any claim against the United States'. The United States is not alone. On 11 June 2008, Canadian Prime Minister Stephen Harper issued an apology to the survivors of the country's century-long programme of effecting the forced transfer of Indigenous children to residential facilities where they were subjected to systematic 'deculturation', but hedged the issue of state liability. In Australia, after a highly publicised official 1996 report concluded that a programme similarly targeting Aboriginal children constituted genocide, the Prime Minister simply announced that there would be no apology. To date, the only country to acknowledge having perpetrated genocide against Indigenous Peoples, and to officially apologise for it, has been Germany with regard to the Namas and Hereros of present-day Namibia in 2004. In 2012, however, when it became apparent that the victims might be entitled to reparations, the acknowledgement was withdrawn. For further background, see Brooks, above n 56.

184 This has been the standard 'remedy' applied in settler-colonial contexts, from South Africa to Australia to Canada. For a penetrating critique, see Roland Chrisjohn and Sherry Young with Michael Maraun, *The Circle Game* (Theytus Books, 1997) esp 12–25, 99–114. See also Neil Funk-Unrau and Anna Snyder, 'Indian Residential School Survivors and State-Designed ADR: A Strategy for Co-Optation?' (2007) 24 *Conflict Resolution Quarterly* 285. More broadly, see Leigh A Payne, *Unsettling Accounts* (Duke University Press, 2008).

185 For explication, see Churchill, *Acts of Rebellion*, above n 153, 247–62. A more comprehensive critique will be found in Ward Churchill, 'Unthinking Eurocentrism: The Indigenist Alternative to Marxian "Anti-Imperialism"' in Deepa Naik and Trenton Oldfield (eds), *Critical Cities* (Middlecourt Press, forthcoming).

186 For a thorough demystification, see Teshale Tibebu, *Hegel and the Third World* (Syracuse University Press, 2011).

187 I have explored this prospect more fully in Churchill, *Acts of Rebellion*, above n 153, 263–74.

scholars such as Sharon Venne and Irene Watson,[188] are governed by conceptions of law radically at odds with that which has defined the malignant history traced herein, retaining their integrity and viability despite concerted efforts of the colonisers to extinguish them.

In such resilience can be discerned what Marcuse described as 'the Archimedean point for a larger emancipation'.[189] Insofar as they exemplify ways in which relations not only between humans, but between humans and the rest of the natural order, can be arranged in a non-statist and sustainable fashion – thus serving as what, in Marcusian terms, might be described as 'counter-models'[190] – the successes of a host of desperate, protracted and typically 'invisible' struggles of Indigenous Peoples to maintain their societies as living entities is truly fortunate for the growing segment of the settler population purporting to embrace one or another variant of anarchism (or 'anti-authoritarianism', as has been the preferred term in some circles since the late 1960s).[191]

There is little need for the settler opposition to squander its energies theorising how sustainably egalitarian socio-political/economic relations 'might work in practice' (unless they are as afflicted as those they purportedly oppose with the

188 Sharon Helen Venne, *Our Elders Understand Our Rights* (Theytus Books, 1999); Irene Watson, *Aboriginal Peoples, Colonialism and International Law* (Routledge, 2015).

189 Herbert Marcuse, 'Repressive Tolerance' in Robert Paul Wolff, Barrington Moore Jr and Herbert Marcuse, *A Critique of Pure Tolerance* (Beacon Press, 1965) 95, 111.

190 In his *Essay on Liberation*, Marcuse called for 'a methodological disengagement from and refusal of the Establishment, aiming at a transvaluation of values', observing that: 'Such practice involves a break with the familiar, the routine ways of seeing, hearing, feeling, and understanding things so that the organism may become receptive to the potential forms of a nonaggressive, nonexploitative world.' He implies that the best approach might be exploration of what Carl Boggs termed 'prefigurative relations' through actualisation of countermodels – or 'counter-institutions' – serving as 'the embodiment within the ongoing political practice of the movement, of those forms of social relations, decision making, culture, and human experience that are the ultimate goal'. Entirely Eurocentric, both theorists were oblivious to the possibility that the alternatives they were seeking might already exist outside the western paradigm. Nonetheless, their ideas continue to figure prominently in the thinking of Euro-american oppositionists. For the passages quoted, see Herbert Marcuse, *An Essay on Liberation* (Beacon Press, 1971) 6; Carl Boggs, 'Marxism, Prefigurative Communism, and the Problem of Workers' Control' (1977) 11 *Radical America* 100. See also Daniel Murray, 'Prefiguration or Actualization? Radical Democracy and Counter-Institution in the Occupy Movement', *Berkeley Journal of Sociology*, 3 November 2014 <http://berkeleyjournal.org/2014/11/prefiguration-or-actualization-radical-democracy-and-counter-institution-in-the-occupy-movement/>.

191 Rudi Dutschke, 'On Anti-Authoritarianism' in Carl Oglesby (ed), *The New Left Reader* (Grove Press, 1969) 243.

longstanding eurosupremacist compulsion to pretend to have invented what has been appropriated from other cultures[192]). What *is* necessary is for the settler society's self-proclaimed oppositionists to overcome the staggering sense of entitlement that allows them to demand that 'equality of oppression' be acknowledged as a precondition to their participation in alliances. With all due respect to Audre Lorde, the settler colonial state, being by its very nature hierarchical, has *of course* spawned a 'hierarchy of oppression'.[193] Abolishing it requires that a hierarchy of another sort – 'something like an order of priorities'[194] – be adopted by any movement serious about accomplishing the task.

Certain realities present themselves. Absent the land upon which they have constructed and maintain themselves, every square inch of which has been expropriated from the peoples Indigenous to it, settler states would not – indeed, *could* not – exist. Absent the ongoing dispossession/internal colonisation of Indigenous Peoples, the oppression by the state upon various sectors of the settler society, both historically and currently, would have been and remains impossible. A few of the very real oppressions suffered by the bulk of the non-Indigenous populace as a consequence of the white supremacist/corporatist/militarist/authoritarian structures of existing settler/police states might be diminished without reversing the 'original sin' bound up in those states' creation and consolidation.[195] However, pursuing such reformist objectives

192 For a compact survey of the duration and magnitude of Europe's cultural imperialism, see Ward Churchill, 'Indigenous Peoples and Imperialism' in Immanuel Ness and Zak Cope (eds), *The Palgrave Encyclopedia of Imperialism and Anti-Imperialism* (Palgrave Macmillan, 2016) vol 2, esp 1266–75, 1278–80.

193 See Audre Lorde, 'There is No Hierarchy of Oppression' (1983) 14 *Homophobia and Education* 9. Recognising that oppression is both layered and differentiated does nothing to nullify either the obligation to oppose it in *all* forms or the need for solidarity among those oppressed in whatever form. It *is*, however, to insist that genocide and, say, wage discrimination are by no means equivalent oppressions.

194 Terry Eagleton, *The Illusions of Postmodernism* (Blackwell, 1996) 93.

195 It is a commonplace in the United States to refer to slavery – meaning the enslavement of black people imported as chattel from Africa and subsequently 'bred' there for commercial purposes – as having been the country's 'original sin'. It does nothing to diminish the horror or magnitude of criminality embodied in the US slave system to observe that, but for the genocide *already* inflicted upon American Indians in the Atlantic coastal regions – a significant dimension of which was their large-scale enslavement by English colonisers, both as a 'domestic' source of labour and as a lucrative export in trade with the West Indies – and concomitant seizure of their land, there would have been nowhere for African chattel to have been imported *to*. For a classic iteration of the standard black/white/slavery framing, see Roger Cohen, 'Beyond America's Original Sin', *New York Times*, 20 March 2008 <http://www.nytimes.com/2008/03/20/opinion/20cohen.html>. A fuller rendering will be found in Jim Wallis, *America's Original Sin* (Brazos Press, 2016) (of the book's 226 pages of text, *three* are devoted to 'Native Americans'). On black chattel slavery in the United States,

would not only be abysmally self-serving,[196] but strategically short-sighted and self-defeating.

Even if such efforts were successful in the near term, the states would remain the same genocidal, colonising entities they have been from the outset. Whatever abatements in the system of racial/class/gender oppression might be attained, it will have been conceded only as a means of containing/co-opting 'social unrest', thereby minimising disruption of business as usual.[197] With nothing *fundamentally* altered, the systemic oppressions alleviated will simply

including commercial breeding, see the works cited above n 172. On the enslavement of Indigenous people in North America that began earlier, lasted into the nineteenth century, and initially extended northward into New England, see Alan Gallay, *The Indian Slave Trade* (Yale University Press, 2002) esp 288–314.

196 The record of 'the' feminist movement in the United States – often referred to as 'the white women's movement' by people of colour – is instructive. The implications of 'talk[ing about] glass ceilings without making sure that everyone's in the building first' are glaringly obvious. As Marjorie Romeyn-Sanabria concludes, feminism 'is for white women [and by] "white" I'm not talking exclusively about race. I'm talking about native-English-speaking, upper-middle-class, educated women. They're the only group of women for whom feminism has any relevance or long-term benefit.' See Sarah Jaffe, 'Trickle-Down Feminism', *Dissent*, Winter 2013 <https://www.dissentmagazine.org/article/trickle-down-feminism>; Marjorie Romeyn-Sanabria, 'Feminism Is for White Women', *Arts.Mic*, 12 August 2013 <https://mic.com/articles/60319/feminism-is-for-white-women#.TqCEErdtJ>.

197 Consider the example recently offered by the US version of the so-called Occupy Movement. While its targeting of the concentrated personal wealth wielded by the '1 per cent' of the population comprising the true financial/corporate élite responsible for a plethora of social and economic oppressions was quite appropriate, and the juxtaposition reflected in its claim to represent the interests of 'the other 99 per cent' made for a spate of catchy slogans, the implications attending its insistence upon casting the latter as an undifferentiated blob rendered it unsustainable. Occupy's 'analysis', effectively placing corporate executives receiving 'compensation' of a quarter of a million dollars a year 'in the same boat' as homeless people living in utter destitution, was from the outset deeply repellent to poor communities – especially those of colour – thereby sharply constraining the movement's ability to expand and gain momentum. The proverbial death knell was sounded within weeks of the movement's nominal inception, as the relatively few organisations of colour willing to explore the possibility of forming alliances were repeatedly informed by Occupy's existing core groups of predominantly young, white, relatively affluent, stylistic anti-authoritarians that introducing issues of race 'would be divisive' (thus was an Indigenous delegation rebuffed in Albuquerque, New Mexico). Having dissipated only months after claiming the international spotlight, the purportedly 'radical' movement's legacy will consist of a handful of liberal reforms of banking regulations, tax codes, student loan programmes and perhaps the health care system. For an effusively self-congratulatory overview advanced in the moment, see Sarah van Gelder and the Staff of YES! Magazine, *This Changes Everything: Occupy Wall Street and the 99% Movement* (Berrett-Koehler, 2011).

re-emerge, likely in a more virulent and intractable form.[198] Having undergone several major and any number of lesser repetitions over the past century and a half,[199] the cycle is not – or at least should not be – especially mysterious. To contend that yet another iteration might finally yield the desired result is to advocate the political equivalent of alchemy.

Only by attacking the hierarchy at its root, eliminating the base or foundation upon which the structure of oppression is contingent, can it be abolished. Only through decolonisation of the Indigenous 'nations within' every settler state can the multifaceted non-Indigenous societies hope to free themselves from the array of oppressions they confront.[200] Only resumption of genuinely self-determining rights by internally colonised Indigenous Nations – specifically, their ability to 'freely determine their political status and freely pursue their economic, social and cultural development' by controlling and 'freely dispos[ing] of their natural wealth and resources'[201] – entails the

198 To cite one example, the concessions ending the Jim Crow (apartheid) mode of racial oppression in the United States during the 1960s had, by the mid-1970s, effectively quelled the black insurgency. By the early 1980s, such material gains had been reversed to such an extent that the objective conditions suffered by the black population had actually worsened, although black political participation markedly increased. The trend has continued into the present moment, with the result that while unprecedented numbers of African Americans hold elected office and state positions, the annual income of black people overall averages 40 per cent less than that of whites, and they are unemployed at more than double the rate of whites and incarcerated at six times the rate. The median accumulated wealth of a black family is presently $8,348, while that of a white family is $111,146. See Manning Marable, *Race, Reform, and Rebellion* (University of Mississippi Press, 1984) 168–99; 'Distribution of Household Income by Race', *Infoplease* (2012) <http://www.infoplease.com/ipa/A0104552.html>; Bruce Drake, 'Incarceration Rate Widens between Whites and Blacks', *Fact Tank* (Pew Research Center), 6 September 2013 <http://www.pewresearch.org/fact-tank/2013/09/06/incarceration-gap-between-whites-and-blacks-widens/>; Laura Shin, 'The Racial Wealth Gap: Why a Typical White Household Has 16 Times the Wealth of a Black One', *Forbes*, 16 March 2015.

199 The rise and fall of the US labour movement is a prime example. Following the 1935 Roosevelt administration's package of concessions, previously militant unions consciously abandoned any broader social or political agenda, becoming what Steven Fraser has termed 'private welfare states'. A half-century ago, nearly a third of the US labour force was unionised; the proportion is now barely 10 per cent, and many of the benefits for which they traded their integrity – pensions and subsidised health care – have largely evaporated. See Steven Fraser, *The Age of Acquiescence* (Little, Brown, 2015) 202. For a deeper critique, emphasising how the exclusionary anti-black/anti-Mexican/anti-Asian racism consistently displayed by the labour movement contributed greatly to its demise, see J Sakai, *Settlers* (Morningstar Press, 1989).

200 The phrase in quotation marks is borrowed from Vine Deloria Jr and Clifford M Lytle, *The Nations Within* (University of Texas Press, 1984).

201 Article 1(1) and 1(2) of the *International Covenant on Economic, Social and Cultural Rights*, 21 UN GAOR, Supp 16, 49, UN Doc A/6316 (1967), reiterated in Art

physical/jurisdictional deconstruction of the states themselves. Only that literal sort of dismantlement can provide the space to revitalise traditional and still-functioning non-statist forms of socio-political organisation while simultaneously undermining the states' internal coherence and material capacity to wield power.[202]

A complete reordering of the priorities displayed by the settler opposition is thus called for. No longer can the rights of Indigenous Peoples be treated as a peripheral issue, by those purportedly seeking to transform the existing order.[203] Nor will it suffice to simply 'include' Indigenous groups within 'broader' – namely, settler – coalitions and/or integrate 'Indigenous planks' into 'broader' oppositional agendas. The liberation of Indigenous Nations encapsulated within the settler states must be taken as the *first* priority of the movement as a whole. This is not to say that it should be the *only* priority, simply that it is the essential ingredient without which none of the others can be met. This priority is fully deserving of the 'privilege' it must be accorded, as are the Indigenous Peoples who have, by every objective standard, suffered the greatest degree of oppression under settler colonial rule.[204]

1(1) and 1(2) of the *International Covenant on Civil and Political Rights*, 21 UN GAOR Supp 16, 52, UN Doc A/6316 (1967). For critique, see the special issue of the *Griffith Law Review* (2011) devoted to the declaration.

202 Returning for a moment to the notion of 'prefigurative relations' (Marcuse, above n 189), the endurance and continuity embodied in Indigenous practice stands in stark contrast to the 'immediatism' reflected in the 'temporary autonomous zones' envisioned by Hakim Bey and others. The tactical utility of this 'ontological' approach is as strategically barren as Timothy Leary's acid-drenched 'new age' commune in Millbrook, New York, during the mid-1960s. See Hakim Bey, *TAZ: The Temporary Autonomous Zone, Ontological Anarchy, Poetic Terrorism* (Autonomedia, 1991); Hakim Bey, *Immediatism* (AK Press, 1994).

203 An especially disheartening example is that of Black Lives Matter (BLM; now the Movement for Black Lives), a promising coalition of more than 60 organisations formed to confront the greatly disproportionate number of unarmed African Americans, especially young men, killed by police across the United States, and broadening its scope to address other issues, hoping to 'rebuild the Black Liberation Movement'. Unfortunately, while BLM has noted that Latinos are also murdered by the police at a disproportionate rate, it has neglected to mention that 'the racial group most likely to be killed by law enforcement is Native Americans'. See 'About the Black Lives Matter Network' (2012) <http://blacklivesmat–ter.com/about/>; Matt Agorist, 'Police are Killing Native Americans at a Higher Rate than Any Race, and Nobody is Talking About It', *Free Thought*, 2 August 2015.

204 As with disproportionate rates of police violence (see ibid), the rate and degree of impoverishment is another area in which American Indians are consistently excluded from progressive analyses in the United States. A recent overview produced by the Institute for Policy Studies devotes exactly two sentences of its thirty pages to 'Native American Households', while the situation of 'Asian-American and Pacific Islanders' is addressed in eight sentences. The rest of the study focuses entirely upon growing wealth disparities between whites and African Americans and Latinos. American Indians were excluded from the

None of this is to say that placing 'first peoples first', as the saying goes, will make the struggle either quick or painless. Quite the contrary: since it goes far deeper than anything that has preceded it, it will undoubtedly be protracted and exceedingly bitter. Each step taken, however, will be a step towards, rather than away from, Marcuse's 'larger emancipation'. In the alternative, should the various elements of the non-Indigenous population continue to place a greater priority upon strategies intended mainly – or solely – to increase their own comfortability *within* the extant order of settler-state colonialism, they will simply remain what they claim to oppose, the steadily evolving system of global domination will complete itself and the malevolence of the Washingtonian/Hitlerian vision will at last be fulfilled. By now, the implications are not only genocidal but truly omnicidal. The choice seems obvious.

comparison. The results turn out rather differently when the rate/depth of impoverishment suffered by the groups in question is compared to that of the reservation-based Indigenous population in the United States, where 'extreme poverty' – federally defined as per capita income of less than $3,000 annually – has run six times the national average since 2000. On the San Carlos Apache Reservation in Arizona, one in four people try to subsist on that pittance; on the Tohono O'odam Reservation in Arizona, one in five are forced to do the same. On the Pine Ridge Sioux Reservation in South Dakota, where two-thirds of the population fall well below the poverty line, per capita income in the town of Allen was $1,539 in 2010. Buffalo County, the poorest in the United States, is on the nearby Crow Creek Sioux Reservation, also in South Dakota. Such data are indicative. See Dedrick Asante-Muhammed, Chuck Collins, Josh Hoxie and Emanuel Nieves, *The Ever-Growing Gap* (Institute for Policy Studies, 2016) <http://www.ips-dc.org/wp-content/uploads/2016/08/The-Ever-Growing-Gap-CFED_IPS-Final-2.pdf>; US Bureau of the Census, *American Indian and Alaska Native Census 2000 Data for 539 Tribes* <http://www.census.gov/aian/census_2000/census_2000_data_for_ 59_ tribes.html>; US Bureau of the Census, *American FactFinder* <https://factfinder.census.gov/faces/nav/jsf/pages/community_facts.xhtml>; Cara Hetland, 'South Dakota has Country's Poorest County', *Minnesota Public Radio*, 1 October 2002 <http://news.minnesota.publicradio.org/features/ 200210/02_het–landc_census-m/>; Ojibwa, 'Indians 101: Reservation Poverty', *Daily Kos*, 6 December 2012 <http://www.dailykos.com/story/2012/12/6/1167663/-Indians-101-Reservation-Poverty>. See also Harvard Project on American Indian Economic Development, *The State of the Native Nations* (Oxford University Press, 2007) 238–9.

Chapter 5

First Nations, Indigenous Peoples: our laws have always been here

Irene Watson

Introduction

I write this chapter from a critical First Nations centre.[1] I honour and remember my mother who always brought me back to centre – whom I am – and the Elders. As my mother advised, 'elders are meant to be the *wave makers* and they should make the waves which will bring the change', so that we can move from mere survival to living the lives we are here to live. In order to live beyond the state of bare survival which colonialism would afford us, the re-centring of First Nations laws, knowledges and relationships to land is essential. It is essential that we become free 'in keeping with the original and independent existence of our ancestors'.[2]

Meanwhile, in the colonised space which we occupy, our lives are being harvested for assimilation by the colonial beast – the muldarbi.[3] The states call it 'development' and 'progress', but the name we give to this absorbing, colonising process is genocide.[4] The gatekeepers of the state and internationally have realised that they are vulnerable to accusations of genocide, and they are wide open to them. There is no shortage of evidence. So they are working hard to disable the avenues that First Nations Peoples could use to prosecute the crime of genocide. First, a successful prosecution might result in

1 Taking up the idea of Aboriginal Law occupying the centre, see Irene Watson, *Aboriginal Peoples, Colonialism and International Law: Raw Law* (Routledge, 2015).
2 Steven Newcomb, 'The UN Declaration on the Rights of Indigenous Peoples and the Paradigm of Domination' (2011) 20(3) *Griffith Law Review* 578, 606.
3 In the language of the Tanganekald, muldarbi means demon spirit. In this context I have applied muldarbi to mean the project of colonialism.
4 For a discussion on the obstacles presented by states against a claim of genocide made by First Nations, see Irene Watson, 'Genocide, the State, and Original First Nations' in Vincent Negri and Isabelle Schulte-Tenckoff (eds), *Towards International Normativity: Between Mimetism and Dissemination* (A Pedone, 2016) 171. See also Tamara Starblanket, *Genocide: Indigenous Nations and the State of Canada* (Masters Thesis, University of Saskatchewan, 2014) for a comprehensive critique of residential schools and the contemporary position of First Nations in Canada.

DOI: 10.4324/9781315628318-6

some remedies; and, second, it might halt the crime from continuing. Well, that is the idea, but the reality of international law's complicity with the colonial project places many obstacles in the way of achieving a successful prosecution. I maintain that international law is complicit, but in fact the historic origins of international law are in colonialism.[5]

So First Nations' futures remain uncertain. This has been so since the beginning of colonialism, but even more in these contemporary times: they are made even more difficult due to this nexus between international law and colonialism.

By re-centring First Nations we can unsettle the dominant state paradigm, the 'mainstream',[6] and the Euro-centred legal systems founded on the violence of *terra nullius*.[7] First Nations, occupying a critical Indigenous standpoint, affirm that 'we were here first', and we still carry the authority which is imbued with obligations to care for our worlds, as we have always done. In the journey to re-centre ourselves we retract from the idea of a mainstream within which we have no place, to instead become the mainstream, no longer on the fringes of colonialism and progress. Becoming more independent and true to whom we are, we occupy and centre our lives as First Nations Peoples. I have argued[8] that the existing colonising 'mainstream' models are the underpinnings of the contemporary body of the colonial project, and because of this they are conflicted and unable properly to determine the content of Indigenous Peoples' futures. Indigenous Peoples' futures are beyond the contemporary assimilationist agendas of the states. The way of the future belongs to First Nations' laws to determine, interpret and translate. The colonial story of power certainly has another take on First Nations' futures, and this chapter will tell the story of the conflict between authority and power.[9] Authority is in the hands of First Nations Peoples and is law, while power is held by states by way of a violent foundation. Violence by way of military force constitutes the laws of colonial states. Our future lies in following proper lines of authority that derive from ancient laws, laws which are still carried and known to First Nations Peoples, our territories and the worlds we occupy.

5 Antony Anghie, *Imperialism, Sovereignty and the Making of International Law* (Cambridge University Press, 2008); China Miéville, *Between Equal Rights: A Marxist Theory of International Law* (Haymarket Books, 2005); see also Watson, *Raw Law*, above n 1.
6 Sharon Venne brought my awareness to how concepts such as the 'mainstream' can be used to embed state dominance over First Nations: Sharon Venne, *Our Elders Understand Our Rights* (Theytus Books, 1998).
7 I apply the term *terra nullius* throughout the chapter, and also acknowledge that the doctrine of discovery as it was applied to North America over five hundred years ago intended the same eliminatory results.
8 Watson, *Raw Law*, above n 1.
9 I acknowledge many conversations with Mary Graham and our interpretations given to 'power' and 'authority' when we centre a First Nations vision.

In our journey to de-centre from the domination of the colonial project, we considered the drafting of the United Nations *Declaration on the Rights of Indigenous Peoples*[10] (UNDRIP), which began in the early 1980s.[11] Our hope was that it might provide a reprieve from the genocidal impact of colonialism. However, it has proven a disappointment. Steven Newcomb and Charmaine White Face among others have queried whether or not the UNDRIP has any capacity to 'end the dehumanising paradigm of domination against nations and peoples termed "Indigenous"'.[12] My reading of the UNDRIP is that it is a bit like states having their cake and eating it too in its approach to the recognition of First Nations. That is, on the one hand it recognises the right of First Nations to self-determination and, on the other hand, it limits self-determination to being exercised in accord with state power.[13] Likewise, the contemporary colonialist approach to recognition of Indigenous Peoples is that you see it in the one hand, and in the other hand it disappears. So we can identify inherent blockages within UN processes and the UNDRIP in particular, and it might be useful to unpack 'measures of recognition' further. In doing this, the purpose would be to consider how the language of international law is deployed to construct Indigenous Peoples' laws and lives with both an historic and contemporary understanding of colonial subjugation and domination. The processes of drafting the UNDRIP, and the call for its implementation by the United Nations High Level Plenary Meeting held in New York in September 2014, illustrates the continuing semantic domination of the states.[14] These international law 'developments' do very little if anything to monitor the domination and subjugation of Indigenous Peoples by colonial states.[15] But while the language and philosophy of empires continue to be applied in the ongoing domination and subjugation of First Nations Peoples, the language and philosophies of First Nations continue to centre our lives and our survival. Drawing on the wisdom of our old people and First Nations

10 *United Nations Declaration on the Rights of Indigenous Peoples*, GA Res 61/68, UN Doc A/RES/61/295 (13 September 2007).

11 For a history of the process, see Sharon Venne, 'NGOs, Indigenous Peoples and the United Nations' in Aziz Choudry and Dip Kapoor (eds), *NGOization: Complicity, Contradictions and Prospects* (Zed Books, 2013) 75, 87–93.

12 Newcomb, 'UN Declaration', above n 2, 581; see also Charmaine White Face, *Indigenous Nations' Rights in the Balance: An Analysis of the Declaration on the Rights of Indigenous Peoples* (Living Justice Press, 2013).

13 White Face, ibid 26–29, 39–41.

14 Newcomb, 'UN Declaration', above n 2, 578–607.

15 Ongoing colonialism exists within the Australian government's Northern Territory response and intervention, and the continuing plunder of First Nations' natural resources without (if it could even be obtained and given lawfully) free, prior and informed consent. China Miéville, 'Anxiety and the Sidekick State: British International Law After Iraq' (2005) 46 *Harvard International Law Journal* 441 argued that human rights interventions are used as an axis upon which the abnegation of sovereign borders occurs.

centres, this chapter will talk up the language of the land and the laws of our ancestors for the future possibilities of good lives for First Nations. And we challenge those narratives which have worked to marginalise our ancient legal systems. They have been marginalised almost to the point of juricide, but still the law lives and it will outlive the lives of humans, for it just is; that is the law.

Kaldowinyeri, that is the law[16]

We are ancient peoples who have held relations between our hundreds of First Nations for thousands of years or forever.[17] We are by our names and connections to country evidence of our relations with each other. We are the First Peoples of place who first realised inter-nation relationships. We are the first internationals. But come the time of colonial states, our inter-national co-operation with each other was ignored. The invaders attempted to bury our laws with their myth of *terra nullius*, which has been legally construed to ignore the fact of our existence in any form at all.[18]

In the time when the law was sung across the lands, our peoples came to know that the law is everywhere and we are related to ruwe, the land, and when science discovers us yet again it will find the connection and relationship with land. The evidence is in our DNA. Indigenous Peoples already know this, just as we always knew the earth was not flat. My mother told the story of a time in the mid-1980s when she and her cousin[19] were visitors to the Arrernte People's territories, close to the centre of Australia. My mother and her cousin were walking the streets of Alice Springs, enjoying the warm night air when they came across a group of white fellers having a barbecue. These men turned to them and in what my mother considered to be a patronising tone, they asked, 'Can we help you? Are you lost?' My mother, not one to be patronised, replied, 'We are not the ones who are lost, it is you who are the lost ones', and she and her cousin continued to walk on. My

16 This term means a long time ago, a time which was translated into English as the 'Dreaming'. It is a time we knew as all time, that is time now, in the past and the present, time as being in cycles, as everywhere and ever-present. There is no beginning or ending; we are who we are, for we have arrived and we are not wanting or waiting to progress to an end-point in time.

17 When measured by scientific methods, and forever in Aboriginal time and law. For further discussion, see Ambelin Kwaymullina and Blaze Kwaymullina, 'Learning to Read the Signs: Law in an Indigenous Reality' (2010) 34(2) *Journal of Australian Studies* 195.

18 See C Black, 'Maturing Australia through Australian Aboriginal Narrative Law' (2011) 110 *South Atlantic Quarterly* 347 for further discussion on Aboriginal law and its ancient origins.

19 They were both of the south-east of South Australia of the Tanganekald and Meintangk Peoples, and while away from their ruwe they were mindful and respectful of protocols when visiting the country of other First Nations.

mother told me the story as yet another account of white racist patronisation. Some might struggle to find the racist content in this story – one could argue that the context was caring, and just helping the lost to find their way. But by my mother's way of seeing and knowing, it was a routine attempt to put the 'natives' back within the controlled perimeters of the colonial project.

Russell Means[20] and Sharon Venne[21] have told a similar but very different story about why and how they travelled to the United Nations in Geneva in 1977.[22] It was not a journey of the lost and 'backward native' seeking recognition, but rather an assertion of First Nations existence across time and the continuing present. In general, it was a statement about First Nations Peoples surviving on territories that continue to be stolen and plundered, but importantly it was a message that was led by the law, as described by Venne:

> The main speaker for our Peoples is our sacred pipe given to us by the Creation. It leads the way. We used our own laws and traditions to enter that meeting. We were not bound by the protocols of the UN to enter quietly and without ceremony. Our Nations walked proudly.[23]

Indigenous Peoples remain connected to country, and we are not going away: we have nowhere to go, for we are already home. The dialogue between First Nations and states is usually patronising, for the states generally assume that we are peoples of limited intelligence and know very little about international law; that we are lost in the wilderness of international law, and either in need

20 Russell Means was an Oglala Lakota activist and philosopher who attended the 1977 UN Conference: see Russell Means and Bayard Johnson, *If You've Forgotten the Names of the Clouds, You've Lost Your Way* (Treaty Publications, 2012).

21 Venne, 'NGOs, Indigenous Peoples and the United Nations', above n 11, 83–6.

22 The International NGO Conference on Discrimination Against Indigenous Populations in the Americas, held at the United Nations' offices in Geneva on 20–23 September 1977, was the first UN conference where Indigenous Peoples attended and spoke with the law for their nations. The following resolution from that meeting was not a call for recognition but the provision of evidence of the claim of genocide against First Nations and a call to stop the destruction: 'The representatives of the indigenous peoples gave evidence to the international community of the ways in which discrimination, genocide and ethnocide operated. While the situation may vary from country to country, the roots are common to all: they include the brutal colonization to open the way for the plunder of their land and resources by commercial interests seeking maximum profits; the massacres of millions of native peoples for centuries and the continuous grabbing of their land which deprives them of the possibility of developing their own resources and means of livelihood; the denial of self-determination of indigenous nations and peoples destroying their traditional value system and their social and cultural fabric. The evidence pointed to the combination of this oppression resulting in the further destruction of the indigenous nations.' 'The Geneva Conference: Official Report' in (1977) 1(77) *Treaty Council News*.

23 Venne, 'NGOs, Indigenous Peoples and the United Nations', above n 11, 84.

of training in international diplomacy, or their advice.[24] This is a species of racism which came with the assumptions of the doctrines of discovery and *terra nullius*, the idea that we do not exist within our own laws, and that the best that can be done is to help with a little bit of recognition of our individual human rights, steering us to eventual assimilation and genocide. Problem solved. It is assumed that we need help to 'reconcile' ourselves to this process, so we are invited to participate in a dialogue which serves to obliterate us.

We already know and have known forever whom we are, *we were here first*, and we already know the land and each other. We have our own stories of whom we are and how we came to be, but now we are in a dialogue about our future and survival, about genocide. We do not need help: we need white fellers to understand and act against their own racism.[25] In the place we now call Australia and before the advent of the lies of *terra nullius*, we comprised more than two hundred First Nations. The evidence or knowledge of this is coded in our languages and songlines crossing Australia, which are also a record of the agreements with each other entered into by First Nations Peoples. The songs are the evidence of the agreements between peoples which established a way of life we lived for many thousands of years. However, for this way of knowing we are often stereotyped as being trapped in the past and incapable of 'getting over it' and moving on with project progress.[26] My argument here is not about projecting contemporary notions of international law onto the past, but rather asserting that we had our relational ways of being together which enabled respect of each other's freedom and relationship with a superordinate authority in law. Our ancient laws survive and are as valid today as they were at the first song; their value, as always, is to hold our worlds together for the future generations. We did not have formal writing, for we are oral peoples, and we had/have song as a record with which we learn and to follow and live by. Evidence of First Nations' laws goes beyond writing, for it is written in the land and the environment which enfolds our lives.

The colonial mapping of international law excludes Indigenous Peoples from being subjects in colonial international law; only the 'state' qualifies as a subject of international law.[27] Accordingly, First Nations are to be absorbed into and by the state. At a First Nations centre this position is resisted by

24 See letter from Mogens Lykketoft, President of the United Nations General Assembly, 16 May 2016 <https://www.docip.org/fileadmin/documents/Docip/Documents_temporaires/pga-consultations-draft-two.pdf>, which included recommendations from advisors on how to improve the participation of Indigenous Peoples. I have included this reference to provide an example of the control and direction exercised over Indigenous Peoples when participating in UN forums.

25 Jimmie Durham considers frequent internet references to Indigenous Peoples as 'being in need of help'. See Jimmie Durham, 'Against Internationalism' (2013) 27 *Third Text* 29.

26 Miéville, *Between Equal Rights*, above n 5, 159, 165.

27 Ibid 161.

many peoples. We resist the genocide: the assimilation of First Nations into and by the state. Because we know another way, a way in which song is the foundation of law and not violence.[28] And while our laws were denied, the colonialists knew of their existence.[29]

Beginnings or endings, they are all the same. I say beginnings and endings are all the same because life goes on and returns in cycles. Endings and narratives of progress[30] are constructs of the muldarbi, the colonial powers which stole our territories and cast our ancient relationships to country by other names. They called our lands Australia, New South Wales and South Australia, and they drew straight lines on maps of the body of our ruwe. We have always been here and are still today carrying our laws and obligations. There is nothing in our legal systems which denies the continuity of our laws; they go on, there is no end-point or beginning, for they are the laws.

We are the mainstream

Unlike sovereignty, law is known. It is held in the body and the land; it is not elusive like sovereignty – a bare and empty space.[31] While we know that there are Western European discourses on sovereignty which were used to justify colonialism, there are also First Nations discourses on law and sovereignty which pre-existed colonialism. International law scholar Anghie interrogates existing ideas of European supremacy:

> The question of how order is created among sovereign states, however, assumes that states are sovereign. This assumption is valid in the case of European states. Non-European states, however, have been characterized by international law as non-sovereign for several centuries. Within the conventional history of the discipline that uses the 'order among sovereign states' paradigm, then, the history of the non-European states is told principally in terms of the civilizing mission, the process by which non-Europeans acquired sovereignty and could then achieve the status of

28 Benjamin argued that the first function of violence is its law-making function. Violence's second function, he theorises, is its 'law preserving function'. Walter Benjamin, *Reflections* (Schocken Books, 1986) 284. I am grateful to Jo Bird for her comments on the work of Benjamin.

29 Miéville, *Between Equal Rights*, above n 5, 168.

30 See Boaventura de Sousa Santos, *Epistemologies of the South: Justice Against Epistemicide* (Paradigm Publishers, 2014) 48–9 for a discussion of Hegel's idea of a universal history and the becoming of what Santos describes as hegemonic globalisation and a 'normative' trajectory towards an Americanisation of the world.

31 Peter Fitzpatrick, 'Surpassing Sovereignty' in Julie Evans, Ann Genovese, Alexander Reilly and Patrick Wolfe (eds), *Sovereignty: Frontiers of Possibility* (University of Hawai'i Press, 2013) 181, 182. Fitzpatrick references the work of Bataille and Nancy, and their claim that, while sovereignty is nothing, we are doomed to seek it.

> being the equal of European states. Within this framework, furthermore, imperialism ended with the process of decolonization, which by the 1970s had ensured that virtually all former colonial territories had exercised their right to self-determination and become sovereign, independent states. This framework, however, cannot answer the question of how non-European states were determined to be non-sovereign in the first place. Who decided this issue? Using what principles? And what is the relationship between those principles and the major doctrines of international law?[32]

The foundational doctrines of international law were formulated to exclude non-European worlds. Those deemed 'civilised' were sovereign while the 'uncivilised' were not sovereign. Sovereignty was a result of colonial encounters, created in order to affirm European power over invaded and colonised territories.[33] Its framework lives on as the measure of the rise and fall of states. Why then would First Nations Peoples use this framework? We have been here forever; we are the mainstream (not the other way around). Would First Nations use it to fit into the international global order? Why would we not just affirm our own ways: that we were here first and that we are ancient peoples with ancient laws and identities? We are hundreds of First Nations that covered the Australian continent, and likewise First Nations covered other continents also.

But affirmations have been made in the past and we have been massacred for asserting whom we are. Those of us who have survived continue to resist and struggle against the powers which would subject us to genocide. We survive within the same colonising space which intends our demise, while the imperialist character of international law endures. It has not changed with the formal decolonisation[34] of the twentieth century. We continue to observe how international law can be used for both good and bad ends, used to constrain violence and also to legitimise it.[35] We navigate the terrain and assess the extent to which it might be possible to constrain violence levelled against First Nations.

In spite of ongoing colonialism, in the spirit of the future cycles, we affirm again that 'we have always been here and always will be', that 'we are the mainstream'. These could become mantras for those resisters of genocide and activists upholding Aboriginal laws, philosophy and knowledge. Our lives have been 'normalised'/'Europeanised' by the colonial project for more than five hundred years; we are the poorest of the poor 'citizens' of the colonial

32 Antony Anghie, 'Western Discourses of Sovereignty' in Julie Evans, Ann Genovese, Alexander Reilly and Patrick Wolfe (eds), *Sovereignty: Frontiers of Possibility* (University of Hawai'i Press, 2013) 19, 21.

33 Ibid 22–3.

34 Ibid 32.

35 Miéville, *Between Equal Rights*, above n 5, 296.

states. Ward Churchill claims that the United States has sought legitimacy for its ongoing subjugation of First Nations by 'engineering a normalization of such relations in universal legal terms'.[36] Examples of this are found in its translation of language in the UNDRIP, where the term 'internal self-determination' indicates from a state perspective no 'right' of independence or permanent sovereignty over natural resources. As the power of states to normalise colonialism continues, we are left to consider the effects of a rights discourse which is locked into the matrix of coloniality. The UNDRIP is an example of this. Is it possible to move beyond this point of lockdown? What will happen if we do not? Colonialism remains even while Indigenous laws, philosophy and knowledges remain foundational to the lives and laws of First Nations Peoples, and colonialism denies our existence in the face of them. We have a face-off which represents the classic colonial knot of impossibility: impossible to change from a state's perspective, but impossible to live with for all species and the natural world. To date, little headway has been made in progressing a horizontal dialogue between colonialist interests and First Nations, while much of the literature and discussion concerning Indigenous Peoples is based upon an anthropocentrically centred, colonially constructed identity. As a result, a shield has been put up which enables the colonial states to see only what they want to see. And further, anything which might look as if it is repugnant to the state agenda, whether it be repugnant to 'universal human rights', development or to business as usual, falls outside the normalisation processes of the colonial project.

While First Nations' lives and territories are occupied by colonial states, we have our ancient international law systems which, in our ways, are not just of the past but are models for our future survival. The languages and philosophies of empires have been and continue to be applied to dominate and subjugate First Nations Peoples, but at the same time the languages and philosophies of our old people continue to live and to centre First Nations' futures. Our ancient legal systems challenge the narratives of domination, and our ways continue to bring a focus to the language of relationality, enabling us to stand in the face of the ongoing discourses and acts of coloniality. Relationality was and remains our core way of being, our mainstream way of life. To see the world as we see and know our lives and our laws opens space for the possibility of justice. Boaventura de Sousa Santos argues that a world without cognitive justice is a world without any possibility of justice,[37] an idea Steven Newcomb also raised in his discussion of the language of domination as representing cognitive injustice.[38]

36 Ward Churchill, 'The Law Stood Squarely on Its Head: U.S. Legal Doctrine, Indigenous Self-Determination and the Question of World Order' (2002) 81 *Oregon Law Review* 663, 691–2.

37 Santos, above n 30.

38 Steven Newcomb, *Pagans in the Promised Land: Decoding the Doctrine of Christian Discovery* (Fulcrum, 2008).

The spaces and places of injustice are many, and one course of action taken by First Nations to sustain our survival has been to call upon international law for remedies. In the short term we seek aid and support, emergency protection and assistance to survive and transform the spaces and places of genocide, and in the long term to regain freedom, peace and independence. Calls have been made to set in motion UN mechanisms, because there is nowhere else to go. But thus far the UN mechanisms have offered little or no assistance. Often the offending state, a member of the United Nations, simply refuses to change or to stop the behaviour which is the subject of a complaint. An example of the weaknesses in UN processes occurred when a complaint regarding the 2007 Northern Territory Intervention was made to the Committee on the Elimination of Racial Discrimination (CERD).[39] The complaint against the Commonwealth government of Australia alleged breaches of the *Convention on the Elimination of all Forms of Racial Discrimination* (1969), citing that the Northern Territory Intervention was racially discriminatory and that the targeted First Nations were not afforded the principles of free, prior and informed consent[40] when the intervention was being developed.[41] However,

39 Request for Urgent Action under ICERD in relation to the Commonwealth Government of Australia (28 January 2009, updated 11 August 2009) submitted by a group of First Nations Peoples affected by the Northern Territory Emergency Response <http://www.hrlrc.org.au/files/E75QFXXYE7/Request_for_Urgent_Action_Cerd.pdf>, <http://www.hrlrc.org.au/files/Update-to-CERD-ll-August-2009.pdf>. CERD is a United Nations committee of independent experts that monitors the implementation of the *Convention on the Elimination of All Forms of Racial Discrimination* by its state parties.

40 As outlined in Arts 18 and 19 of UNDRIP.

41 The Commonwealth government of Australia established the Northern Territory Intervention in response to a report on violence in Aboriginal communities in the Northern Territory: Rex Wild and Pat Anderson, *Ampe Akelyernemane Meke Mekarle 'Little Children Are Sacred': Report of the Northern Territory Board of Inquiry into the Protection of Aboriginal Children from Sexual Abuse* (Northern Territory Government, 2007). First Nations and supporters protested the discriminatory nature of the intervention, the conversion of collective land rights to individual ownership, removal of power from communities of the right to control entry onto lands, and the introduction of an income management scheme, among other backward provisions supported by the following Commonwealth laws: *Northern Territory National Emergency Response Act 2007* (Cth); *Family, Community Services, Indigenous Affairs and Other Legislation Amendment (Northern Territory National Emergency Response and Other Measures) Act (No 128) 2007* (Cth); *Social Security and Other Legislation Amendment (Welfare Payment Reform) Act (No 130) 2007* (Cth); *Families, Community Services and Indigenous Affairs and Other Legislation Amendment (Northern Territory National Emergency Response and Other Measures) Act 2007* (Cth); *Appropriation (Northern Territory National Emergency Response) Act (No 1) 2007* (Cth); and *Appropriation (Northern Territory National Emergency Response) Act (No 2) 2007* (Cth). In July 2012 at the conclusion of the Northern Territory Intervention, that package of legislation was replaced with the *Stronger Futures in the Northern Territory Act 2012* (Cth); *Stronger Futures in the Northern Territory Act 2013* (Cth); *Social Security Legislation Amendment Act 2012* (Cth). For further critical discussions, see Irene Watson, 'In the Northern

the Commonwealth chose to ignore the CERD complaint and the responses from many human rights bodies, all of whom concluded that the Northern Territory Emergency Response (NTER) was discriminatory.[42] In 2016, almost ten years after the implementation of the intervention, aspects of it survive and remain embedded in the laws of Australia.[43] In 'liberal' Australia, the colonial project survives undiminished by the minimum standards set out in the UNDRIP, particularly when it comes to the rights set out for free, prior and informed consent and the standards set by CERD regarding discrimination. None of these had any influence over the discriminatory enactment and application of the NTER.[44]

Colonial states continue to occupy First Nations' territories and to harvest our lands and natural resources without our free, prior and informed consent. But it is also important to note that the question of consent in many instances could not be answered in accord with Aboriginal Law; for example, giving consent to the development of a nuclear waste dump on First Nations' territory would be a breach of First Nations laws. In this context, the question of consent is not the concern; what is important is the authority in First Nations to say 'no', and having the power to enforce 'no'.

The pressure for development on First Nations territories is high and in Australia there is very little legal and political restraint of those developments. In the mid-1990s, the Kupa Piti Kungka Tjuta[45] formed an alliance

Territory Intervention, What is Saved or Rescued and at What Cost?' (2009) 15 *Cultural Studies Review* 45; Nicole Watson, 'The Northern Territory Emergency Response: Has It Really Improved the Lives of Aboriginal Women and Children?' (2011) 35 *Australian Feminist Law Journal* 147.

42 The following organisations outlined the discriminatory nature of the NTER: Human Rights Committee, *Concluding Observations: Australia*, UN Doc CCPR/C/AUS/CO/5 (7 May 2009) [14]; Committee on the Elimination of Racial Discrimination, Urgent Action Letters to the Australian Government (13 March 2009 and 28 September 2009) <http://hrlc.org.au/northern-territory-intervention-request-for-urgent-action-cerd/>; Committee on the Elimination of Racial Discrimination, *Concluding Observations: Australia*, UN Doc CERD/C/AUS/CO/15–17 (27 August 2010); Committee on Economic, Social and Cultural Rights, *Concluding Observations: Australia*, UN Doc E/C 12/AUS/CO/4 (12 June 2009) [15]; James Anaya, *Observations on the Northern Territory Emergency Response in Australia*, UN Doc A/HRC/15/13/Add4 (4 March 2010).

43 See Larissa Behrendt, 'Back to the Future for Indigenous Australia' in Nick Dyrenfurth and Tim Soutphommasane (eds), *All That's Left: What Labor Should Stand For* (University of New South Wales Press, 2010) 113.

44 For further discussion on the impact of the NTER, see Senate Select Committee on Regional and Remote Indigenous Communities, *Third Report* (2009) <http://www.aph.gov.au/binaries/senate/committee/indig_ctte/reports/2009/report3/a01.pdf>.

45 The Kupa Piti Kungka Tjuta was a group of senior Arabana, Kokatha, Yankunytjatjara and Antikarinya First Nations women formed in the early 1990s. The Kungkas held authority and the responsibility for caring for the lands that were being proposed for development of a nuclear waste dump at Billa Kallina near

with Aboriginal and environmentalist groups to prevent the building of a nuclear waste dump on Billa Kallina in South Australia, a place of importance to women but also important to the health of many generations' ongoing relationships to country.[46] Following a long campaign and in the lead-up to the 2004 federal election, the Kungkas successfully influenced public opinion and the Commonwealth government decided not to go ahead with the nuclear waste dump. Following the re-election of the conservative Coalition and against promises it made not to build a nuclear waste dump, it went ahead with planning for one in the Northern Territory. So without consultation (let alone free, prior and informed consent, if it could even be given) with traditional owners the Warlmanpa People, the promise to the electorate was broken. In 2005, the government enacted the *Commonwealth Radioactive Waste Management Act 2005*, legislation that provides exemptions from Aboriginal heritage protection laws. In 2006, further amendments to the Act enabled the nomination of sites for the dump, again without consultation or consent from traditional owners. In 2007, a site at Muckaty, Northern Territory, was nominated, but as a result of court action initiated by the Warlmanpa People of Muckaty that nomination was repealed in 2014.[47] The Australian government then advertised nationally for a site for a nuclear waste dump in 2015; they offered one lucky farmer in a suitable area a big bag of money if he would let them use a hundred acres or so. An agri-business in the Flinders Ranges of South Australia 'won' the prize, and they are very happy. The farm was not making any money, and now it will. But, again, it is not their land; it is the territory of the Adnyamathanha People, who are saying 'no!' to the storage of nuclear waste on their territories. So, as I write, many of the Adnyamathanha are shaping up for a fight once again to resist the development of a nuclear waste dump on their lands.[48]

In respect of the nuclear waste dump and in the short term international law standards might be an aid. Article 29 of UNDRIP[49] requires that First

Coober Pedy in the north of the state of South Australia. In 2004, the Commonwealth government abandoned plans to build the dump at this site.

46 The campaign against nuclear waste development on First Nations lands is documented at 'Response to Proposed New Muckaty Nuclear Waste Nomination', *Beyond Nuclear Initiative*, 7 November 2014 <http://beyondnuclearinitiative.com/2014/11/>.

47 *Mark Lane Jangala v Commonwealth, Northern Land Council and Others* [2014] FC (unreported).

48 Jane Norman, 'Nuclear Dump: Barndioota Station in SA Earmarked as Site of Waste Facility', *ABC News*, 29 April 2016 <http://www.abc.net.au/news/2016-04-29/nuclear-waste-dump-expected-south-australian-cattle-station/7369346>.

49 Article 29 of UNDRIP: '(1) Indigenous peoples have the right to the conservation and protection of the environment and the productive capacity of their lands or territories and resources. States shall establish and implement assistance programmes for indigenous peoples for such conservation and protection, without

Nations Peoples be fully consulted, but it does not enable or empower peoples to say 'no'. Moreover, the extent to which states will acknowledge and respect the standards of the UNDRIP is yet to be seen. There is no mechanism that could bring the state to account for any action which was taken in conflict with Art 29. Currently, all possibilities are in the hands of the economic and political will of states. Similarly, when our natural environments are threatened by fracking, uranium mining[50] and coal mining,[51] developments which pose wide-scale threats to the territories of First Nations across Australia, UN processes provide no mechanism to mitigate the power and colonial attitudes of the states; that is, they continue to dominate and subordinate First Nations' interests to those of powerful corporate bodies.

First Nations across Australia all have their own stories to tell, stories about having authority but no power to uphold the obligations we carry from our laws. We have responsibilities to care for country, and our laws continue, post-invasion and the almost complete decimation of our peoples. Up until the late 1960s and the early 1970s in Queensland we were subject to the *Aborigines Acts*,[52] but our peoples continued whenever and wherever they could to care for country. When, in the 1980s, my mother held the authority

discrimination. (2) States shall take effective measures to ensure that no storage or disposal of hazardous materials shall take place in the lands or territories of indigenous peoples without their free, prior and informed consent. (3) States shall also take effective measures to ensure, as needed, that programmes for monitoring, maintaining and restoring the health of indigenous peoples, as developed and implemented by the peoples affected by such materials, are duly implemented.'

50 The largest uranium mine in the world, Roxby Downs mine and processing plant, has impacted on the surrounding natural environment and the artesian basin underground waters around Lake Eyre, the land of the Arabana People. While the state advises they have obtained consent, Arabana Elder Kevin Buzzacott has protested the development since the 1980s. The processing plant uses millions of litres of water per day. The water is drawn from ancient underground water ways which connect us all in our future needs and dependencies, and should not be squandered on concentrating heavy metal ores. A new mine is being proposed on the lands of the Martu Peoples in Western Australia. Many of the Martu First Nation claim they have not agreed to the process. In June 2016, the Martu continued their protest against the mine being developed by Canadian company Cameco: Angus Sargent, 'Martu People Leave on 110km March in Protest Against Pilbara Uranium Mine', *ABC News*, 5 June 2016 <http://www.abc.net.au/news/2016-06-04/martu-people-in-the-pilbara-protest-a-uranium-mine/7476440>.

51 The Queensland government's approval of the Adani coal mine has to date been the subject of eight legal challenges.

52 Colonial states controlled First Nations through the following laws known as the '*Aborigines Acts*': *Aboriginals Protection and Restriction of the Sale of Opium Act 1897* (Qld); *Aborigines Protection Act 1886* (Vic); *Aborigines Act 1890* (Vic); *Aborigines Protection Act 1890* (WA); *Aborigines Protection Act 1909* (NSW); *Northern Territory Aboriginals Act 1910* (SA); *Aborigines Act 1911* (SA).

to persuade the local council of Kingston in the south-east of South Australia to move the district rubbish dump from the ruwe in which our ancestors lived and buried our old people, they did so. She was able to lead the restoration of the site. Our ancestors' bodies face the nearby sea and after their burial their spirits passed on to Kangaroo Island and then later travelled further on, to the south. My mother's authority came from our ruwe, and it was her obligation to ensure that a cynical colonial dispossession and deliberate destruction was corrected.

But to each generation new obligations fall, and it is now our responsibility to protect the country of our ancestors at Nora Creina Bay, ruwe on the coast near Robe in the south-east of South Australia. Another of our ancestors' resting places is earmarked for 'development' – a golf course and 'high-end' tourist resort. This development will ruin the ruwe and endanger our ngaitje,[53] some of whom are on the brink of extinction. And the beautiful, bountiful lands of the South Australian south-east, now mainly held by wealthy farmers, are going to be fracked for natural gas. The farmers chafe uncomfortably if we mention that the land they do so well on is actually stolen, but they do not want it to be fracked either. So we join them and say no to the fracking, for fracking might ruin the water which we still share. Our challenges are immense, but although we have the authority to say 'no!' we have no power to uphold it. These are the same challenges facing the territories of hundreds of First Nations Peoples across this continent. They are many and onerous. We have no law which can agree to the destruction and the extinguishment of the law, for that is law.[54]

The Elders have inspired our obligation and commitment for caring for country; that obligation is core to our understandings of whom we are and what we do. That is, it is what those of us who are still standing do, those not imprisoned, stolen by the state 'welfare' and/or just prostrated by inter-generational traumas, the effects of a violent coloniality. The current political and legal frameworks both domestic and international enable the language and philosophy of empire to continue to be applied, but the laws of original First Nations continue to centre our lives and our survival. And, drawing on the centres of knowledge and philosophy and the language of the speaking land, the laws of our ancestors will become louder so as to challenge those narratives which have worked to marginalise our ancient legal systems.

Recognition – but the state cannot see the laws and bodies of First Nations

The 'advancement' of 'rights recognition' through standards set by the UNDRIP is considered a high water mark of international law. The

53 Ngaitje means our relation, and could be animal, plant or natural landscape.
54 Watson, *Raw Law*, above n 1.

declaration takes a human rights approach to our struggles to survive genocide, but how does this approach translate into First Nations' epistemologies and ontologies? Is this approach more about assimilating First Nations into the vocabulary of colonialism and the narratives and rhetoric of states?[55] In the context of UN states founded on colonialism, what is to be recognised? What frameworks are deployed to determine rights? Are the only human rights those determined by the colonial settler state, which holds power to determine what they are? Or could they be determined by First Nations?

We have been here forever; why would we seek recognition from the colonisers? What does it mean to be recognised by the one who has been responsible for land theft and genocide? On recognition, do we become like the settler colonial society? Will we be no longer native and related to the land, instead separated and civilised? What, other than genocide and ecocide, could be recognised? Is there a will within the state to recognise our being beyond that of peoples who can only ever be absorbed and assimilated? Our ancestors responded at the time of the invasion; they stated repeatedly, 'We have always been here!' There is nothing to recognise, we have always been and we will always be Aboriginal peoples on Aboriginal land. We have already arrived.[56]

While there are many questions about processes and the effectiveness of 'rights recognition', are there possibilities for monitoring – beyond the words and symbols of recognition? If First Nations had power, as we had before colonialism and invasion, we would determine all things in our lives and would not be appealing for human rights protection, because we would have it. So what is it we have now in this place of an ongoing coloniality – more of the same, coloniality? Article 3 of the declaration declares that Indigenous Peoples have the right to self-determination,[57]

55 At the time the UNDRIP was voted on in the United Nations General Assembly in September 2007, a handful of Indigenous 'leaders' participated, claiming to be 'representing' millions of First Nations Peoples. Without a poll, and we lack the resources to hold one, I would confidently bet that less than 10 per cent of the global Indigenous population even knew the process was taking place. The question of mandate lies at the feet of the states and their Indigenous 'representatives'. The question to ask is: where does their mandate to speak and give their consent on behalf of global populations of Indigenous Peoples originate?

56 Martii Koskenniemi, 'Human Rights – So 90's' (Public lecture delivered at the University of Oxford, 4 March 2014) <https://www.youtube.com/watch?v=9hFdZRYZhkg>.

57 UNDRIP Preamble: '*Acknowledging* that the Charter of the United Nations, the International Covenant on Economic, Social and Cultural Rights and the International Covenant on Civil and Political Rights as well as the Vienna Declaration and Programme of Action, affirm the fundamental importance of the right to self-determination of all peoples, by virtue of which they freely determine their political status and freely pursue their economic, social and cultural development. *Bearing in mind* that nothing in this Declaration may be used to deny any peoples their right to self-determination, exercised in conformity with international law.'

but the limits made to self-determination render the principle rhetorical and practically inoperable.[58]

We know our own names and who we are

Many First Nations have belonged to our lands from the time of the first sunrise,[59] and we had our own names for the land.[60] Now, post-invasion and dispossession, our natural world is known by other, colonial names: Australia, Canada, the United States of America and New Zealand. We might ask, who drew up the map of the world, with the north at the top and the south at the bottom? We know that, not very long ago, a Eurocentric knowledge had the world as flat; meanwhile, our old people always knew planet Earth for what it really was, a round, cyclical body of law and motion. Some see their world as normative and other ways of knowing as strange. Our old people watched the hawks carrying the fire stick to light the bush to flush out game, and this is where we learnt fire stick farming, from our relations the hawks, for we are one in our sharing of life and knowledges. Stories of hawks carrying fire are known in European history but are considered myth, and do not tell of connection or relationship between hawks and other beings including those who call themselves human. In September 2001 (just days after the 9/11 event in the United States), *The Australian* newspaper reported that Northern Territorians claimed that ancient fire-stick farming practices of local First Nations were akin to acts of terrorism. What is demonstrated here is that colonial settler society has lost the possibility of knowing the story of the hawk and its lessons in how to live with one another. Instead, fire stick-farming is reinscribed as an act of terrorism.[61]

The politics of recognition works to contain First Nations within the confines of settler colonial society's rules and regulations and this is one

Article 3: 'Indigenous peoples have the right of self-determination. By virtue of that right they freely determine their political status and freely pursue their economic, social and cultural development.'

Article 4: 'Indigenous peoples, in exercising their right to self-determination, have the right to autonomy or self-government in matters relating to their internal and local affairs, as well as ways and means for financing their autonomous functions.'

58 White Face, above n 12, 72.

59 Our story of the first sunrise is sung by the magpies, and still today their song is heard just at the sun rising, a song that is sung again and again, will always be sung; while the magpie still sings that is law.

60 Evidence of our philosophy is found in our languages. As Russell Means writes, the Lakota had over fifty words for the naming of clouds, and the English have many words for torture. You would struggle to find one word to translate the concept of torture in Indigenous languages. Means and Johnson, above n 20, 6.

61 Paul Toohey, 'Scheming Blacks Behind Fires: Farmers', *The Australian, Weekend Australian Magazine*, 22 September 2001, 18.

interpretation of Art 46 of UNDRIP. Article 46 ensures that it will remain within the power of UN states to determine what Indigenous Peoples' territories and laws are. On that analysis very little would shift at all. At a domestic level, the colonial states have constructed regimes of recognition, and at the end of the 1990s the Australian government came out with 'native title' which was greeted with some enthusiasm by both Indigenous and non-Indigenous people. Native title recognition of rights to land was a hollow victory emanating from the High Court decision in *Mabo (No 2)*,[62] and was further limited by the *Native Title Act 1993* (Cth). Native title created a right recognised by Australian property law, but it was a lesser right than freehold, a beneficial right to the land. And it did not enable us to take care of country, protecting it from invasive and destructive developments. Voices criticising it in the 1990s were dismissed for being 'too way out', or too naive and dumb to understand the process. Now, decades later, a more critical approach is slowly developing. We belong to ruwe, the land, and reject a colonialist perspective which positions our lands as a commodity or a property right. Some of us have pointed out that native title created a lucrative industry for lawyers, indeed created a 'native title gravy train'. It has certainly created a hierarchy of those who are eating and those who remain starved – literally starved for food, but also starved for the health which country enables. The academy has been well fed: many academic careers have been made aboard the native title gravy train, and many law firms have grown fat from native title work. The Australian government saved face after the 1992 High Court *Mabo* decision by enacting the *Native Title Act 1993*, which effectively diverted international condemnation from falling on its racist colonial foundation – *terra nullius*. These same illusions of recognition were manufactured in the body of Aboriginal title and treaty negotiations across the United States in the 1800s.[63]

Prior to the *Mabo (No 2)* decision, international condemnation of Australia had been building. Paul Coe and others worked for more than a decade to gain an international opinion on *terra nullius* and its ongoing application to Australia.[64] This work followed in light of the *Western Sahara (Advisory Opinion)*[65] and international condemnation of *terra nullius* as a founding principle of colonial empire. However, these efforts were washed away by the

62 *Mabo v Queensland (No 2)* (1992) 175 CLR 1.
63 See Churchill, above n 36, 674–6, a discussion which reveals similarities with the Australian High Court decision in *Mabo (No 2)*. Discovery gave exclusive rights to the discoverer, a power that cannot be questioned. A similar conclusion as to the application of *terra nullius* was reached by the High Court in *Mabo v Queensland (No 2)* (1992) 175 CLR 1, 31–5, 78; for a further discussion, see Watson, *Raw Law*, above n 1, 131–2.
64 Paul Coe, 'Mabo: Confirming Dispossession', *Broadside*, 10 February 1993.
65 *Western Sahara (Advisory Opinion)* [1975] ICJ 12.

spirit of reconciliation and recognition,[66] which the government had fostered after *Mabo (No 2)*, and today we are still bedevilled by the legacy of *terra nullius*. *Terra nullius* still has life post-*Mabo* and post-*Western Sahara*. There was no glitch or pause in the colonial machine; the only change was the assimilation of some 'successful' native title applicants' entré into the Australian law of property. Our continuing effort to care for country remains a struggle and native title does little to relieve that struggle: its main effect is to enable participation in the (from an Aboriginal law perspective) un-lawful activity of wheeling and dealing and selling the land, and to assimilate into the colonial games of 'foundation' and 'recognition'.[67] At the time of writing, the lands of my old people the Tanganekald, Meintangk and Boandik First Nations, our territories now named the south-east of the state of 'South Australia', are being mapped for unconventional gas production (fracking). We have no native title claim over our lands, yet, but the state is working on it. My old people would say 'no' and our obligations to the land mean that we say 'no' to fracking of our ruwe. We have no power under colonial law to veto mining, but native title now opens a space of 'recognition' in which native title holders can wheel and deal; within the native title process they still have no power to say 'no', but native title deals might offer them baubles if they say 'yes'. Under our laws, they have no authority at all to say 'yes'. It is the classic colonial knot.

The reason we would say 'no' in any case is because we are of the land, it is our relation; the land is our future. We have an obligation to our lands and our laws; we know that the quality of our air, water and earth soils cannot be compromised. We know that we cannot go anywhere else; that the land is whom we are and our survival as peoples is wholly connected to it. Without the land we are nothing; we become empty shells and peoples who become disconnected from our being. So while we understand that the colonial project

66 The Council for Aboriginal Reconciliation was established in 1991 by the Commonwealth government to build a united Australia. The council ended in 2001. A united Australia remains a project of assimilation.

67 Here I am referring to negotiations pursuant to the *Native Title Act 1993* (Cth) s 24BA through Indigenous Land Usage Agreements (ILUA). Developments on native title lands are frequently negotiated within an ILUA framework. For example, most large-scale developments, including the Roxby Downs uranium mine, involved an ILUA; note the confidential character of this agreement: Barry FitzGerald and Sarah Martin, '$900m Olympic Dam Windfall to Indigenous Groups', *The Australian*, 5 May 2012 <http://www.theaustralian.com.au/business/m-olympic-dam-windfall-to-indigenous-groups/story-e6frg8zx-1226347243652>. The recent developments of the Cameco Corporation uranium mine at Kintyre in the Pilbara region of WA on the lands of the Martu People was also negotiated as an ILUA in 2012: 'Kintyre', Cameco Australia <https://www.camecoaustralia.com/projects/kintyre>. Many of these agreements have resulted in conflict over who has a mandate for representation and signing off on agreements. As I write, the Martu People are walking the country to bring awareness to their opposition to the uranium mine: Sargent, above n 50.

is ongoing, our resistance to it is also ongoing. There is no end to conflict within the colonial matrix, for we must resist if we are to have a future as the First Nations Peoples.

Resistance across Australia is rising again; we are resisting the pressures of assimilation as it shifts and takes different forms. The politics of recognition are about assimilation, for to be recognised we must assume the poses desired by the colonialists. Many First Nations Peoples live in extreme poverty and this is part of a largely deliberate end game of removal from our homes, the ruwe, and assimilation. It is how the colonial project closes in on its next harvest, developing, progressing and commodifying. The removal of First Nations children has been identified as a historical national scandal, but in the contemporary sphere continues to occur in numbers greater than at any previous time in the colonial history of Australia.[68] Today our children are removed in acts of the state deemed to be in their 'best interest'; or for punishment of minor offences;[69] they are 'humanitarian interventions', contemporary missions for 'recognition of our humanity' and the reformists' need to rescue, placate, civilise and whiten us up. This is the modern face of assimilation and genocide. All across Australia, First Nations communities are being starved of resources, and the Commonwealth and state governments threaten to withdraw funding for social services, education, and housing and health services. Our land and labour provides the resources, but the colonists cannot afford us.[70] These are our homes and we have nowhere else to go. Of course, there are always standing offers for us to get aboard the assimilationist agenda of the states. Apart from having nowhere else to go, we have an obligation to care for the country we are born to, to ensure that there is a future for our grandchildren.

Another angle the states pursue is our incarceration. Incarceration rates of First Nations peoples in Australia are higher than ever before. We could, as we have done for most of the years after 1788, claim the award for the most imprisoned peoples in the world. When the *Aborigines Acts* were in force, the

68 Ronald Wilson, *Bringing Them Home: Report on the National Inquiry into the Separation of Aboriginal and Torres Strait Islander Children from Their Families* (HREOC, 1997). A national movement of senior First Nations women, Grandmothers Against Removal, campaigns to stop the removal of Indigenous children.

69 In detention, First Nations children have been treated in a cruel and inhumane way; recent evidence of this treatment has been exposed by Caro Meldrum-Hanna, 'Australia's Shame', *ABC 4 Corners*, 25 July 2016, <http://www.abc.net.au/4corners/stories/2016/07/25/4504895.htm>

70 A growing debt is owed. In the 1970s First Nations made the claim for 'paying the rent' arguing it was owed for stolen Aboriginal lands. Debt owed to First Nations could also be measured by the displacement of First Nations governance: Stewart Motha, 'The Debt Crisis as Crisis of Democracy' (2012) 8 *Law, Culture and the Humanities* 390–7. On debt characterised as a foundational sovereign debt, see Maria Giannacopoulos, 'Sovereign Debts: Global Colonialism, Austerity and Neo-Liberal Assimilation' (2015) 19 *Law Text Culture* 166–93.

states used reserves and missions (and prisons) to detain us. The prisons alone perform that function today.

In these post-*Mabo*, post-native title, post-reconciliation, post-Rudd-apology[71] times, there is much discussion around the promise of constitutional recognition.[72] This will no doubt fall in a heap, but contemporaneously there is also further talk of a treaty. All this while the colonial project is working on its final grab and theft of our lands and resources: closure of communities. These communities, often old missions and reserves, occupy the remnant scraps of land set aside for us when the bulk of the land was taken.

It should be clear that there are no remedies in the recognition game; it is like the game of snakes and ladders, which goes up and down, but leads to only one ending, our assimilation into the white Australian nation. Genocide: there is currently no other alternative on offer. And this is perhaps why we get no mileage in our arguments that assimilation is genocide; genocide is a powerful word all about the muldarbi power, but the truth is that if assimilation is the only option for First Nations futures, then it is the death of First Nations.

First Nations Peoples have not sought recognition of whom we are; we know who we are. First Nations' dialogue with colonial states, the United Nations and other international institutions has been a process of seeking avenues for peace and survival and relief from the genocidal effects of the colonial project still grinding on.[73] We continue to seek mechanisms which will provide relief from the processes of the colonial states, but the talk of recognition remains just that – talk, and talk which seems to provide no avenue to anywhere but back into the corridors of assimilation into the colonial state. The idea of First Nations seeking 'recognition' from the colonial states negates the truth: we have always been on our territories, and we were here first. First Nations have our own names, our own languages, and our own territories, laws, peoples and ways of being in the world. But this alternative narrative, this 'truth' of the coloniser, continues to be constructed: the

71 On 13 February 2008, the Prime Minister of Australia, Kevin Rudd, apologised for the forcible removal of Aboriginal children, also known as the 'Stolen Generation'.

72 Recognition of First Nations has been an ongoing discussion, from exclusion – as captives of colonial state jurisdiction – to inclusion within Commonwealth constitutional power to make laws for Aboriginal peoples. Evidence of those Commonwealth powers over Aboriginal Peoples has been identified in the NTER. In 2016, at a meeting in Victoria, over five hundred First Nations Peoples voted 'no', almost unanimously, to the Commonwealth government's constitutional recognition campaign. See Hamish Fitzsimmons, 'The Victorian Government Will Enter Talks to Draft Australia's First Treaty with Aboriginal People', *ABC Lateline*, 26 February 2016 <http://www.abc.net.au/lateline/content/2015/s4414840.htm>.

73 Sharon Venne, 'NGOs, Indigenous Peoples and the United Nations', above n 11, 75–101.

'natives' are seeking recognition. Recognition of what? Of our humanity? We know we are human, but we also know that the human is only one part of life; the simple 'rights of the human' cannot exist in isolation. Our ways of thinking are different to those who have led and maintain the colonial project. Why would we appeal for recognition, just to enable a better fit into the assimilatory project of the state?

We are ancient peoples who have shared relations with hundreds of other First Nations and our names and connections to country are evidence of those relations with each other. We are the First Peoples and we originated internation relationships. We are the first internationals – but different from those whom we know now as international states. And again, the evidence of our inter-national cooperation with each other is unacknowledged, buried by the myths of *terra nullius*, another part of ignoring the fact of our existence as subjects in international law.

But we resist, and First Nations' resistance takes many forms. One form is to challenge the idea that the centre of our world is Europe and European epistemologies. This resistance challenges the idea that there is no horizon other than the European colonial matrix which still dominates the human rights agenda. It is also a challenge to the idea of a Eurocentric universal – which is all there is, that is, the only horizon or possibility.

Much of the literature and discussion concerning the recognition of Indigenous rights is anthropocentric and also centred on colonially constructed identities. Our First Nations – before they were enclosed by that which is now called Australia – were bound by songlines. The songs held the peace and the boundaries between the nations, and were respected and upheld: that was the law. But, as we know, at the invasion our laws were translated differently, lumped into '*terra nullius*' and deemed non-sovereign. And the natives were deemed sub-human, and thus fell completely outside colonial frameworks of recognition. Anghie notes: 'the history of the non-European states is told principally in terms of the civilizing mission'[74] and colonial states are still in the business of initiating and controlling discourses on the subject of Indigenous recognition. The current discussion in Australia about possible constitutional recognition of First Nations is out there for public consumption, in an electorate noted for its conservatism. What it means beyond the *terra nullius* narrative is yet unknown, but there is little to suggest that it means much more than the continuation of that same narrative: the *terra nullius* body dressed in the costume of 'recognition'.

Current debates on 'recognition' within the colonists' circles have no interest in acknowledging that the lands stolen – the vast continents stolen – did not belong to peoples in a proprietorial enslaved way, but that we belonged to them, in our ancient relationships with them. There is no interest in acknowledging that discredited doctrines of discovery and *terra nullius*

74 Anghie, 'Western Discourses of Sovereignty', above n 32, 21.

underpin the foundations of all these contemporary settler states. The subject of First Nations' laws still falls outside colonial state discourses of recognition, because it has the potential to unsettle and fracture the states' foundations. So it is avoided.[75]

There are many obstacles to freedom in international relations and law, and recent developments in the discourses of 'Indigenous recognition' are further obstacles, aimed to disempower First Nations' struggles for freedom. For within current recognition frameworks there is no opportunity of freedom which we could take up to decolonise on our terms, languages and frameworks. The only opportunities involve continuing to work inside the frameworks of the colonial state. 'Recognition' is imploding on the ground, but even so recognition is being constructed for the profit of states. The illusion of recognition enables them to appear as if they have given something back, or acted to deconstruct the embedded colonial relationships, to decolonise. Of course, nothing will really have shifted. Illusions of recognition will not impede the dreary, ongoing rhetoric in the racist, patronising discourses on 'our aborigines' as if we were the domestic objects of state colonial desires. Evidently, that is what the eyes of the states still see.

It appears then that the only possibility is assimilation and, while from a First Nations perspective that can only translate as genocide, is there a way out for us? If another way can be mapped, then it would be critical to maintain and centre First Nations' epistemologies. This challenges the idea that there is no horizon other than that set by the colonial matrix. It also challenges the idea of a Eurocentric universal and the trajectory of progress at any cost. We would not be alone with this: most credible evidence indicates that current western models of progress are working at an unsustainable cost to our natural world and a lot of people know this.

Conclusion: why not get over it and assimilate?

While I think this is a dumb question, it continues to be asked on a regular basis. It is still seen by many (as in the eighteenth, nineteenth and twentieth centuries) that realistically no option other than to assimilate exists, and to seriously consider alternatives is seen as irrational. The colonialist view of 'native savagery' was similarly seen as irrational, in much the same way as opposition to assimilation is depicted as irrational. It is as if we are treading water – still under pressure to be absorbed by the invading colonial settler society, the same one which has dispossessed us from the beginning. Always there has been this demand to assimilate; however, to do this would be to relinquish our laws and lives and also the obligations we carry as First Nations Peoples. And where, in the end, would it get us? Say, for example, if we were to simply join the treadmill of rights recognition, for a meagre native

75 *Mabo v Queensland (No 2)* (1992) 175 CLR 1, 30 (Brennan J).

title right 'handout' this would absorb us into Australian property law, and further the commodification of our lands and waters, but it would be an unlawful act from an Aboriginal law perspective. In gaining 'rights' from the processes of colonialism, we would breach the laws of our nations.

Carrying out the obligations to our laws means opposition and resistance to the invaders, a resistance that requires understanding of where the enemy lies. Where does the pressure to make us disappear originate from? Obviously, it is still to rid the settlers of 'troublesome natives' and to secure their flocks and mining leases once and for all, but we are still here, and still a trouble to the colonial state. And it looks as if it could go on for hundreds of years more. So perhaps another way is called for – that is, to unpack, decolonise and continue to be the peoples we have always been.[76] But colonial attitudes are so heavily set that to do this is seen as impossible, and the colonists revert to the question: what about the rule of law? (That is the same rule of law which stole Aboriginal lands from under our feet and fenced our lives in.[77])

But if we could imagine a world in which the colonial states were really decolonised, that they could relinquish power over First Nations' territories and laws, this could be the spot or the place from where we turn away from the trajectory of progress and its dire prospect of an ending, and move towards a positive transformation of the global status quo.[78] It could be a transformative process which enables the transformation of the United Nations statist system, and decentring the United States from performing at its core.[79] The dominant counter argument is fuelled by the fear of a loss of the rule of law, but this does not necessarily follow.[80] It is more likely to be a liberation for everyone. Fear and greed are certainly behind a system which continues to commit genocide across the globe, with a body count estimated to lie at millions of corpses and growing daily from wars alone over the past fifty years.[81]

The fear of a loss of the 'rule of law' implies there is nothing else other than the violent colonial foundations which have constituted colonial legal systems. In the colonial context, the rule of law is an assertion of power without authority, as authority is with First Nations Peoples. It is a fear that negates

76 Churchill, above n 36, 696, discusses how we might liberate ourselves from the endless knot of colonialism, and unpack or untie ourselves from an unlawful foundation.

77 Natsu Taylor Saito, *Meeting the Enemy* (New York University Press, 2012) 42: the rule of law, having the 'force of law' with its inherent colonial violence, holds the power to include or exclude non-Christian peoples entirely on the terms of the invading colonial body. And it is also paramount: ibid 82–3.

78 Churchill, above n 36, 697.

79 Ibid 702–6.

80 See Miéville, *Between Equal Rights*, above n 5, 304–8, on the need to critically evaluate the tensions of humanitarian intervention and its underpinning of a liberal-cosmopolitan defence of the rule of law.

81 Churchill, above n 36, 704.

the fact of First Nations laws. Our nations had laws to provide a remedy for greed and power; our ancient ancestors managed to settle the drought and release the water so as to replenish the land and all life forms. This was done without violence; the law led the way. The frog who grew and grew, outgrowing all other life forms, was encouraged to laugh and let go of the all the Earth's water. The community of animals brought the giant frog to laugh, and in laughing the frog let go of all the world's water, filling those dry depleted spaces, so we could all drink again. It was also decided the one big frog would become many, and the many shared and accessed the world's waters. No wars, no violence, a laugh and a letting go. That is the law. Whether we come to it sooner or later, the law just is.[82]

82 I have reflected on the frog across a number of works and most recently in Watson, *Raw Law*, above n 1, 16–17, 87.

Chapter 6

Law and politics of Indigenous self-determination: the meaning of the right to prior consultation[1]

Roger Merino

Introduction

In June 2009, the town of Bagua in the Peruvian Amazon was the scene of one of the most important political events in recent Peruvian history. Amazonian Indigenous Peoples blocked the Curva del Diablo highway for two months, protesting against a governmental package of decrees approved by President García which favoured the exploitation of natural resources in the Amazon. As a result of police repression, hundreds of people were wounded and 33 people died.

After this political event, known as the Baguazo, a social consensus emerged that Peru needed to launch new intercultural policies that recognised and valued Indigenous cultures and, in this way, would reduce social conflict. Law No 29785 of September 2011, the *Law of the Right of Prior Consultation of Indigenous Peoples, Recognized in the ILO Convention 169*,[2] best known as the 'Prior Consultation Law' (*Ley de Consulta Previa*), was the legal mechanism that supposedly would achieve these aims. This law was based on the *Indigenous and Tribal Peoples Convention* No 169 (ILO Convention No 169[3]), which establishes the obligation to consult Indigenous Peoples before approving any administrative or legal norm that can affect their collective rights. This Prior

1 I am very grateful for comments on earlier drafts of this chapter to Ana Dinerstein (University of Bath), Sara Motta (University of Newcastle, Australia) and Irene Watson (University of South Australia). Thanks too to the colleagues who participated in the Annual Conference of the Society of Latin American Studies, University of Sheffield (Sheffield, 18–20 April 2012); the Postgraduates in Latin American Studies Annual Conference, Department of International Development, University of Oxford (Oxford, 25–27 June 2012); and the Institute for Global Law and Policy Workshop, Harvard Law School (Doha, January 2013) for their generous comments. I especially thank the University of Bath for financial support through a University Research Scholarship.

2 Ley No 29785, *Ley del derecho a la consulta previa a los pueblos indígenas u originarios, reconocido en el convenio 169 de la organización internacional del trabajo* (OIT).

3 International Labour Organization, *Indigenous and Tribal Peoples Convention* 1989 (No 169) (entered into force 5 September 1991).

DOI: 10.4324/9781315628318-7

Consultation Law is the first of its kind in Latin America. Although it did not fully follow the higher standards of the *Declaration on the Rights of Indigenous Peoples* of 2007 (UNDRIP) and the Inter-American Court of Human Rights jurisprudence, it was considered an advance in the protection of Indigenous rights in Peru by politicians, international organisations, civil society organisations and the business sector.

In this chapter, I argue that the Prior Consultation Law is embedded in 'coloniality' because it does not properly recognise Indigenous Peoples' self-determination.[4] Coloniality denotes that, even though colonial rule has ended in formal legal and political terms, power remains distributed according to a colonial ontology and epistemology. This explains why social, legal and economic relationships regarding Indigenous Peoples still respond to an inclusion–exclusion paradox. After colonisation, the political and economic elites constructed states under European models according to which the state was the legal and political expression of a homogeneous social collective (a 'nation'). Therefore, Indigenous Peoples have to be either included within these new nation-states (denying their different social, political and economic arrangements) or excluded from them (which meant in some contexts the legal and material elimination of these peoples). Thus, in the new state model 'Indigenous Nations' were not accepted.

This political tension rooted in colonisation is a paradox that continues today. Thus, when Latin American constitutions recognise the right of self-determination or autonomy for Indigenous Peoples, they actually refer to the right of each Indigenous community to govern themselves within a specific space legally protected with property entitlements. There is no recognition of the self-determination of a whole Indigenous Nation with territorial rights, only the recognition of specific communities of individuals 'included' in the political and economic logic of the nation-state.

The inclusion–exclusion paradox responds to the colonial denial of two key aspects of Indigenous law and politics: the denial of their territories and the denial of their character as nations. Thus, juridical innovations to recognise Indigenous rights have always relied on western standards. According to the dominant liberal theory, Indigenous Peoples must be integrated, included, assimilated or accommodated within the liberal framework as ethnic minorities with proprietary entitlements, so they can 'participate' in the benefits of 'development', instead of seeing Indigenous Peoples as nations with territorial rights that pursue their own models of development.

4 Although the concept of 'self-determination' is rooted in the project of modernity and political liberalism, from a decolonial perspective (which I will expose in the next section), it is possible to understand this and other political concepts from different ontologies and epistemologies, giving new meanings and political potentials.

For this reason, Indigenous Peoples maintain a tense and ambiguous relation with liberal legal systems: they use private property, human rights and consultation law for territorial defence, but at the same time they criticise the limitations of this legislation to grant complete self-determination. Thus, Indigenous Peoples struggle for social emancipation by appropriating and 'going beyond' liberal law, and in this way they dispute the state logic of either inclusion or exclusion. In other words, they reject the logic by which the state either deploys legal and institutional mechanisms to assimilate Indigenous Peoples (compulsory use of Spanish, aggressive diffusion of Christianity and economic arrangements) or exclude them (the requirement that voters must be able to read, the prohibition of use of their language and culture, amongst other things).

In this chapter, I explore these issues by engaging with the implementation of the Prior Consultation Law in Peru. First, I analyse the meaning of self-determination as an essential concept to understand the potential and limitations of the right to prior consultation and its differences from the right to provide free prior and informed consent. Then, I analyse the legal and political foundations of this right and its relation to coloniality, and unpack the Prior Consultation Law in order to show its dark side. Lastly, I explain the tensions between Indigenous territorial rights, self-determination and the 'national interest'.

Indigenous self-determination and the inclusion–exclusion paradox

The relation between Indigenous rights and the state's laws has always been ambiguous, because for Indigenous Peoples the state system has meant both domination and resistance. Thus, Silvia Rivera explains how domination over Indigenous Peoples did not mean a lack of agency since they have strategically appropriated the liberal legal system to defend their rights.[5] Thus, after the process of independence in Bolivia (1810–25), some Indigenous Peoples used colonial legislation[6] that recognised some special rights for Indians to challenge the liberal state. This strategic use of the law is part of the long memory of Indigenous resistance that continues today in the different struggles for territorial rights.

The legal system, then, has always been an instrument to mediate Indigenous politics of self-determination, understood as the collective freedom from colonial powers. However, liberal laws have never been able to express

5 S Rivera Cusicanqui, 'The Notion of "Rights" and the Paradoxes of Postcolonial Modernity: Indigenous Peoples and Women in Bolivia' (2010) 18(2) *Qui Parle: Critical Humanities and Social Sciences* 29.

6 By 'colonial legislation' I mean the Indian Law or *Leyes de Indias*, a body of laws and decrees issued by the Spanish Crown in order to regulate the interactions between the settlers and natives in its American and Philippine colonies.

Indigenous reality completely because, by imposing Eurocentric conceptions of 'nation'[7] and individual rights, they have always subjected Indigenous Peoples to the inclusion–exclusion paradox.

This paradox means that, by constructing 'one nation' and making the Indigenous Nations in former Latin American colonies invisible, the Indigenous population was subjected to two options: to be included in the new nation-state under European liberal laws, which meant losing territorial and self-determination rights but gaining property entitlements and citizen rights; or to be excluded from the new nation-state logic, which meant being subjected to practices of slavery, deprivation and genocide.

The dividing line between inclusion and exclusion is complex because in many contexts practices of recognition of rights for assimilation (inclusion) and denial of rights (exclusion) were applied simultaneously or consecutively. Thus, in the past if Indigenous Peoples rebelled against assimilatory practices such as forced conversion to Christianity or abusive taxation, they were objects of exclusion through military repression of the revolts.[8] (Today, if Indigenous Peoples oppose the extractive industries that express the 'inclusion' to a specific development model, they are also objects of repression.) Inclusion and exclusion were simultaneously applied, for example, when Indigenous Peoples were recognised as citizens but under conditions that in practice deny the exercise of rights (for example, the requirement to read to be able to vote).[9]

In order to understand the conceptual boundaries of the inclusion–exclusion paradox fully, it is important to review the meaning of 'statehood'. The literature on international law defines the state as composed by substantial and formal aspects.[10] The substantial aspect refers to a political community that shares cultural features, a territorial space, political aims and an identity, whereas the formal aspect refers to its legal configuration and recognition by the international community. The first aspect expresses the self-determination of peoples or the 'nation' that is the material basis of the state, and the second aspect expresses state sovereignty as a capacity to rule within a territorial space and to be protected by, and given obligations under, international law. The state and the nation are then two different concepts although deeply

7 For discussions of the European concept of 'nation', see Benedict Anderson, *Imagined Communities: Reflections on the Origin and Spread of Nationalism* (Verso, rev edn, 1991); Partha Chatterjee, *The Nation and its Fragments: Colonial and Postcolonial Histories* (Princeton University Press, 1993); Homi Bhabha, *Nation and Narration* (Routledge, 1990).

8 D Sanders, 'The UN Working Group on Indigenous Populations' (1989) 11(3) *Human Rights Quarterly* 406.

9 This requirement was eliminated in Peru just four decades ago with the Political Constitution of 1979.

10 See references in M Craven, 'Statehood, Self-Determination and Recognition' in Malcolm Evans (ed), *International Law* (Oxford University Press, 3rd edn, 2010) 203.

related. The state is the juridical-political expression of the 'nation' (a socio-cultural concept) and the European model of the 'nation-state' expresses this relation.

However, Indigenous Peoples were not considered 'nations' in these terms. In some contexts they were considered a second category of nations subjected to an imperial power (in North America) or as simple tribes (in Central America). Therefore, they were not allowed to be states and subjects of international law. The consequence of this is that, even though they could be recognised as political communities, their lack of statehood made them legally vulnerable to the imperial powers' domination.

After independence from the British, Spanish and Portuguese empires in the eighteenth and nineteenth centuries, the new political units in America obtained the formal aspects of statehood, and the substantial aspect of self-determination had to entail the construction of a 'nation' in which the Indigenous Nations had to be either included or excluded.[11] The new nation-states were constructed as European, Catholic and white countries with no place for autonomous Indigenous Peoples.[12] The political dynamics have obliged a rethink of the notion of self-determination and a re-elaboration of legal and political arrangements.

The notion of Indigenous self-determination has a rich genealogy that began with the imperial history of colonisation,[13] but an important milestone was the discussions around the decolonisation of Africa.[14] Thus, around the First World War, self-determination became a powerful political discourse from which notions of statehood were derived.[15] When the United Nations was created, 'the self-determination of peoples' was included in the founding principles of the UN Charter.[16] In 1960, the United Nations General Assembly adopted the *Declaration on the Granting of Independence to Colonial Countries and Peoples*, referring to self-determination in relation to formal

11 J Galindo, 'Cultural Diversity in Bolivia: From Liberal Interculturalism to Indigenous Modernity' in M Janssens (ed), *The Sustainability of Cultural Diversity: Nations, Cities and Organizations* (Edward Elgar Publishing, 2010) 80.

12 F Arocena, 'Multiculturalism in Brazil, Bolivia and Peru' (2008) 49(4) *Race & Class* 1.

13 See P Fitzpatrick, 'Necessary Fictions: Indigenous Claims and the Humanity of Rights' (2010) 46(5) *Journal of Postcolonial Writing* 446; A Pratt, 'Treaties vs. Terra Nullius: "Reconciliation", Treaty Making and Indigenous Sovereignty in Australia and Canada' (2004) 3 *Indigenous Law Journal* 43.

14 Craven, above n 10.

15 D Philpott, 'In Defense of Self-Determination' (1995) 105(2) *Ethics* 352; C Fromherz, 'Indigenous Peoples' Courts: Egalitarian Juridical Pluralism, Self-Determination, and the United Nations Declaration on the Rights of Indigenous Peoples' (2008) 156(5) *University of Pennsylvania Law Review* 1341; A Peang-meth, 'The Rights of Indigenous Peoples and Their Fight for Self-Determination' (2002) 174(3) *World Affairs* 101.

16 V Napoleon, 'Aboriginal Self Determination: Individual Self and Collective Selves' (2005) 29(2) *Atlantis* 1.

colonial rule.[17] The 'peoples' in this declaration were colonised peoples dominated by foreign powers. For them, self-determination meant independence from the colonial authority.

However, to derive statehood from self-determination was problematic because not all states in the world had the two aspects of statehood (the substantial and formal aspects previously mentioned) in the same way. Although all states alleged international political recognition and sovereignty, inside many 'postcolonial' states lived different Indigenous Nations. In this context, international scholars differentiated between 'external self-determination' and 'internal self-determination'.[18] The former refers to a situation in which a specific nation has the right to be an independent republic in front of the international community, and the latter refers to a situation in which different nations coexist within a specific state and maintain some degree of political autonomy, however, under a unitary legal and political framework.

When international legal instruments and most scholars refer to Indigenous self-determination, they are referring to 'internal self-determination' as the right to maintain their ancestral territory and their specific cultural and social norms as Indigenous Peoples within a specific state.[19] This version of self-determination has been recognised in the *International Covenant on Economic, Social and Cultural Rights* and the *International Covenant on Civil and Political Rights*, adopted by the United Nations General Assembly in 1966. These are the sources of Art 3 of UNDRIP, which recognises the 'right of self-determination', although respecting the principle of political unity of the sovereign state.[20]

17 *United Nations Declaration on the Granting of Independence to Colonial Countries and Peoples*, GA Res 1514/15, UN Doc A/RES/1514(15) (adopted 14 December 1960). See A Muehlebach, 'What Self in Self-Determination? Notes from the Frontiers of Transnational Indigenous Activism' (2003) 10(2) *Identities: Global Studies in Culture and Power* 241.

18 The conceptual origins of the right of self-determination for Indigenous Peoples can be found in the imperial history of colonisation. In North America, the British Royal Declaration of 1763 established that the only authority that could negotiate with Indigenous Peoples (considered as nations) and secure property to the settlers was the Crown. After independence, Chief Justice Marshall in *Worcester v State of Georgia* 31 US 515 (1832) alleged that Indigenous property and government were legally recognised, though under the *imperium* of the settler nation. Thus, although Marshall recognised American Indian nations as sovereign, this recognition applied only to the relationship between Indian nations and other states, not with the federal government. Therefore, even though some celebrate the Royal Declaration and the Marshall jurisprudence as the basis of Indigenous self-determination, in practice the common law has aimed to eliminate Indigenous territorial rights. See Fromherz, above n 15; S Dodds, 'Justice and Indigenous Land Rights' (1998) 41(2) *Inquiry: An Interdisciplinary Journal of Philosophy* 187.

19 S Errico, 'The Draft UN Declaration on the Rights of Indigenous Peoples: An Overview' (2007) 7(4) *Human Rights Law Review* 741.

20 E Daes, 'An Overview of the History of Indigenous Peoples: Self-Determination and the United Nations' (2008) 21(1) *Cambridge Review of International Affairs* 7; Peang-meth, above n 15; Muehlebach, above n 17.

The legal recognition of internal self-determination has been celebrated by some scholars[21] because it would make Indigenous Peoples subjects rather than objects of international law. In that sense, Anaya argues that the recognition of Indigenous 'self-determination' has been central to their demands at an international level: self-determination is a foundational principle that encompasses the constellation of Indigenous rights; for him this means that, under the human rights approach, Indigenous Peoples, with their own social and political institutions, must be equal participants in all the levels of the government under which they live.[22]

However, in practice the recognition of 'internal self-determination' has meant the reinforcement of state power over Indigenous territory in exchange for some degree of autonomy. The reason for this is that, in order to negotiate 'self-determination' successfully with the states at UN forums, Indigenous Peoples had to accept the human rights framework under the paradigm of the unitary nation-state, instead of the decolonial framework in which 'self-determination' was born, namely, as a specific collective political right rooted in the resistance against colonisation.[23]

But it seems problematic to accept that self-determination can only be understood in terms of a liberal conception of the nation-state and human rights, and that it must be detached from decolonial struggles. On the contrary, 'self-determination' must be understood from Indigenous perspectives through a conceptual turn that in decolonial theory is called 'border thinking'.[24] According to this view, decolonial epistemology does not mean a fundamentalist rejection of all western categories, but the acknowledgement that there are non-western theoretical frameworks that must be grasped on their own terms; only then is it possible to start a dialogue and exchange. Thus, it does not reject the use of western categories but invites us to rethink those categories from non-western epistemologies.[25] Border thinking, therefore, allows a

21 P Keal, *European Conquest and the Rights of Indigenous Peoples: The Moral Backwardness of International Society* (Cambridge University of Press, 2003); J Gilbert, 'Indigenous Rights in the Making: The United Nations Declaration on the Rights of Indigenous Peoples' (2007) 14 *International Journal on Minority and Group Rights* 207.

22 J Anaya, 'Derecho de los pueblos indígenas a la libre determinación tras la adopción de la Declaración' in Claire Charters and Rodolfo Stavenhagen (eds), *El desafío de la declaración: Historia y futuro de la declaración de la ONU sobre pueblos indígenas* (IWGIA, 2009) 194.

23 K Engle, 'On Fragile Architecture: The UN Declaration on the Rights of Indigenous Peoples in the Context of Human Rights' (2011) 22(1) *European Journal of International Law* 141.

24 R Grosfoguel, 'A Decolonial Approach to Political-Economy: Transmodernity, Border Thinking and Global Coloniality' (2009) 6 *Kult* 10.

25 W Mignolo and M Tlostanova, 'Theorizing from the Borders: Shifting to Geo- and Body-Politics of Knowledge' (2006) 9 *European Journal of Social Theory* 205; R Grosfoguel, 'World-Systems Analysis in the Context of Transmodernity, Border Thinking, and Global Coloniality' (2006) 29(2) *Review of the Fernand Braudel Center* 167.

redefinition of western concepts and devices such as democracy, human rights and self-determination.

In that sense, Indigenous self-determination from a decolonial perspective entails two options for Indigenous Peoples: integrating state political and economic institutions or enacting their own political and economic arrangements in relation to the state (which can mean the re-emergence or reinvention of pre-colonial legal and political frameworks). Thus, it can entail a variety of institutional arrangements, from decentralisation and social participation to total independence and autonomy. Its implementation depends on the political and social context of each situation. Nonetheless, in all cases Indigenous self-determination must be conceived in legal-political and ontological/epistemological terms as a foundational right: the right to transcend the inclusion–exclusion paradox.[26]

This right has never been fully recognised. Indigenous Peoples' rights in Latin American countries have been enacted through top-down legal recognition of specific 'Indigenous communities' in the case of Peru or 'Indigenous *resguardos*' in the case of Colombia.[27] These spatial units of colonial legacy are composed by segments of Indigenous Peoples that were organised in specific areas during the colonial era. When Latin American multicultural constitutions recognise the right of self-determination or autonomy, what they are recognising is the right of each community to govern themselves within that specific space (in political, economic and juridical terms). They are not recognising the self-determination of a whole Indigenous Nation, but the 'pluriculturalism' by which Indigenous Peoples are autonomous units *within the national political community*.[28] The difference between plurinationalism and pluriculturalism is relevant here. Plurinationalism recognises the existence of different nations under a state legal and political framework, whereas pluriculturalism only celebrates the 'cultural diversity' of a country without recognising Indigenous Peoples as nations.

Another institutional arrangement suggests that Indigenous Peoples have the inherent right to be recognised not as units within a nation but as different nations. This does not mean denying state sovereignty but recognises the fact that they are not going to be assimilated into a dominant nation. The models of federal Indigenous Nations proposed by Tully[29] and the recent plurinationality implemented in Bolivia express this kind of

26 On the notion of 'foundational rights', see R Merino, 'Critical Human Rights and Liberal Legality: Struggling for "The Right to Have Communal Rights"' (2013) 3(3) *Philosophy Study* 246.

27 These are recognised in the current political constitutions: Political Constitution of Peru (1993) and Political Constitution of Colombia (1991).

28 D Van Cott, *The Friendly Liquidation of the Past: The Politics of Diversity in Latin America* (University of Pittsburgh Press, 2000).

29 J Tully, *Strange Multiplicity: Constitutionalism in an Age of Diversity* (Cambridge University Press, 1995).

self-determination.[30] It is important to note that these different political arrangements entail different degrees of self-determination. The anthropologist Richard Smith has accompanied Indigenous movements for decades and has found that self-determination refers to the right of a people to choose the type of relationship it wants to maintain with a dominant state.[31] There are, of course, some radical proposals such as Ward Churchill's claim for the constitution of an Indian nation independent from the United States.[32] However, most academic and political proposals range from some degree of autonomy through decentralisation within a dominant nation such as the liberal multiculturalism in Latin America, to political projects that recognise Indian nations within the state.

However, even in decolonial projects or any other project in which there is a dominant nation-state, Indigenous self-determination is affected by norms of exception and national interest that allow the reconstitution of liberal law and the political economy of extraction. For example, the recognition of Indigenous collective property is limited because the state (or transnational corporations with concession rights) can always exploit the natural resources located under Indigenous land on behalf of the 'national interest'.[33] Therefore, the liberal legal system must be decolonised. Indigenous Peoples appropriate legal tools which accord to their own political agendas but at the same time move beyond legal boundaries towards the recognition of more profound Indigenous rights: territory, nationality and consent are the final aims of the struggles for property, communality and consultation.

Prior consultation: between inclusion and exclusion

The recognition of Indigenous rights is not new in Peruvian history. President Leguia (1908–12 and 1919–30) promoted the legal recognition of 'Indigenous communities' in the Constitution of 1920[34] and pro-Indigenous legislation for their integration into the national society. President Velasco (1968–75) enacted laws to recognise Indigenous communities as peasant and native communities and promoted a project of Indian modernisation through a co-operative agrarian model.[35] Indigenous Peoples have been treated as subjects to be modernised and

30 B Santos, 'La reinvención del Estado y el Estado plurinacional' (2007) 8(22) *OSAL* 25.

31 R C Smith, 'Los indígenas amazónicos suben al escenario internacional: Reflexiones sobre el accidentado camino recorrido' in F Morin and R Santana (eds), *Lo transnacional: Instrumento y desafío para los pueblos indígenas* (Abya-Yala, 2003) 203.

32 W Churchill, *Struggle for the Land: Native North American Resistance to Genocide, Ecocide, and Colonization* (City Lights Books, 2002).

33 Eg Art 21b of Law No 26834, 1997; Art 5c of Law No 28736, 2006.

34 Constitution of the Republic of Peru of 1920, approved by the National Assembly in December 1919.

35 See L Del Castillo, '¿Tienen futuro las comunidades campesinas?' (1992) 14 *Debate Agrario* 39; J Matos, 'Comunidades indígenas del área andina' in J Matos

each legal device that has recognised their rights has been accompanied by norms that reinforce the state's power in their territory on behalf of the 'national interest'.

The Prior Consultation Law is a new legal innovation for the recognition of Indigenous rights in the context of multiculturalism, which was inaugurated by Fujimori's government (1990–2000). During the 1990s the multicultural trend led to the constitutional recognition of Peru as a multi-ethnic society, but at the same time the weakening of Indigenous rights: the 1993 Constitution[36] removed the remaining norms in favour of Indigenous Peoples from Velasco's legislation,[37] including the inalienability of Indigenous lands, and reasserted the state's absolute control over natural resources, promoting at the same time the selling, leasing and mortgage of Indigenous land (Decree No 653[38]). The recognition of multiculturalism included formal recognition of Indigenous activism in a space allocated to political and economic elites (they become *indios permitidos*), and some important achievements related to cultural recognition, but undermined the possibility of articulating other fundamental claims.[39] Therefore, multiculturalism is an instrument to ensure the power of neo-liberal governments, rather than a real commitment to Indigenous Peoples' rights to territory and self-determination.[40]

The right to free, informed and prior consultation fits within this logic. This right was first recognised by the ILO Convention No 169 (1989) as a right of Indigenous Peoples to be consulted before the approval of any measure that affects their collective rights.[41] According to the convention, in general it is only necessary to *consult* and not to obtain *consent* (with the exception of displacements[42]).

(ed), *Hacienda, comunidad y campesinado en el Perú* (Instituto de Estudios Peruanos, 1976) 179.

36 Articles 88 and 89 of the Political Constitution of Peru, Title 3 'Economic Regimen', Chapter 6 'Agrarian Regimen of Peasant and Native Communities'.

37 The main Indigenous legislation of Velasco's government was Decree 17716, *Law of Agrarian Reform* (1969) and Decree 20653, *Law of Native Communities and Agricultural Promotion of the Amazonian and Low Amazonian Regions* (1974).

38 D Leg No 653, *Law of Promotion of Investment in the Agrarian Sector*.

39 C Hale, 'Neoliberal Multiculturalism: The Remaking of Cultural Rights and Racial Dominance in Central America' (2005) 28(1) *Political and Legal Anthropology Review* 10.

40 R Sieder, '"Emancipation" or "Regulation"? Law, Globalization and Indigenous Peoples' Rights in Post-war Guatemala' (2011) 40(2) *Economy and Society* 239; L Horton, 'Contesting State Multiculturalisms: Indigenous Land Struggles in Eastern Panama' (2006) 38(4) *Journal of Latin American Studies* 829.

41 Article 6(1) of the ILO *Indigenous and Tribal Peoples Convention* No 169 (1989): 'In applying the provisions of this Convention, governments shall: (a) consult the peoples concerned, through appropriate procedures and in particular through their representative institutions, whenever consideration is being given to legislative or administrative measures which may affect them directly.'

42 Ibid Art 16(2): 'Where the relocation of these peoples is considered necessary as an exceptional measure, such relocation shall take place only with their free and

Scholars have criticised the notion of consultation because it becomes a business device for companies to achieve the status of social responsibility.[43] It has been appropriated and repackaged by public and private global institutions such as the World Bank, the Inter-American Development Bank and the International Council on Mining and Metals, amongst others, which inserted it into a global political economy that recognises the right of consultation but not the right of Indigenous Peoples to provide consent.[44] Others criticise the idea that prior consultations prevent and resolve social conflicts when in reality they generate tensions between local visions of development and state economic goals.[45]

The UNDRIP[46] went further by emphasising that the processes of consultation should be directed to obtain the 'free, prior and informed consent' of Indigenous Peoples,[47] and expressly recognising the necessity of consent in cases of displacement, storage or disposal of hazardous materials in Indigenous territory, and the use or occupation of Indigenous material and immaterial property and territory.[48] However, the right to consent in the declaration is

informed consent. Where their consent cannot be obtained, such relocation shall take place only following appropriate procedures established by national laws and regulations, including public inquiries where appropriate, which provide the opportunity for effective representation of the peoples concerned.'

43 C Rodríguez-Garavito, 'Ethnicity.gov: Global Governance, Indigenous Peoples, and the Right to Prior Consultation in Social Minefields' (2011) 18(1) *Indiana Journal of Global Legal Studies* 263.

44 D Szablowski, 'Re-empaquetando el CLPI: las conexiones globales y el debate sobre el consentimiento indígena para la extracción industrial de recursos' (2010) 28 *Anthopologica* 217.

45 Almut Schilling-Vacaflor, 'Rethinking the Link between Consultation and Conflict: Lessons from Bolivia's Gas Sector' (2014) 35(4) *Canadian Journal of Development Studies/Revue canadienne d'études du développement* 503.

46 *United Nations Declaration on the Rights of Indigenous Peoples*, GA Res 61/295, UN Doc A/RES/61/295 (adopted 13 September 2007).

47 Ibid Art 19: 'States shall consult and cooperate in good faith with the indigenous peoples concerned through their own representative institutions in order to obtain their *free, prior and informed consent* before adopting and implementing legislative or administrative measures that may affect them.'

Article 32(2): 'States shall consult and cooperate in good faith with the indigenous peoples concerned through their own representative institutions in order to obtain their *free and informed consent* prior to the approval of any project affecting their lands or territories and other resources, particularly in connection with the development, utilization or exploitation of mineral, water or other resources.'

48 Ibid Art 10: 'Indigenous peoples shall not be forcibly removed from their lands or territories. No relocation shall take place without the *free, prior and informed consent* of the indigenous peoples concerned and after agreement on just and fair compensation and, where possible, with the option of return.'

Article 11(2): 'States shall provide redress through effective mechanisms, which may include restitution, developed in conjunction with indigenous peoples, with respect to their cultural, intellectual, religious and spiritual property taken without their *free, prior and informed consent* or in violation of their laws, traditions and customs.'

not yet fully recognised because, apart from these situations, the state has the power to decide in cases when an agreement between the government and Indigenous Peoples is not reached. As full consent is an expression of full self-determination, the lack of recognition of the latter affects the former.

In the judicial arena there have not been enough achievements. In the most important decision on the right of consent (*Saramaka v Suriname*[49]), the Inter-American Court of Human Rights asserted that consent is necessary in cases of 'large-scale development or investment projects' that would have a 'major impact' on 'a large part of their territory', whereas the UNDRIP establishes that the states shall consult in order to obtain free and informed consent prior to the approval of *any project affecting their lands or territories and other resources.* The argument of the Court is less protective than the UNDRIP because, according to it, if extractive industries do not affect a significant area of Indigenous territory, it is enough to undertake processes of consultation, not of consent.[50] The Court's most recent decision on the issue (*Sarayaku v Ecuador*[51]) does not go any further in the recognition of the right of consent.

Therefore, it is important to distinguish between the current consultation standard, the consent standard and consent as an expression of Indigenous self-determination. The two former are expressly recognised by international law whereas the latter is rooted in the historical struggles for decolonisation although not yet completely recognised by national and international standards.

Article 28(1): 'Indigenous peoples have the right to redress, by means that can include restitution or, when this is not possible, just, fair and equitable compensation, for the lands, territories and resources which they have traditionally owned or otherwise occupied or used, and which have been confiscated, taken, occupied, used or damaged without their *free, prior and informed consent.*'

Article 29(2): 'States shall take effective measures to ensure that no storage or disposal of hazardous materials shall take place in the lands or territories of indigenous peoples without their *free, prior and informed consent.*'

49 *Case of the Saramaka People v Suriname* (Inter-American Court of Human Rights, 28 November 2007). In the 1990s, Suriname granted logging and mining concessions to private companies within the traditional Saramaka People's territory without their consent. In 2000, the petitioners complained to the Inter-American Commission of Human Rights and argued that, despite the fact that they were not in possession of a title for the territory, they had the right to use and possess the territory for their cultural, religious and economic activities. The case went to the Inter-American Court of Human Rights in 2006. The Court decided that the Saramaka People did not need a title in order to own the lands and asked the Suriname government to 'delimit, demarcate and grant a collective title over the territory of the members of the Saramaka people, in accordance with their customary laws, and through previous, effective and fully informed consultations'.

50 J Pasqualucci, 'International Indigenous Land Rights: A Critique of the Jurisprudence of the Inter-American Court of Human Rights in Light of the United Nations Declaration on the Rights of Indigenous Peoples' (2009) 27(1) *Wisconsin International Law Journal* 51, 90.

51 *Case of the Kichwa Indigenous People of Sarayaku v Ecuador* (Inter-American Court of Human Rights, 27 June 2012).

Consultation and the limited application of consent are not only trapped in the logic of multicultural liberalism; they also explain the permanence of the inclusion–exclusion paradox. In spite of consultation processes, Indigenous Peoples' territory is still subjected to extractive exploitation on 'behalf of the national interest', with the argument that it will bring modernisation and development to Indigenous communities and the whole country. Namely, Indigenous Peoples are included into the extractivist political economy in order to exclude their own model of development that may be different from extractive exploitation.

Thus, the promotion of extractive projects requires a legal framework that recognises Indigenous rights as only being related to social and economic participation in the project,[52] and not rights of self-determination and territoriality expressed in their right to provide consent. The economic policies are implicitly based on the premise that Indigenous Peoples do not have the capacity to manage their own territory properly according to the 'national interest'. In sum, the extractivist economic policies and laws embody the prejudices of colonial governments which saw Indigenous Peoples as primitives who should be civilised and eventually incorporated into western culture.[53]

Critiques of the Prior Consultation Law

The Prior Consultation Law is the legal implementation of ILO Convention No 169, which was ratified by the Peruvian state in 1994. Since then, a few state agencies such as the Ministry of Energy and Mines have implemented a weak version of consultation under the name of 'informative workshops'. That is why in the last decade civil society and Indigenous organisations have strongly requested the correct implementation of consultation processes, reverting to court action and political activism.[54]

In the social arena, this law was the outcome of the Baguazo and other protests against national policies that ignored the ways in which Indigenous Peoples are affected by extractive industries. Ollanta Humala became President in 2011 under a 'social inclusion' banner, and the Prior Consultation Law was one of his first measures passed by the Congress. As the legislators felt compelled to implement ILO Convention No 169 and not the declaration (which is seen as a symbolic document rather than a normative one), they emphasised 'consultation' more than 'consent'. Thus, partially taking

52 M Satterthwaite and D Hurwitz, 'The Right of Indigenous Peoples to Meaningful Consent in Extractive Industry Projects' (2005) 22(1) *Arizona Journal of International & Comparative Law* 1.

53 S Davis and A Wali, 'Indigenous Land Tenure and Tropical Forest Management in Latin America' (1994) 23(8) *Journal of the Royal Swedish Academy of Sciences* 485.

54 See J Ruiz, *La implementación del derecho a la consulta previa de los pueblos indígenas: Una mirada constitucional* (IDL, 2011).

international standards into account, the law regulated the right to 'prior, free and informed consultation' instead of the right to prior, free and informed consent (as established in the declaration).

The original enthusiasm about the law was quickly abandoned in favour of criticism of its process of implementation through regulation (*Reglamento*),[55] which established very polemical rules, such as the exemption from consultation of infrastructure projects to provide health, education and 'public services' in general (this norm is very dangerous because these projects usually have major impacts on the Indigenous population), or the limited recognition of the right to provide consent. Indigenous Peoples only hold the right to provide consent when the state seeks to displace them to other territories, and when there is an attempt to keep dangerous materials on Indigenous land.[56] In any other cases the state only has to consult, and if there is a disagreement it is solved unilaterally by the state.

These limitations of the right to consultation have been exposed by activists who have formulated legal interpretations that enlarge the right to consultation;[57] however, to focus on consultation as a key element of Indigenous Peoples' legal status and political agenda is misleading. Even more, a deep analysis of the Prior Consultation Law and its regulations leads us to question its very foundations. Let us start by observing the structure of the consultation process. It is a process of 'dialogue' between the state and the peoples (with no intervention from companies); it is led by the public entity that enacted a law or administrative norm (including licences for extractive activities) that would affect Indigenous collective rights. Then, the process may have six stages (Arts 14–23 of the regulation): identification (of the people affected and the norm enacted); publicity (about the norm); information (the state informs Indigenous Peoples about the measure); internal evaluation (the community will evaluate the convenience of the measure); intercultural dialogue (which emerges only if there is no agreement after the internal evaluation); and decision. This process has a very short duration of 120 days.

As can be observed, the whole process is designed as a mechanism to inform and convince Indigenous Peoples of a decision already made; the 'intercultural dialogue' only appears if Indigenous Peoples are not persuaded. But should it not be the other way around? An intercultural dialogue should be the first stage in a state that is respectful of Indigenous Peoples, in order to identify their priorities and aspirations and undertake a mutually enriching dialogue.

This does not mean that Indigenous Peoples hold a unique position on the idea of development; indeed, the complexity of the processes of consultation

55 Bylaw (*Reglamento*) of the Law 29785, *Law of the Right of Prior Consultation of Indigenous Peoples Recognised under Convention 169 of the International Labour Organization (ILO)*, approved by Supreme Decree No 001–2012-MC, 3 April 2012.

56 This article is based on Art 29(2) of the UNDRIP.

57 See Ruiz, above n 54.

also responds to the plurality of Indigenous politics. Among the Awajun people, Indigenous leaders, Indigenous organisations and Indigenous intellectuals usually hold contrasting visions regarding globalisation and extractive industries.[58] For Greene, these tensions must be seen as forms of active negotiation with the state and market actors.[59] Rather than interpret them as contradictions, these are the diverse paths on which the Awajun construct their different projects. Indeed, these contrasting visions do not mean the renunciation of Indigenous self-determination. Themes such as territoriality and a strong environmental concern are still crucial in the general Indigenous agenda. Most discussions do not deny those ideals, but aim to define the ways in which engagement with the capitalist political economy and liberal legal system would end up affecting them. Therefore, what Indigenous Peoples want to negotiate in the processes of consultation is not the renunciation of their self-determination, but how this self-determination will interact with the market and the state.

However, the current law does not allow a complete exercise of self-determination because opposition to extractive industries is not an option. Nonetheless, Indigenous Peoples do not abandon the processes of consultation and this explains the process of appropriation and 'going beyond' the liberal legal system. Indigenous Peoples are very critical of the Prior Consultation Law; they strongly opposed the exclusion of the right of consent, but at the same time they are using the judicial system to demand more processes of consultation.[60] This apparent contradiction is in reality an expression of Indigenous politics: consultation is an available liberal tool to be used until the complete recognition of Indigenous self-determination is achieved. This also explains why consultation processes are so complex and contentious.

For this reason, the different engagements with consultation and other liberal devices must not be seen from the epistemological position of the West that usually portrays Indigenous Peoples as 'liberals' if they engage with consultation and human rights; as 'potential entrepreneurs' if they use property

58 In 2012–13, I did fieldwork with the Awajun people in northern Amazon and the Interethnic Association for the Development of the Peruvian Amazon (AIDESEP). The Awajun is one of the 52 Indigenous Peoples officially recognised by the Peruvian state (Official Data Base of the Ministry of Culture, 2014). According to the Vice Ministry of Intercultural Affairs, the census of Indigenous communities of the Amazon of 2007 estimated there were 55,366 people self-identified as Awajun, inhabiting native communities and *centros poblados* located mainly in the departments of Loreto, Amazonas, San Martin and Cajamarca. Most Awajun organisations are part of AIDESEP, the most important Amazonian Indigenous organisation.

59 S Greene, *Customizing Indigeneity: Paths to a Visionary Politics in Peru* (Stanford University Press, 2009).

60 See all the cases in J Ruiz, 'Problemas Jurídicos en la Implementación de la Consulta Previa en el Perú' (2014) 42 *Derecho & Sociedad* 179.

entitlements to defend their territory; and as 'radical Left terrorists' if they oppose extractive activities. Usually, the liberal legal system is a means to mediate Indigenous politics with the final aim of obtaining more spaces for self-determination.

Prior to prior consultation: territorial rights and the politics of Indigenous self-determination

I contend that the Prior Consultation Law's rationality is rooted in coloniality because it does not allow the exercise of Indigenous Peoples' self-determination: they can participate in the process but not oppose state decisions. Indeed, the hope of some companies and technocrats was to institutionalise conflicts within the Prior Consultation Law, and through this process – of passing information and persuasion – legitimise the policy, 'If properly obtained previous consent should allow large extractive industry projects to go forward in a less conflicted atmosphere'.[61] In sum, the law and its regulation is aimed at freezing Indigenous politics into new extractivist policies.

In addition to this, the expectations and propaganda raised by the Prior Consultation Law make us forget other important rights that have historically been part of Indigenous Peoples' agenda. Thus, academics and activists tend to conceptualise Indigenous rights around the right of consultation,[62] so other rights are simply treated as emerging rights that someday might be recognised by the law. However, crucial rights such as territoriality are not emerging claims; they have a long history of affirmation and resistance embedded in the politics of Indigenous self-determination.

In Peru, Arts 89 and 149 of the Constitution[63] recognise self-determination as the autonomy of peasant and Indigenous communities (which involves the right of autonomous organisation, communal work, use and free disposition of land, and economic, administrative and jurisdictional autonomy within the 'law'). Nonetheless, as this autonomy does not mean that Indigenous Peoples hold a complete power of decision making over their land (and they have no right over the resources of the subsoil), they often direct their claims towards decolonial projects. A decolonial project, as in the case of Bolivia, would mean the recognition of Indigenous Peoples not as 'communities' but as 'nations' and the recognition of their vital spaces not as 'land rights' but as 'territorial rights'.

61 L Laplante and S Spears, 'Out of the Conflict Zone: The Case for Community Consent Processes in the Extractive Sector' (2008) 11 *Yale Human Rights & Development Law Journal* 69, 71.

62 See E Salmón, 'The Struggle for Laws of Free, Prior, and Informed Consultation in Peru: Lessons and Ambiguities in the Recognition of Indigenous Peoples' (2013) 22(2) *Pacific Rim Law & Policy Journal* 353.

63 Political Constitution of Peru of 1993.

In fact, the key concept of territory has specific features that make it different from property. Economic and political theory obscure the fact that Europeans imposed systems of property on the colonies, and that Indigenous Peoples were already there, living with their own tenure systems.[64] In fact, Indigenous Peoples vindicate the concept of territory as a geo-political space that includes a communal system of land and resources tenure rather than property.

The literature on Indigenous territory has explained how it consolidates a singular set of social networks among the different beings that share the environment;[65] since it is a place for identity reproduction it is more than an economic issue. The territory possesses social, cultural and spiritual dimensions,[66] which are preconditions for Indigenous material and cultural survival.[67] This does not mean that Indigenous territories are given or static; indeed, their constitution responds to internal and external negotiations within the communities and the state.[68] That is why a politics of space or cartographic disputes are emerging between Indigenous claims to reinvent their territorialities and the state reaffirmation of its absolute power over Indigenous vital spaces.[69]

As previously mentioned, self-determination must be understood as the main right for Indigenous Peoples, a *foundational right* in the sense that it is the basis of a whole legal, political and economic system rooted in non-western ontologies and epistemologies.[70] Self-determination and territoriality support the right of consent, wrongly called 'right to veto' because it does not derive from a special power conferred to Indigenous Peoples due to their hegemonic position in the democratic system (as is the case with the presidential veto power), but it is an expression of their self-determination as peoples. Self-determination also supports the right to use and obtain direct benefits from the

64 J Tully, 'Aboriginal Property and Western Theory: Recovering a Middle Ground' (1994) 11 *Social Philosophy and Policy* 153.

65 P García and A Surrallés, *Tierra Adentro: Territorio indígena y percepción del entorno* (A Surrallés and García Hierro eds, IWGIA, 2004).

66 E Daes, 'An Overview of the History of Indigenous Peoples: Self-determination and the United Nations' (2008) 21(1) *Cambridge Review of International Affairs* 7; R Roldán, 'Models for Recognizing Indigenous Land Rights in Latin America' (Biodiversity Series, Paper No 99, World Bank Environment Department, 2004).

67 L Sweptson and R Plant, 'International Standards and the Protection of the Land Rights of Indigenous and Tribal Populations' (1985) 124(1) *International Labor Review* 91; E Stamatopoulou, 'Indigenous Peoples and the United Nations: Human Rights as a Developing Dynamic' (1994) 16(1) *Human Rights Quarterly* 58.

68 J Erazo, *Governing Indigenous Territories: Enacting Sovereignty in the Ecuadorian Amazon* (Duke University Press, 2013).

69 J Wainwright and J Bryan, 'Cartography, Territory, Property: Postcolonial Reflections on Indigenous Counter-Mapping in Nicaragua and Belize' (2009) 16 (2) *Cultural Geographies* 153.

70 Merino, above n 26.

land or the right of peoples to establish their own views of development, among other rights that contrast with new Indigenous rights that have been recognised in the last decades by international standards, such as ILO Convention No 169 and the jurisprudence of the Inter-American Court of Human Rights.

Indeed, many of these new rights are responses to western logic: the right of consultation (Arts 6(1), 6(2) and 15(2) of ILO Convention No 169), for example, has as a premise that a state is going to affect Indigenous self-determination and it needs at least to ask Indigenous Peoples their opinion; the right of Indigenous Peoples to participate in economic benefits obtained by extractive industries (Art 15(2) of ILO Convention No 169) responds to the fact that companies are exploiting (or are going to exploit) Indigenous land and resources.

This does not mean that there is no recognition of foundational rights at international level (indeed, ILO Convention No 169 timidly recognises the right to territory and the UNDRIP recognises a weak version of the right of self-determination); or that many Indigenous Peoples, because of their historical process, are closer to the discourse and practice of the new rights (such as consultation and economic benefits). It does mean rather that the problem of coloniality is still alive and hidden behind an optimistic discourse of globalisation of Indigenous rights.

This situation generates practical consequences. After enacting the Prior Consultation Law, the Peruvian government had to decide which would be the first process of consultation. The Quichua of Pastaza were elected as the first communities to be consulted because they had suffered from the environmental impacts of extractive industries for decades and had received considerable media attention. The consultation was planned at the commencement of exploitation activities of the oil concession 1AB located close to the communities. The Quichua of Pastaza, however, argued that before any process of consultation they wanted the recognition of their territorial rights and the remediation of sixty years of environmental impacts on their territory. The government, first, had to delay the process of consultation, and then undertake a rapid process of consultation whose results are not recognised by most Indigenous organisations. This example shows how new rights such as 'consultation' can be confronted with foundational rights, such as territoriality.

The problem of focusing on consultation is that it can obscure foundational rights that are components of today's Indigenous agenda. The most important Indigenous organisation in Peru (AIDESEP) and one of the most important non-governmental organisations that supports Indigenous rights (the Institute of the Common Good, Instituto del Bien Comun), for example, are promoting the notion of 'integral territory'. One of the experts in the institute is an Awajun who has developed this concept technically and theoretically.[71] According to him, the problem is that native communities' titling covers small parcels in which they live (as in the Andes) without taking into account

71 Interview with Ermeto Tuesta, Lima, 4 April 2013.

the whole territory that includes spaces for fishing, hunting and collecting. Then, huge areas become 'free spaces' that are given for extractive activities without consultation. To face this problem, communities are starting to claim title over territorial habitats instead of specific plots; they are demarking their territory in a long-term strategy until its comprehensive legal recognition.

Therefore, whereas Indigenous politics could be represented – paraphrasing Silvia Rivera[72] – as a long-term politics which entails the pre-eminence of a long memory (anticolonial struggles, pre-Hispanic order), many state officials and technocrats (and some activists as well), in contrast, associate Indigenous politics with the agrarian reforms of the 1960s and claims for statism and land redistribution which today would mean underdevelopment. Thus, this short memory (the fear of state intervention in the market) and short-term politics (undertaking strong extractivism to obtain fast economic growth) seems irreconcilable with the long memory (a history of coloniality) and long-term politics (with strategies such as integral territory).

That is why Indigenous self-determination is still affected by norms of exception that ensure the inalterability of the political economy and a specific view of development on behalf of the 'nation'. Indeed, the application of these norms has always been connected to the expansion of the extractive industries. As Orihuela asserts, the rise of the modern extractive industries is connected to Indigenous exploitation and dispossession, in the mines of the Andes and the rubber plantations of the Amazon.[73] It is therefore natural that in countries with a colonial past, land rights are not well defined and the state owns all underground resources: this allows the legal displacement of communities in the name of the greater public good.

By exception the state can then exploit resources in areas that are protected because of their environmental fragility (Art 21b of Law No 26834, 1997), and even in reserves for Indigenous Peoples in voluntary isolation (Art 5c of Law No 28736, 2006) because the untouchable character of the reserves can be broken by the state on behalf of the public interest.[74] Therefore, by designing policies from the logic of coloniality, the government completely controls peoples' vital spaces and the reduction or violation of Indigenous rights is a necessary sacrifice given the promise of development.[75] This power

72 S Rivera Cusicanqui, *Oprimidos pero no vencidos: Luchas del campesinado Aymara y Qhechwa 1900–1980* (WA-GUI, 4th edn, 2010).

73 J C Orihuela, 'The Making of Conflict-Prone Development: Trade and Horizontal Inequalities in Peru' (2012) 24 *European Journal of Development Research* 688.

74 M Finer, C Jenkins, S Pimm, B Keane and C Ross, 'Oil and Gas Projects in the Western Amazon: Threats to Wilderness, Biodiversity, and Indigenous Peoples' (2008) 3(8) *Plos One* 1; N Hughes, 'Indigenous Protest in Peru: The "Orchard Dog" Bites Back' (2010) 9(1) *Social Movement Studies* 85.

75 G Stetson, 'Oil Politics and Indigenous Resistance in the Peruvian Amazon: The Rhetoric of Modernity Against the Reality of Coloniality' (2012) 21(1) *Journal of Environment and Development* 76.

over Indigenous Peoples is usually justified as an expression of state sovereignty (the argument that Indigenous Peoples cannot have a 'veto power' over the state) or the necessity of economic development and the fulfilment of the government's social responsibilities.[76]

However, there is a historical connection between the political economy of extraction and the power to exploit Indigenous territories on behalf of the national interest. This connection expresses the logic of coloniality by which certain peoples can be exceptionally sacrificed on the ground of the alleged economic benefits for all (economic argument) and the national cohesion (sovereignty argument). But what is obscured is that the people sacrificed usually have been ranked as the less civilised and constructed as those who urgently need to be integrated into modernisation.

Indeed, these arguments are rooted in the colonial denial of Indigenous self-determination and territoriality and are expressed in the Prior Consultation Law. For that reason, the liberal legal system should be understood as a means to mediate Indigenous politics, not as an end in itself. Indigenous Peoples criticise and at the same time engage in the processes of consultation with the aim of pushing for their agenda of self-determination beyond consultation. The final aim is to transcend the inclusion–exclusion paradox towards the recognition of different nations with territorial rights and the reconstitution of the state. The challenges in this are tremendous. It entails not only policy innovations, but also overcoming the elite's ideology and the political economy embedded in coloniality, namely, the view that resource extraction and 'integration' of Indigenous Peoples to this logic is the only path to development. The politics of Indigenous self-determination obliges us to question these premises.

Conclusion

In this chapter I have explained one crucial consequence of the colonisation process that has implications today: the double denial of Indigenous Peoples, the denial of their territories and communal tenure and the denial of their character as 'nations'. These denials mean that Indigenous Peoples are conceived, at best, as landowners (able to hold property rights) and citizens (able to hold political rights of participation) who belong to ethnic minorities instead of being conceived as a people with territorial rights who belong to a specific nation.

The chapter also revealed the meaning of the inclusion–exclusion paradox: Indigenous Peoples are either included into the logic of the liberal capitalist state or excluded from it. Indigeneity is tolerated insofar it does not contradict the political and economic fundamentals of this system. Thus, participatory and economic rights of Indigenous Peoples are articulated in terms of the

76 Laplante and Spears, above n 61.

political economy of extraction: Indigenous Peoples are consulted about the way in which an unavoidable extractivism must be undertaken, and they have the right to obtain economic benefits from extractive activities.

Many Indigenous Peoples seek to transcend the inclusion–exclusion paradox by proposing a politics of self-determination. I suggest that Indigenous self-determination means that Indigenous Peoples have the right to enact their own legal, political and economic systems. This principle does not deny the interrelation of Indigenous Peoples with the state and the market nor the plurality of Indigenous politics; it entails that Indigenous Peoples should have the option to decide about the future of their territory and the way they want to implement their own view of 'development'.

That is why I conceive of self-determination as a 'foundational right'. I differentiate between Indigenous foundational rights (such as self-determination and territoriality) that are ontologically located beyond the inclusion–exclusion paradox and therefore support the whole Indigenous system, and 'new Indigenous rights', such as the right of consultation or the right to obtain economic benefits from extractive activities. Instead of foundational rights that are rooted in non-western principles, the new Indigenous rights are situated in the context of the global political economy of extraction and do not question the two denials of Indigenous Peoples mentioned above.

I have demonstrated that coloniality survives in the Prior Consultation Law by conceiving of Indigenous Peoples as minorities with proprietary entitlements that can 'participate' in the benefits of 'development'. This explains why the liberal legal framework cannot contain the whole Indigenous cosmology and why Indigenous Peoples use this legal system and move beyond it in a project of social emancipation that seeks to reinvent the state structure in order to recognise Indigenous territorial rights and self-determination.

Chapter 7

How governments manufacture consent and use it against Indigenous Peoples

Sharon Venne

Introduction

This chapter is not written from the position that the colonisers are the repositories of knowledge. It is shaped from our Indigenous point of view, using our own knowledge to analyse issues and respond to the colonisers. Our Elders teach us that the Creation gave us a beautiful gift: a mind.

Indigenous Peoples have been subjected to the coloniser's education system for more than five hundred years. The state and churches took our children and tried to teach us to be servants of the colonisers. Those institutions did not even teach basic skills other than cooking, cleaning, taking care of animals and obedience to their weapons of punishment. The churches instilled hypocrisy, worship and idleness, and tried to stop our critical thinking so that we could no longer be inventive. Then, they returned those surviving broken children to their families. The colonisers wanted our children to be non-inventive, only to repeat the lies of the colonisers. The colonisers were holding the pens to write a history that favoured their narrative. Our histories that the colonisers did not like were suppressed and rewritten to favour them. The colonisers wanted to be the masters so that they could continue to abuse our territories and resources. This is not a new invention. It is a repeat. The colonisers' repeat is corruption. They construct the story based on their values and try to construct the narrative to fit their view of created history. This history is full of myths and lies. Nonetheless, it is used as an effective means to spread hatred and racism.

This age-old tactic has become very visible in two recent manifestations. Domestically, legislation in Canada called the *First Nations*[1] *Financial*

1 During the constitutional discussions in Canada in the late 1970s and early 1980s, the English and French settlers started calling themselves the founding nations. The Indigenous Peoples in response started to call themselves the First Nations of Great Turtle Island. Since that time, it is an accepted practice to be referred to as First Nations Peoples. In this chapter, the term 'First Nations' is interchanged with 'Nations' and I use 'citizen' rather than 'member'. I will use these terms where I am not copying or reproducing source materials.

DOI: 10.4324/9781315628318-8

Transparency Act[2] (known widely across Canada as C27) tried to undermine our treaty governments. Canada attempted to paint a picture that the citizens of our Nations did not know what was happening with our finances and needed the federal government to act to protect the citizens. This was false. The citizens of the Indigenous Nations have always had access to the audits – either at the office of the Nation or at the nearest office of the Department of Indian Affairs and Northern Development (DIAND). At the international level, a high-level plenary of the United Nations General Assembly (GA) was branded the 'World Conference on Indigenous Peoples'. These two examples will be explored in this chapter.

Canada's version of transparency was to expose our Peoples to racism and hatred. There was a perceived idea that our Peoples are not accountable. Canada's transparency exposed our Nations to the carpetbaggers who mined information online to target our Nations while the high-level plenary allowed only one Indigenous individual to address the GA. Both of these processes were orchestrated and manipulated by states for specific purposes. There were lots of collaborators who were more than happy to play along with the games. What were their rewards? It seems the reward was to get their names in the media. They had no thought for the seventh generations[3] and the effect that their action would have on the rest of the Creation. Indigenous governments who were opposed to the process were branded unco-operative and punished for non-compliance.

Manipulation of Indigenous Peoples continues unabated. Governments of states have organised their own groups of Indigenous Peoples who have been recognised by their political masters to make 'decisions' for Indigenous Peoples. Controllers have been used by governments to enact regressive domestic legislation and to push an international agenda.

Canada and 'real transparency'

Canada is a state created by an Act of the British Parliament in 1867.[4] In relation to the history of Great Turtle Island, it is very new. Canada is a

2 Bill C27 was enacted by the Parliament of Canada and received Royal Assent on 27 March 2013.

3 Within our traditional laws our Peoples are directed to think of the seventh generation – those that are not yet born. We are asked to consider the implication of our decisions on them. In this way, we are separating decisions from ourselves and the immediate future. It gives us a longer view of things rather than 'me me' thinking. The concept of seventh generation is widely held by Indigenous Peoples and Nations of the Americas.

4 *British North America Act 1867*, 30 & 31 Vict, c 3 (UK). As part of the colonisation process, our island was rebranded North America by the colonisers. Our Creation stories put us on this floating island called Great Turtle Island. As part of our decolonisation process, we must take back our names for our island. North America is Great Turtle Island.

product of colonisation. The British Crown sent representatives across the oceans to the shore of our island. What they saw, they wanted. There was only one problem. The lands and resources were being used by our Nations. The British Crown enacted the *Royal Proclamation of 1763*[5] to govern the subjects of the Crown in accessing Indigenous territories. There are three important aspects of the Royal Proclamation: (1) in order to access the lands and territories of 'Indian Nations or Tribes', there needed to be an agreement or a treaty; (2) if the Crown's subjects were within the territories of the Indian Nations or Tribes, the Crown was obligated to remove them (they would be considered squatters); and (3) agreements or treaties would be made if the Indians 'so desired'. This makes treaties a prerequisite to the Crown's subjects legitimately moving into the territories of Indigenous Nations.

Treaties that were made by the British Crown were passed to Canada to implement. Treaties have been recognised internationally as a source of rights, for example by Special Rapporteur Miguel Alfonso Martinez in his ten-year study of treaties made between Indigenous Nations and states.[6] Alfonso Martinez wrote:

> In the case of Indigenous Peoples having concluded treaties or other legal instruments with the European settlers and/or their continuators in the colonization process, the Special Rapporteur has not found any sound legal argument to sustain the position that they have lost their international juridical status as nations.[7]

His conclusions were similar to Lord Denning's in *The Indian Association of Alberta v Foreign and Commonwealth Secretariat*[8] in 1982.

However, the created state of Canada did not want to recognise the rights of our Nations. Indigenous Nations govern with our own laws that are distinct and separate from what the federal government of Canada imposes on us through its laws, policies and legislation, including the '*Indian Act*'.[9] The *Indian Act* tries to restrict and limit the way in which Indigenous Nations govern our affairs in our territories. The territories of the Nations include, but are not limited to, those territories recognised and designated as 'reserved' or

5 Issued by King George III of Great Britain and Ireland on 7 October 1763.

6 United Nations Economic and Social Council, *Study on Treaties, Agreements and Other Constructive Arrangements between States and Indigenous Populations: Final Report by Miguel Alfonso Martinez, Special Rapporteur*, UN Doc E/CN.4/Sub.2/1999/20 (22 June 1999).

7 Ibid [265].

8 *R v The Secretary of State for Foreign and Commonwealth Affairs, ex parte The Indian Association of Alberta, Union of New Brunswick Indians, Union of Nova Scotian Indians* [1982] QB 892 (CA).

9 See Sharon H Venne, *Indian Acts and Amendments 1868–1975: An Indexed Collection* (University of Saskatchewan Press, 1981).

'reserve' lands. However, these recognised 'reserved lands' are only one small part of the larger traditional territories of the Nations. It is necessary to understand the extent to which the state of Canada has attempted to restrict our movements and use of our territories. Legislation and policies imposed restrictions such as the pass system, the need for permits to dispose of our produce, and to cut and sell timber from our lands, and restricting foods to force our children into residential schools. In Sarah Carter's book *Lost Harvests* she documents the non-Indian farmers who protested the ability of the Indians to farm collectively and undermined their efforts.[10] These protests led to changes in the *Indian Act*[11] which was a federal law that prohibited Indians from selling produce without a permit from the federal government's DIAND. This practice continued until the 1960s. Now, there is a new process to control and monitor the Indians. The latest tool designed to control and restrict the Indigenous Nations is Contribution Agreements (CAs).[12]

In the early 1960s, Canada started to make funds available to the Nations for social assistance. Over time, the number of programs that were offloaded onto the Nations to administer has increased but the funds have not kept pace. In the 1980s, Canada unilaterally imposed a 2 per cent cap on funding, without consulting the Nations.[13] This cap is still in place, despite the statements made by the new Liberal Government that the cap would be removed. Canada controls the funds voted by the Treasury Board through CAs. These agreements are wide-ranging and control the use of the funds through the terms and conditions. The CAs can range from one to five years depending on the government's assessment of the ability of the Nation to manage those funds. The CAs require First Nations to provide detailed financial information to the government. A failure to provide the necessary

10 Sarah Carter, *Lost Harvests* (University of McGill Press, 1993). See also Bruce Dawson, *Better than a Few Squirrels: The Greater Productions Campaign on the First Nations Reserves of the Canadian Prairies* (Master's Thesis, University of Saskatchewan, 2002). In a well-documented thesis, Dawson points out that Indian lands have been used to enrich the officials of DIAND at the expense of the Indians.

11 The *Indian Act* was amended in 1880 to ban the selling of produce and to prohibit anyone from purchasing such products from Indians.

12 A complete history of the CAs was filed at the United Nations with the Special Rapporteur James Anaya in response to questions asked. This document is available from Ermineskin Cree Nation who prepared and submitted the materials. Ermineskin had filed a complaint with the Special Rapporteur on the unilateral and arbitrary implementation of terms and conditions that were considered a violation of the treaty relationship.

13 First imposed by a Liberal government in 1996, the 2 per cent cap was a limit that DIAND placed on annual increases to First Nations' budgets. When it was first announced, the cap was greeted with protest. It meant that, despite inflation and a fast-growing population, funding for First Nations communities, programmes and services could only increase by 2 per cent each year. The government said that they would lift the cap in the new budget expected in the spring of 2016, but this had not happened as of February 2017.

information could lead to the cancelling of the agreement or to a manager being imposed to manage those federal dollars. It is a well-established process. CAs are governed by onerous reporting requirements spelt out in a reporting guide that the government changes on a yearly basis without any consultation with First Nations. These changes spell out in detail the level of reporting required for the funds allocated from Ottawa. It is a myth that these monies are not regulated by Ottawa.

There are hundreds of reports due in every calendar year. If there is a failure to account for the funds properly, then DIAND has many options available, as spelt out in the CAs, including putting in place a manager of the funds. During the standing committee discussions on C27, Mrs Carol Hughes (Algoma-Manitoulin-Kapuskasing, NDP) noted, 'Auditor General's report from December 2006, it basically said the unnecessary reporting burden placed on first nations communities needed to be reduced, and it noted that AANDC alone obtains more than 60,000 reports a year from over 600 first nations.'[14]

The Reporting Handbook of DIAND was used to implement the legislation.[15] A unilateral amendment to the Reporting Handbook imposed the criterion that all recent legislation must be respected and honoured. A failure to comply was a breach of the agreement. In the Reporting Handbook, the salaries of the Chief and Council[16] must be reported as part of the annual audit done for DIAND. It was another myth that this information was unknown to members of the community. All audits are available either at the offices of the Nation or at DIAND. All a member needs to do is make an appointment and look at the audit. In addition, many Nations have their own finance laws in place that are much more stringent that anything that applies to non-Indigenous People across the country. The posting of the consolidated audits on a 'public'[17] website was designed to expose the Nations to every carpetbagger from around the world.

There are some examples of auditors targeting Indigenous Peoples because they could see on the website that they had a source of income outside the government monies. In addition, I have lost count of the number of lawyers who have called me offering to work for various Nations. It might be a

14 Report of the Standing Committee, 31 October 2012.
15 The annual Reporting Handbook is available on the DIAND website, <https://www.aadnc-aandc.gc.ca/eng/1385559716700/1385559777677>.
16 Schedule of Salaries, Honoraria, Travel Expenses and Other Remuneration – Elected or Appointed Officials.
17 For example, Onion Lake Cree Nation has a website where their audits are posted for their members to review – all they need to do is log on to the website and review the audit. However, this website is only open to citizens of Onion Lake. The Government of Canada wanted to have the audits put on the DIAND website, which would allow anyone with access to a computer and an internet connection to view those audits. Onion Lake has always maintained that their public is their citizens. This was not acceptable to the Government of Canada.

coincidence that the offers to work are only for Nations with independent monies. People from other countries have tried to contact the Nations with offers of business opportunities. In one instance, there was an offer to set up an embassy for the Nation – of course, the person wanted to act as a paid advisor to said embassy. There is no end to the schemes and scams that are being floated, all exposed by the 'trustee' of Indians – the government of Canada.

Only the treaty peoples can change our status – so the states are trying to manufacture 'consent' in order to bring our lands and resources within the state. This is without the consent of the Indigenous Nations. 'Individuals' who are not accountable to the Nations are used to ensure that the voices of the Nations are pushed aside and not considered. Worse than this, the true voices of the land are left outside of the process as the state pushes its agenda.

Transparency and the attack on our Nations' governments mean that our governments are treated differently to other organisations. For example, private sector businesses have accountability to their shareholders, but they do not necessarily have accountability to the media or have their private accounts posted on the world wide web. Canada helped the process by giving funds to individuals who worked with organisations such as the Canadian Taxpayers Federation (CTF)[18] that promoted the legislation. They would not listen to any discussion on treaty rights. The rallying cry was: these are taxpayers' dollars and we need to know what you are doing with them.[19] Two things spring to mind: DIAND has a complete accounting of the funds through its extensive reporting requirements. This leads to the second observation: CTF do not believe that their own government is capable of creating a process of accountability. Instead of dealing with their own problems, there was an attempt to destroy the treaty relationship and undermine the privacy rights of Indigenous Peoples by publishing confidential financial information. Why?

Bill C27

Bill C27, An Act to Enhance the Financial Accountability and Transparency of First Nations (short title: the *First Nations Financial Transparency Act*), was introduced and received its first reading in the House of Commons on 23 November 2011. On 7 November 2012, Indian Affairs Minister John Duncan imposed closure on the Bill to stop further discussions. It was passed by the

18 The CTF is a federally incorporated, not-for-profit citizen's group dedicated to lower taxes, less waste and accountable government. The CTF was founded in Saskatchewan in 1990 when the Association of Saskatchewan Taxpayers and the Resolution One Association of Alberta joined forces to create a national taxpayers organisation (copied from their website).

19 In the documents filed in a case against Onion Lake, Sawridge, Athabasca Chipewyan, Thunderchild and Ochapowace in the Federal Court of Canada, the federal government stated that these were not taxpayer dollars.

House of Commons and sent to the Senate. Chief Craig Makinaw on behalf of the Confederacy of Treaty Six appeared before the Senate asking the Senators to send the Bill for constitutional review as the Bill was unconstitutional and a violation of the treaties. Despite the Chief's appeal, the majority of the Conservative Senators approved the Bill. It received Royal Assent on 27 March 2013.

The legislation, which applies to over six hundred First Nations communities defined as 'Indian bands' under the *Indian Act*, provides a legislative basis for the preparation and public disclosure of First Nations' audited consolidated financial statements and of remuneration, including salaries and expenses, that a First Nation or *any entity* that it controls pays to its elected officials.[20] The legislation also requires the publication of this information on a website maintained by or for the First Nation, and on the DIAND website. There are additional provisions in the legislation to allow for the application of court remedies and administrative measures to enforce compliance with its requirements. The government of Canada used both measures to try to force the Nations into legislation that the treaty peoples considered to be a violation of the treaties.

Anyone who reads the list of reports and other materials that are required by DIAND will see that the First Nations must disclose their revenues and funding from all sources including 'private enterprises'. This has been part of the Reporting Handbook for many years. It was only the Federal Court of Canada decision in the *Montana*[21] case that prohibited the federal government from releasing this 'private and confidential' information.

The CTF made a lot of noise about 'band members' needing the CTF to advocate for them. This is untrue. If the CTF wanted to be helpful to their public, they should have directed those band citizens to go to the nearest DIAND office and look at the audits that have been available for years for any member to see.

There are some key elements of the law that are contrary to the rights of Indigenous Peoples. Under section 2 of the law, consolidated financial statements must include 'the assets, liabilities, equity, income, expenses and cash flows of the First Nation and of those entities that are required by those principles to be included are presented as those of a single economic entity'. If there is any doubt as to the meaning of entity, there is a definition in the law, 'a corporation or a partnership, a joint venture or any other unincorporated association or organization' (s 2). In other words, all the activities of the

20 All of these components are part of the reporting requirements set out in the DIAND Reporting Handbook.

21 *Montana Band of Indians v Canada (Minister of Indian and Northern Affairs)* [1989] 1 SC 143 (TD). In this case a journalist requested a band's financial information from DIAND, but was denied on the basis that the information was confidential for the purposes of para 20(1)(b) of the *Access to Information Act* because the journalist's interests were not consistent with those of the band.

Nation outside of the federal dollars must be reported to the government. Failure to report is a violation of the CA.

The consolidated financial statements are to be prepared in accordance with 'generally accepted accounting principles, the primary sources of which are the handbooks – including the handbook respecting public sector accounting – of the Canadian Institute of Chartered Accountants' (s 5(1)). As was identified above, the schedules required in the Reporting Handbook relate to the salaries and honorarium of Chiefs and Councils. This has been a standard requirement of DIAND for many years. However, the Federal Court decision in *Montana* prohibited the release of the materials to third parties to protect the privacy rights of Indigenous Peoples. This legislation stripped away those rights. There was no discussion with the Nations about the loss of their right of privacy. It was assumed that the government of Canada could deny them rights that all other people living within the state would automatically enjoy. This is the nature of the colonial mindset. When Ermineskin Cree made an access to information request to determine what the Department of Justice had advised the Department of Indian Affairs on the issue of privacy and First Nations, the documents sent were whited out – except for one page that had a note at the bottom, 'Have a nice weekend'.

The legislation perpetuates the myth that First Nations are corrupt and incapable of maintaining our own affairs. The legislation erodes our sovereignty and our ability to assert our own principles of self-determination as the legislation undermines our traditional forms of government. In the Senate debate on this Bill, the Hon Senator Dennis Glen Patterson made the following statements regarding First Nations leaders and governments:

> [T]hey work to keep this information hidden, if not from all members, from those who oppose them. As reported by some witnesses before the committee considering this bill in the other place, intimidation has occurred in some communities when a member asked for access to this basic financial information.[22]

Senator Patterson's statement implies that all First Nations governments utilise corrupt tactics and assumes that First Nations leaders need legislation to keep them accountable to their members, further eroding our ability to develop our own governments through our inherent Indigenous rights. The statement further perpetuates the colonial narrative that First Nations leaders and governments are corrupt and incapable of maintaining our affairs, a narrative that belittles our ability to implement our own governance structure through practising self-determination.

22 Canada, *Parliamentary Debates*, Senate, 4 December 2012 (Dennis Glen Patterson) <http://www.parl.gc.ca/Content/Sen/Chamber/411/Debates/125db_2012-12-04-e.htm#37>.

At the hearings in the House of Commons, the majority Conservative government invited persons who were in favour of the legislation to appear on the record. The government invited people who had problems with their own First Nations; Chiefs who wanted to appear were not invited. It was a bit galling to have the Crown tell Mr Justice Barnes in August 2015 that if the First Nations objected to the legislation they should have appeared before the committees. It is hard to appear when not invited. The First Nations members who did appear supporting the legislation were not told that they could have gone to the nearest office of DIAND to look at the audit.

Onion Lake Cree Nation from the Treaty Six Territory chose to challenge the legislation in November 2014. In December 2014, the DIAND Minister Bernard Valcourt brought a suit against five First Nations: Onion Lake, Sawridge, Athabasca Chipewyan, Thunderchild and Ochapowace. There was a sixth named First Nation but they submitted their audit and were subsequently dropped from the action. Onion Lake and Sawridge brought an action for a stay against the Minister's application. It was heard in August 2015. In October 2015, the Federal Court granted a stay against the Minister's application. The monies halted by DIAND were returned to the Nation two and a half months after the decision of the Federal Court. The Ministerial Loan Guarantee for housing of low income and needy families was not released until March 2016.

During the court hearing on C27, Canada called an expert witness, a chartered accountant who made a name for himself during the disputes in Attawapiskat.[23] Allan Mak appeared before the Standing Committee supporting the legislation. Then he was hired by the Department of Justice as an expert witness on the legislation. His statement before the Standing Committee that he supported the punitive clauses[24] in the legislation did not garner a challenge to his independence as an expert witness for the Crown. It might have given him the necessary federal credibility to be called as an expert. He did not know anything about the DIAND Reporting Handbook or the reporting that First Nations needed to do under the CAs, but he was

23 CBC News reported: 'While that may be a big improvement, Deloitte's findings for 2010–11 are still a "serious problem," investigative accountant Alan Mak told CBC News. Mak is with the firm Rosen and Associates in Toronto.' Daniel Schwartz, 'Inside Attawapiskat's Financial Troubles', *CBC News*, 9 January 2013 <http://www.cbc.ca/news/canada/inside-attawapiskat-s-financial-troubles-1.1359658>.

24 While appearing before the Standing Committee as an invited guest who was reimbursed for his travel and related expenses on 13 February 2013, Mr Mak said: 'I believe that it does provide a further obligation to comply simply because it is a matter of shedding light on the financial affairs of a First Nation. Even though some might not be inclined to comply, this obligation is now legislated, and there is the very fact that, if they do not, there are consequences. Being required to follow GAAP and having to be audited, with the limitations that I pointed out, still *creates a threat*, if you will. On that basis, I think it does improve corporate governance' (emphasis added).

given a space at the Standing Committee and paid to appear as an expert witness before the Federal Court hearing.

It was during the examination of Mr Scott Stevenson that the federal government's plans to enforce compliance to the legislation became known.[25] As the Associate Deputy Minister, Mr Stevenson was hired by the department to implement the legislation. He had a team of seven people across the country to check on compliance. In his examination in mid-July, he was able to scope out the department's approach to the legislation. On major issues such as treaty rights and violation of privacy, he was not able to answer. Stevenson was in the department for one year and eleven months (October 2013 to August 2015), leaving the department and government shortly after his examination.[26]

On 23 October, the Federal Court issued a stay against the legislation, a request filed by Onion Lake and supported by Sawridge. The other First Nations were present at the hearing in August 2015. It took the Department of Indigenous Affairs until the beginning of January 2016 to release the monies halted by the department. These monies had been part of the CAs but deemed by the department to be 'halted'. Mr Stevenson tried to characterise these monies as halted and not withheld so as to force compliance with the legislation. This was a new term not used before in relation to these monies. Stevenson said that Onion Lake could have gone into the marketplace and borrowed monies against the halted funds. This would have been difficult considering that the government did not provide any letters to indicate that these were monies owed to Onion Lake.

The concerns about the legislation are still not resolved. The legislation is still on the books in Ottawa and has not been repealed. The government has indicated a review but, at the same time, the Canadian Taxpayers Association (CTA) and other non-Indigenous 'think tanks' are calling for its implementation as the band members need to know what is happening with their monies. The CTA declared, 'Canadians need to know what is happening with their monies', despite the documents filed in the Federal Court about the character of those monies. There is a lull in the battle. There is no such lull at the United Nations: things are being pushed along without the Indigenous Nations.

25 In the Federal Court of Canada rules, an affidavit needs to be presented with the statement of claim to begin a legal action. In the case of Minister Valcourt's action, Scott Stevenson signed the affidavit and he could be examined on his affidavit. This is not a cross-examination as this procedure occurred outside the courtroom. The examination is based on his sworn affidavit and only on his affidavit and its contents.

26 At this time, Mr Stevenson was a senior fellow at the University of Ottawa in the Graduate School of Public and International Affairs. Prior to his work at the Department of Aboriginal Affairs, he was in the Department of National Defence and with Finance Canada.

'World conference' (so-called)

On 3 March 1995, the Commission on Human Rights[27] started to unravel the right of the Indigenous Nations to speak for ourselves. The Intersessional Working Group was created to review the *Declaration on the Rights of Indigenous Peoples*, and in the process removed the ability of the Nations to represent ourselves. The resolution to elaborate a draft declaration set out the criteria for the participation of Indigenous Peoples and Nations in the process.[28] The direction of the commission was based on para 5 of GA Resolution 49/214:

> Encourages the Commission on Human Rights to consider the draft United Nations declaration on the rights of indigenous peoples, contained in the annex to resolution 1994/45 of 26 August 1994 of the Subcommission on Prevention of Discrimination and Protection of Minorities, with the *participation of representatives of indigenous people*, on the basis of and in accordance with appropriate procedures to be determined by the Commission, with a view to achieving the adoption of a draft declaration by the General Assembly within the Decade.[29]

Instead, the commission set out a process for accreditation that limited the ways in which Indigenous Peoples could participate. The annex to the commission resolution set out the procedures that were to be used solely for the participation of Indigenous Peoples who did not have consultative status or non-governmental organisational (NGO) status within the UN system.[30] In 1984, the Working Group on Indigenous Populations (Peoples) had adopted the rule that Indigenous People could speak and contribute to the work without belonging to a recognised NGO.

The thousands of Indigenous People who came to Geneva to participate in the drafting of the declaration came representing their Nations. Their voices and contributions made the declaration a true work of the grassroots. The members of the working group heard our voices. However, the commission chose not to follow this lead. It was possible for the commission to allow the

27 The Commission on Human Rights was replaced by the Human Rights Council in 2006.
28 Commission on Human Rights Res 1995/32 (3 March 1995).
29 GA Resolution 49/214 (23 December 1994) (emphasis added).
30 See Sharon Venne, 'NGOs, Indigenous Peoples and the United Nations' in Aziz Choudry and Dip Kapoor (eds), *NGOization, Complicity, Contradictions and Prospects* (Zed Books, 2013) 75. In this chapter, I explore the problems of NGOs and the role of our Nations in trying to push for decolonisation, which cannot be accomplished from an NGO position. In the early 1980s, the Nations were allowed to speak for ourselves. The result was the initial declaration. See also the analysis done by Charmaine Whiteface in her book *Indigenous Nations' Rights in the Balance: An Analysis of the Declaration on the Rights of Indigenous Peoples* (Living Justice Press, 2013), where she explores the three different version of the declaration and the changes to the text.

same process to continue in the review of the declaration, but state governments did not want Indigenous Peoples and Nations to determine the direction of the declaration. It was possible for the commission to adopt rules that would have allowed Indigenous Peoples to participate fully in their own right. The GA permission to allow for participation of Indigenous Peoples 'in accordance with appropriate procedures to be determined by the Commission' was not followed.

The commission's decision is set out in greater detail in the annex to their resolution. The resolution identifies Indigenous People – individuals – not representatives of their Peoples. The 's' has been removed from the process. In the many years of drafting the declaration, Indigenous Peoples fought hard to have the 's' on 'Peoples'. Peoples have a right of self-determination. Without the 's', it refers to individuals who do not have a right of self-determination that relates directly to our lands and territories. In order to participate in the working group of the commission, an application process was to be followed. The annex is set out in part below:

3 Organizations of indigenous people not in consultative status wishing to participate in the Working Group may apply to the Coordinator of the International Decade of the World's Indigenous People. Such applications must include the following information concerning the organization concerned:

   (a) The name, headquarters or seat, address and contact person for the organization;
   (b) The aims and purposes of the organization (these should be in conformity with the spirit, purposes, and principles of the Charter of the United Nations);
   (c) Information on the programmes and activities of the organization and the country or countries in which they are carried out or to which they apply;
   (d) A description of the membership of the organization, indicating the total number of members.

4 Upon receipt of applications, the Coordinator of the International Decade should consult with any State concerned pursuant to Article 71 of the Charter of the United Nations and paragraph 9 of resolution 1296 (XLIV) of the Economic and Social Council. The Coordinator should promptly forward all applications and information received to the Council Committee on Non-Governmental Organizations for its decision.

5 Authorization to participate shall remain valid for the duration of the Working Group subject to the relevant provisions of part VIII of resolution 129 (XLIV) of the Economic and Social Council.

6 The activities of organizations of indigenous people authorized to participate in the Working Group pursuant to these procedures shall be governed by rules 75 and 76 of the rules of procedure of the functional commissions of the Economic and Social Council.

7 Organizations of indigenous people authorized to participate in the Working Group will have the opportunity to address the Working Group, consistent with the relevant provisions of paragraphs 31 and 33 of Council resolution 1296 (XLIV), and are encouraged to organize themselves into constituencies for this purpose.
8 Organizations of indigenous people may make written presentations which, however, will not be issued as official documents.
9 States having indigenous populations should take effective measures to bring the invitation to participate and these procedures to the attention of organizations of indigenous people potentially interested in contributing to and participating in the Working Group.

The criteria are not based on our Nations and our governmental structures. The use of the term 'organization' rather than Indigenous governments or representatives of our Nations carries a predetermined bias. The organisations need to have the approval of the state – the colonial state that is occupying our territories and lands must give their approval before the special accreditation can be granted.

In the process, Indigenous People with the specially created accreditation were allowed into the room for the discussions. However, their written submissions were not added to the official documents. Indigenous People became silent ghosts in the process. They lacked any real ability to create a written record of their concerns. Is this a real process that would affect the lives of the millions of citizens of Indigenous Peoples and Nations? It was the start of the discounting of Indigenous Peoples and Nations. The special accreditation process used for the intersessional working group was adopted by the Permanent Forum on Indigenous Issues[31] and the Expert Mechanism.[32] Since 3 March 1995, Indigenous Peoples and Nations have had to comply with the rules of the state governments. In reality, the colonisation process was adopted by the United Nations. The coloniser states got to pick and choose the representatives of the state-recognised organisations or groups.[33] The state governments got to manufacture the consent of the 'Indigenous Peoples and

31 The Permanent Forum is an advisory body to the Economic and Social Council established by Resolution 2000/22 on 28 July 2000. The forum has the mandate to discuss Indigenous issues related to economic and social development, culture, the environment, education, health and human rights.
32 The Expert Mechanism on the Rights of Indigenous Peoples (EMRIP) was established by the Human Rights Council, the UN's main human rights body, in 2007 under Resolution 6/36 as a subsidiary body of the council. The EMRIP provides the Human Rights Council with thematic advice, in the form of studies and research, on the rights of Indigenous Peoples as directed by the council. The EMRIP may also suggest proposals to the council for its consideration and approval.
33 See Appendix B of this chapter, which sets out the flow chart of the various bodies associated with the 'world conference'.

Nations' using state-recognised organisations. The real voice that Indigenous Peoples sought by picking and choosing our own representatives and having those representatives accepted by the United Nations was effectively finished in 1995. Now, the state governments control and manipulate the process. The 1995 decision led to the creation of the organisational representatives from the state-recognised groups who planned the high-level meeting in 2014.

What is a world conference?

In examining the international effort on the world conference, we should ask: what is a real world conference and what goes into the process of convening a real world conference? Since its inception after the Second World War, the United Nations has convened many world conferences. Usually, they are at least a week long and have specific goals and objectives, such as the Fourth World Conference on Women, held in Beijing, China, in September 1995. At that world conference, after two weeks of political debate, exchange of information on good practice and lessons learned, and sharing of experiences, representatives of 189 governments agreed to commitments that were unprecedented in scope. More than 30,000 people also participated in the NGO forum. Women had four UN conferences by 1995. Indigenous Peoples have had none – yet we have been subjected to more than five hundred years of colonisation. The United Nations is in its fourth decade of combatting racism without any end in sight. The idea of the world conference was born in the minds of Indigenous Peoples in the 1980s.

In order to see how Indigenous Peoples were short changed with a high-level plenary, one needs to ask: What is a high-level plenary within the UN system? A high-level meeting is the name given to meetings that occur outside the GA agenda. Usually, the high-level meetings, held over one or two days, are thematic, for example focusing on refugees, economic matters, climate change, environmental issues and so on. These meetings usually take place within the GA hall but are not GA meetings. High-level plenary meetings usually take place prior to the start of a GA meeting or else the GA meeting is suspended to allow for a high-level meeting to occur. It is not a world conference because the rules of participation are set by the president of the GA. The list of speakers and their length of speeches are predetermined by the rules of procedure. Allowing Indigenous People to occupy the whole space and time would require the suspension of the rules of the GA. This did not occur for the three-hour high-level plenary that took place in the GA hall. The rest of the day and a half was spent in round table discussions away from the main hall. The round tables were not part of the official high-level meeting but a side event with reports to the GA. So, there was no world conference – no focused ten days of discussion on the rights of Indigenous Peoples. It was a sideshow, or even a bit of a hoax.

In December 2010, the GA adopted a resolution to convene a high-level meeting, but to call it a 'World Conference'. The GA:

> *Decides* to organize a high-level plenary meeting of the General Assembly, to be known as the World Conference on Indigenous Peoples, to be held in 2014, in order to share perspectives and best practices on the realization of the rights of indigenous peoples, including to pursue the objectives of the United Nations Declaration on the Rights of Indigenous Peoples, and invites the President of the General Assembly to conduct open-ended consultations with Member States and with representatives of indigenous peoples *within the framework* of the Permanent Forum on Indigenous Issues, as well as with the Expert Mechanism on the Rights of Indigenous Peoples and the Special Rapporteur, in order to determine the modalities for the meeting, including the participation of indigenous peoples in the Conference.[34]

So how did the high-level plenary fall short of a process to recognise the rights of Indigenous Peoples who have been and continue to be colonised?

To understand these moves, we must remember the movement that began in the 1980s by the Indigenous Peoples who came to the Working Group on Indigenous Peoples. There was a call to have 1992 set aside within the UN system as the International Year on the Rights of Indigenous Peoples. The United Nations regularly sets years to highlight different themes. Indigenous Peoples wanted to have 1992 set aside to call attention to the five hundred years of colonisation in the Americas. Their call met with great resistance from western governments especially the United States and South and Central American states. The Roman Catholic Church was 'celebrating' five hundred years of evangelism in the Americas. So, the United Nations offered 1993 as the International Year of Indigenous People – no 's'. Indigenous Peoples soundly condemned the United Nations for pushing the year onto us, and then for adding insult by removing the 's' off 'Peoples'. The only thing that the United Nations managed to do in the year was to create a single-sheet calendar. We did not even merit a postage stamp, which was a usual procedure for commemoration of an international year. By contrast, for the International Year for Old People, Canada created a working body chaired by former Premier Lougheed to promote it. Canada did nothing to promote the International Year of Indigenous People. Even the International Year of the Potato garnered a cookbook on the potato. Indigenous Peoples got a calendar. In order to deal with the backlash from the hundreds of Indigenous Peoples who were insulted by the whole international year, there was an attempt to right the wrong. In 1993, the United Nations announced a decade – 1994 to 2004 – on the rights of Indigenous Peoples. Then the United Nations did absolutely

34 GA Resolution 65/198 (21 December 2010) (emphasis added).

nothing except move to get rid of the Working Group on Indigenous Peoples. The working group had a twofold mandate: to receive information on recent developments within the Indigenous territories and to develop standards on the rights of Indigenous Peoples. The *Declaration on the Rights of Indigenous Peoples* was one standard. There was ongoing work related to intellectual property, land rights, free, prior and informed consent, rights of Indigenous Peoples in small island Nations and relocation of Indigenous Peoples as a result of climate change. A lot of ongoing work was left on the table when the Working Group was dissolved in 2006. With nothing done in the first decade, the United Nations decided to have a second decade with a 'promise' of a 'world conference' at the end, which would fall in 2014.

The United Nations replaced the Working Group on Indigenous Peoples with the Expert Mechanism on Indigenous Issues, which reports to the Human Rights Council. The Expert Mechanism does not have any mandate to develop any new standards or an ability to draft a convention on the rights of Indigenous Peoples. At present, there is no process within the United Nations to create a binding convention.

It seems that the 'high-level' process was designed to distract people away from the real issues. It was designed from the beginning to give the appearance that Indigenous Peoples were giving their consent to the United Nations agenda. There were no real discussions on the way for our Nations to decolonise. There was no real discussion on the implementation of self-determination within our territories. It was manufactured to give the appearance of movement when none occurred.

How did it get started? There was the resolution passed by the GA in December 2010.[35] The resolution allowed for organisations of Indigenous People to have a planning meeting. The delegates were selected during the summer of 2011 at the Expert Mechanism meeting held in Geneva. The people who had accreditation following the process set out in 1995 were self-selected as a representative group. There was no regional process to allow for Indigenous Peoples or Nations to select their own representatives. The GA resolution limited the process for participation, stating that the:

> President of the General Assembly [is] to conduct open-ended consultations with Member States and with representatives of indigenous peoples *within the framework* of the Permanent Forum on Indigenous Issues, as well as with the Expert Mechanism on the Rights of Indigenous Peoples and the Special Rapporteur.

On 12–13 January 2012, a brainstorming workshop was organised by the Greenland Self Rule Representation in Copenhagen, the Saami Parliament of

35 Appendix A of this chapter sets out the GA Resolution.

Norway and the International Work Group for Indigenous Affairs.[36] The two-day meeting held in Copenhagen was to discuss Indigenous Peoples' participation in the planning of the UN World Conference on Indigenous Peoples.[37] At the brainstorming session (now renamed the Indigenous Global Coordinating Group) John Henriksen (representative of the Saami Parliament of Norway) was appointed as co-facilitator. Who set the mandate for a co-facilitator? Who chose the reporting process for the Indigenous Peoples and Nations? There was nothing in place. There was no place or space for Indigenous Peoples or Nations to participate in the approval. In the end, the self-selected group appointed a co-facilitator without asking whether Indigenous Peoples accepted the idea of a high-level meeting rather than having a real world conference. There was no process from within the regions.

From the meeting in Copenhagen, the Indigenous Global Coordinating Group had several meetings with the office of the President of the GA and with some government delegations in New York. Their aim was to promote the conclusions and recommendations agreed in the Copenhagen meeting. The group pushed for the appointment of the Indigenous co-facilitator in order to ensure the full and effective participation of Indigenous Peoples in the preparatory process towards the UN World Conference on Indigenous Peoples.

The question remained: how do Indigenous Peoples have full and effective participation in the process when they have been excluded from the outset? On 5 April 2012, in a letter sent to all Permanent Missions to the United Nations, the President of the GA announced the appointment of Ambassador Luis Alfonso de Alba (Mexico) and Mr John Henriksen (Saami Parliament, Norway) as facilitators for consultations with governmental delegations and representatives of Indigenous Peoples. There was supposed to be a process to decide the format, organisational issues and possible outcomes of the World Conference on Indigenous Peoples.

The decision taken by the President of the GA to appoint an Indigenous co-facilitator was a response to the demands made by the group. His job apparently was to ensure the full and effective participation of Indigenous Peoples working towards the high-level meeting. If it was a real world conference, there would have been regional meetings where Indigenous Peoples and Nations would be able to participate and make decisions on the outcomes that they would like to have from a world conference. In the normal course of

36 There was a limited list of invited Indigenous representatives. There were four from North America – seven regions with four representatives per region. Two other people, one from Hawaii and one from Alaska, turned up at the meeting and were met with a cool reception. The final communique contains a single note that Ronald Barnes from Alaska did not agree with the final wording. A copy is on file with the author.

37 Leon Sui, Foreign Affairs Minister for the Kingdom of Hawai'i, went to the meeting without an invitation and filed their objections to the process. His letter is reproduced in Appendix C.

events within the UN system, there are regional preparatory meetings well in advance of a world conference that allow for many voices to contribute to the outcome documents. In addition, all the specialised agencies of the United Nations contribute papers and conferences on the theme of the world conference. It would be truly a global initiative, unlike what actually happened. There was no full and effective participation of Indigenous Peoples because there was no real attempt to involve the Nations.

Great Turtle Island response

The North America Indigenous Peoples Caucus (NAIPC) from our Great Turtle Island had problems with the construction of the GA resolution and the rebranding of the 'world conference' as a high-level plenary. The process for selecting representatives was questioned. At the meeting held in Niagara Falls in March 2012, there were two representatives[38] appointed to attend meetings, listen and gather information. The appointment of two people did not mean that the caucus was giving its consent to the process. They were to act as fact finders to report to the next NAIPC meeting. There were a lot of discussions at the caucus meetings including the reasons that Indigenous People from Great Turtle Island went to the United Nations in the first place in 1977 and to the League of Nations in 1923.[39] Strategies for the next steps were carefully considered and documents prepared for each stage of the discussions.

After the meeting at Niagara Falls, the NAIPC decided to take a careful and vigilant approach to the 2014 UN High-Level Plenary Meeting, which was 'to be known as a World Conference on Indigenous Peoples'. That stance by the NAIPC resulted in the following 'Caucus Strategy' statement:

> It was observed that the word 'participate' was dividing the room and a suggestion was made that 'participate' and 'participation' be replaced with the position that NAIPC is going to 'explore' or is 'exploring' what the UN HLPM [high-level plenary meeting] is all about. Suggested text was offered by the North American Representative to the UNPFII [United Nations Permanent Forum on Indigenous Issues]. After a brief

38 Chief Randy Kapashesit of MoCreebec Council of Cree Nation and Kenneth Deer of Kanestake, Mohawk Territory. In April 2012, Chief Kapashesit passed away suddenly leaving Kenneth Deer along with the co-convenors of the NAIPC – Debra Harry and Art Manuel – as the alternative representatives until the next gathering of the NAIPC.

39 For a brief outline of the work of Indigenous Peoples in these international bodies, see Debra Harry and Sharon H Venne, 'The Road to the United Nations and Rights of Indigenous Peoples' (2011) 20(3) *Griffith Law Review* 557. See also Sharon H Venne, *Our Elders Understand our Rights: Evolving International Law Regarding Indigenous Peoples* (Theytus Press, 1998).

> discussion, the word 'participate' was removed from two places in the suggested text, and replaced with the words 'exploring' and 'explore.'
>
> What led to NAIPC's cautious and vigilant approach, is the expressed concern that full 'participation' in the HLPM process, at this stage, can be viewed as providing active or tacit consent for states to proceed with their HLPM and outcome document, which will be controlled by state governments, and which might well retreat from the successes of our work as nations and peoples over the past forty years, and might lead to an erosion of the provisions of the UN Declaration on the Rights of Indigenous Peoples that advance the rights and protections of Indigenous Nations and Peoples. Another expressed concern was whether Indigenous peoples' 'participation' is even possible given the constraints of the HLPM framework.
>
> The result, arrived at by consensus, is after an outcome document has been produced at the Indigenous Peoples' gathering in Alta, Norway, that document will be reviewed by the NAIPC 'to explore and assess' the possible positive and negative impacts of the HLP/WCIP [high-level plenary/World Conference on Indigenous Peoples], and, after having explored and assessed, the NAIPC will decide ('determine') at its gathering next year, 2014, its 'future involvement' with regard to the HLP/WCIP.
>
> Having arrived by consensus on a Caucus Strategy with regard to the HLP/WCIP, a decision was made to attend Indigenous Peoples' gathering in the Alta, Norway, but to attend as 'Peoples and Nations with rights equal to all other Peoples,' with 'the inalienable right of and to self-determination are expressed in various international instruments (the Universal Declaration of Human Rights, Article 1 of the Human Rights Covenants, and U.N. Resolution 1514).'

The Alta Conference held on 10–12 June 2013, a planning conference leading to the high-level meeting known as the 'world conference', was hosted by the Saami Parliament. An outcome document was produced but this was not a consensus document to mandate going forward with negotiations. As Steve Newcomb wrote in *Indian Country Today* on 8 July 2013:

> We have to keep our wits about us by staying on top of every detail, and not see the repeat of an historical pattern. It does not make sense to select one person to 'negotiate' on behalf of 370 million people. To do so would be the height of folly, no matter how many qualifications that person might possess.
>
> The North American Caucus delegation arrived at the Alta gathering with a ceremonially bundled document developed at the NAIPC meeting at the Sycuan Resort in the Kumeyaay Territory. It states that the Caucus will attend the Alta gathering on an exploratory basis to see 'where this

> can go,' 'this' referring to the entire High Level Plenary of the UN General Assembly to be known as 'the World Conference on Indigenous Peoples.'
>
> Additionally, the North American Caucus delegation attended the Alta gathering based on our original free existence to protect and advance the right of self-determination in international law, as well as on the basis of those international treaties that provide the potential means of liberating our nations and peoples. We have not wavered from that position.[40]

From the conference in Alta, there was a lead-up to the conference in New York in September 2014. The documents from the United Nations did not get into the hands of the Nations despite the numerous requests. The UN process kicked into high gear under the rules of the GA, now chaired by John Ashe. John Henriksen was not able to advance the right of self-determination and open the process up to the representatives of the Indigenous Nations who had entered into treaties with Europeans to allow for settlement on Great Turtle Island.

What happened?

The high-level meeting proceeded according to the rules of the United Nations. There was an opening at ten as is the custom of the United Nations. There were addresses by various speakers as prescribed by the rules of the GA, which allowed one Indigenous person – the Faithkeeper of the Haudenosaunee – to speak. The rest of the speakers were functionaries within the UN system. At the end of the day, the process produced a state-adopted paper on the steps forward. Indigenous Peoples, who do not vote in the UN system, were not able to exercise any free, prior and informed consent. In that adoption, the United Nations violated the *Declaration on the Rights of Indigenous Peoples* and violated the resolution that set in place the high-level plenary. The GA resolution called for the full participation of Indigenous Peoples. That did not occur.

What was the outcome of the high-level meeting? John Ashe, President of the GA, who could have opened the process to Indigenous Nations and Peoples, was indicted for:

> accepting more than $1.3 million in bribes from Chinese businesspeople in exchange for advancing their interests in the U.N. Among the interests was support for a planned U.N. conference center in Macau, a Chinese

40 Steven Newcomb, 'The Alta Outcome Document and the Issue of Interpretation', *Indian Country Today*, 8 July 2013 <http://indiancountrytodaymedianetwork.com/2013/07/08/alta-outcome-document-and-issue-interpretation>.

> special administrative region, and development in the Caribbean, authorities claim.[41]

Subsequently, Secretary-General Ban Ki-Moon appointed Wu Hongbo to coordinate the outcome document's implementation within the UN system. Why was Mr Wu appointed to this position? Is there a link between Mr Ashe and China? Wu's appointment could not have been coincidental. China has a lot of interests in the territories of Indigenous Peoples around the world. This is an unexplained and unexplored area of the 'world conference'. Were Indigenous Peoples set up? Were we used?

The resolution from 1995 by the Commission on Human Rights is now being implemented within the whole UN system. Indigenous representatives are ensuring that the outcome of the high-level plenary meeting continues to be advanced in the United Nations. Our old people constantly remind us that organisations are not rights holders. In Canada, the Assembly of First Nations (AFN) is told by the Chiefs that they are not a rights-based organisation. They are an organisation with a limited mandate. The AFN cannot make decisions that affect the rights of our Nations. Our governments who made treaties are still in place. The detrimental language in the outcome document that attempts to create special rules of participation for 'representative institutions' of Indigenous Peoples is a violation of our right of self-determination and contrary to the Charter of the United Nations. These new standards – that only those who have state recognition and approval will be allowed to speak at the United Nations – are not acceptable. How can our Nations decolonise if they must operate within the colonial structures of the colonial state? The high-level plenary was designed to manufacture 'consent' to a process to undermine our sovereignty. The state governments are using the UN organisation to undermine and discredit our Nations and Peoples and pushing us back to before the 1977 conference in Geneva, Switzerland. The 1977 conference was meant to deal with the systemic racism directed at the Indigenous Nations and Peoples of the Americas. It is not a new position. It is the position of state governments such as Canada that 'representative institutions' are preferred. They are easier to control.

There was an attempt to use Indigenous organisations and groups to give some legitimacy to the process of a 'world conference'. The elements of our Nations have not been disrupted. Our right of self-determination remains intact. In the drafting of the declaration, Indigenous Peoples and Nations pushed the right of self-determination. We are Peoples with our own

41 Rebecca Davis O'Brien, Christopher M Matthews and Farnaz Fassihi, 'Former United Nations General Assembly President Charged in Bribery Scheme', *The Wall Street Journal*, 6 October 2015 <http://www.wsj.com/article_email/former-u-n-general-assembly-president-charged-in-bribery-scheme-1444141619-lMyQjAxMTE1MjA2NzUwODc5Wj>.

territories, laws, government and histories. We were in our place when the colonisers arrived. In the last five hundred years, our Peoples have never relinquished our responsibility to our territories. Our Peoples continue our original instructions as given to us by the Creation. The outcome document never addressed these instructions.

Our territories remain our territories. It does not matter to us that there are cities on the land – we are still responsible for our territories. The colonisers do not understand these instructions, but we are raised with the protocols and obligations. From our territories, we maintain our right to give our free, prior and informed consent to use our territories. The peace and friendship treaties made with the British Crown guaranteed our rights in our territories. These issues were not addressed by the outcome document.

Now what?

What is the role of the United Nations in the process at this point? As Steve Newcomb wrote in *Indian Country Today* on the high-level meeting:

> a number of conclusions can be drawn from that recent UN meeting. First, our Nations are not being recognized *as Nations* at and by the UN. Second, in its interventions at the UN, the United States is characterizing our *Nations* as 'tribes' and 'tribal governments' that the U.S. deems to be 'domestic' to its dominating political system. Third, the US has evidently begun to interpret 'indigenous peoples' to mean merely 'individuals' and 'communities.' This diverts attention away from our political identity as originally free and independent *Nations*, as *Nations* that began originally free and independent of the political domination of the United States.[42]

This has been a goal of states like Canada since 1969. In the 1969 White Paper, Canada proposed to get rid of the treaties and incorporate Indigenous Nations and our territories into the fabric of the colonial state of Canada.[43] On the last day of the conference, Canada explicitly stated that it would not support free, prior and informed consent because Canada refuses to relinquish its presumed supremacy over Indigenous Nations. This goal is not possible if we remember that we have the right to consent. Indigenous Peoples and Nations who have been colonised and continue to be colonised cannot have our rights undermined by manufactured consent. The state governments tried everything to manufacture consent to the high-level meeting and the outcome

42 Steven Newcomb, 'The U.S.'s Interpretation of the UN High-Level Outcome Document', *Indian Country Today*, 12 October 2014 <http://indiancountrytodaymedianetwork.com/2014/10/12/uss-interpretation-un-high-level-outcome-document>.

43 *Statement of the Government of Canada on Indian Policy (The White Paper, 1969)*, Indigenous and Northern Affairs <http://www.aadnc-aandc.gc.ca/eng/1100100010189/1100100010191>.

document. A self-selected group from the 'recognised organisations' under the state process established in 1995 became the gatekeepers for the colonisers. The Indigenous Nations and Peoples who did not go along with the programme were marginalised. There were meetings held without inviting them to participate, or if the representatives managed to get to the meetings they were not invited to eat with the rest of the people. What was not understood by the self-selected group was this fact: our representatives were selected by our Nations to represent our position. They did not create their own position. They had a mandate, unlike most of the people who were in the room. In the NAIPC caucus, there was a real attempt to be inclusive. Long days were spent in discussion and debate on the merits of the proposals related to the United Nations. At one time, I was told by a senior official of the United Nations that 'if you want to come into our house, know the rules'. It was a simple fact that most of the people leading the process had not studied the rules and procedures and allowed themselves to be led along the path.

Glen Morris observed:

> As it became clear that the indigenous gatekeepers could not achieve a global consensus for indigenous peoples' collaboration in the HLPM plan, the UN simply began to exclude and silence the opposition. When the North American Indigenous Peoples' Caucus (NAIPC) decided that it was not going to accept subordination and inequality in the 'world conference' design, NAIPC representatives (both adult and youth) were systematically excluded from any debates or decisions regarding the meeting.[44]

Our NAIPC representative[45] from the northern part of Great Turtle Island witnessed first-hand the exclusion and the silencing that was taking place.

Conclusion

The 524 struggle to be decolonised and have our Nations recognised remains a goal of our Peoples. It is our inherent authority in our territories and our responsibility to future generations to analyse these processes so that future generations can learn the tricks of the colonisers. They use divide and conquer tactics – within and outside the state. In a way, nothing has changed. The colonisers still want access to our lands and resources and will do

44 Glen Morris, 'Invader-States Hijacked UN World Conference on Indigenous Peoples', *Indian Country Today*, 16 October 2014 <http://indiancountrytodaymedianetwork.com/2014/10/16/invader-states-hijacked-un-world-conference-indigenous-peoples>.

45 Janice Makosis, Cree, Saddle Lake Cree Nation.

anything to manufacture 'consent' to get at our lands and resources. Indigenous Peoples continue to follow our ancestors' teachings. All my relations.[46]

Appendix A

Resolution adopted by the General Assembly on 21 December 2010
[*on the report of the Third Committee (A/65/453)*]
65/198. Indigenous issues

The General Assembly,

Recalling all relevant resolutions of the General Assembly, the Human Rights Council and the Economic and Social Council relating to the rights of indigenous peoples,

Recalling also its resolution 59/174 of 20 December 2004 on the Second International Decade of the World's Indigenous People (2005–2014),

Recalling further the 2007 United Nations Declaration on the Rights of Indigenous Peoples,[47] which addresses their individual and collective rights,

Recalling the 2005 World Summit Outcome[48] and the outcome document of the High-level Plenary Meeting of the General Assembly on the Millennium Development Goals,[49]

Recalling also Human Rights Council resolution 15/14 of 30 September 2010,[50] by which the Council decided to extend the mandate of the Special Rapporteur on the rights of indigenous peoples, and resolution 15/7 of 30 September 2010 on human rights and indigenous peoples,[51]

Noting the first Peoples' World Conference on Climate Change and the Rights of Mother Earth, hosted by the Plurinational State of Bolivia in Cochabamba from 20 to 22 April 2010,

Concerned about the extreme disadvantages that indigenous peoples have typically faced across a range of social and economic indicators and about the impediments to their full enjoyment of their rights,

46 This is a reference to all of the Creation. The Creation is the responsibility of those born on Great Turtle Island, and it is the law amongst Indigenous Peoples around the world, which became well known in the process of drafting the declaration.
47 Resolution 61/295, annex.
48 See Resolution 60/1.
49 See Resolution 65/1.
50 See UN GAOR, 65th sess, Supp No 53A, UN Doc A/65/53/Add.1, ch 2.
51 Ibid ch 1.

1. *Welcomes* the work of the Special Rapporteur on the rights of indigenous peoples, and takes note with appreciation of his report on the situation of human rights and fundamental freedoms of indigenous people[52] and his report on the Second International Decade of the World's Indigenous People;[53]

2. *Also welcomes* the report of the United Nations High Commissioner for Human Rights on the status of the United Nations Voluntary Fund for Indigenous Populations;[54]

3. *Decides* to expand the mandate of the United Nations Voluntary Fund for Indigenous Populations so that it can assist representatives of indigenous peoples' organizations and communities to participate in sessions of the Human Rights Council and of human rights treaty bodies, based on diverse and renewed participation and in accordance with relevant rules and regulations, including Economic and Social Council resolution 1996/31 of 25 July 1996;

4. *Urges* Governments and intergovernmental and non-governmental organizations to continue to contribute to the United Nations Voluntary Fund for Indigenous Populations and the Trust Fund for the Second International Decade of the World's Indigenous People, and invites indigenous organizations and private institutions and individuals to do likewise;

5. *Encourages* those States that have not yet ratified or acceded to the International Labour Organization Indigenous and Tribal Peoples Convention, 1989 (No. 169) to consider doing so and to consider supporting the United Nations Declaration on the Rights of Indigenous Peoples, and welcomes the increased support by States for the Declaration;

6. *Takes note* of the report of the Secretary-General on the midterm assessment of the progress made in the achievement of the goal and objectives of the Second International Decade;[55]

7. *Calls upon* States to consider the recommendations contained in the midterm assessment of the implementation of the Second International Decade and to enhance national and international efforts, including international cooperation for the solution of problems faced by indigenous peoples in such areas as culture, education, health, human rights, the environment and social and economic development by means of action-oriented programmes and specific projects, increased technical assistance and relevant standard-setting activities;

52 See A/65/264.
53 See A/64/338.
54 See A/65/163.
55 A/65/166.

8. *Decides* to organize a high-level plenary meeting of the General Assembly, to be known as the World Conference on Indigenous Peoples, to be held in 2014, in order to share perspectives and best practices on the realization of the rights of indigenous peoples, including to pursue the objectives of the United Nations Declaration on the Rights of Indigenous Peoples, and invites the President of the General Assembly to conduct open-ended consultations with Member States and with representatives of indigenous peoples within the framework of the Permanent Forum on Indigenous Issues, as well as with the Expert Mechanism on the Rights of Indigenous Peoples and the Special Rapporteur, in order to determine the modalities for the meeting, including the participation of indigenous peoples in the Conference;

9. *Requests* the Secretary-General, in consultation with Member States, relevant United Nations organizations and mechanisms and other stakeholders, including organizations representing indigenous peoples, to submit to the General Assembly at its sixty-seventh session a report that evaluates the progress made in the achievement of the goal and objectives of the Second International Decade and its impact on the achievement of the Millennium Development Goals;

10. *Decides* to continue consideration of the question at its sixty-sixth session under an item entitled 'Rights of indigenous peoples'.

71st plenary meeting
21 December 2010

Appendix B

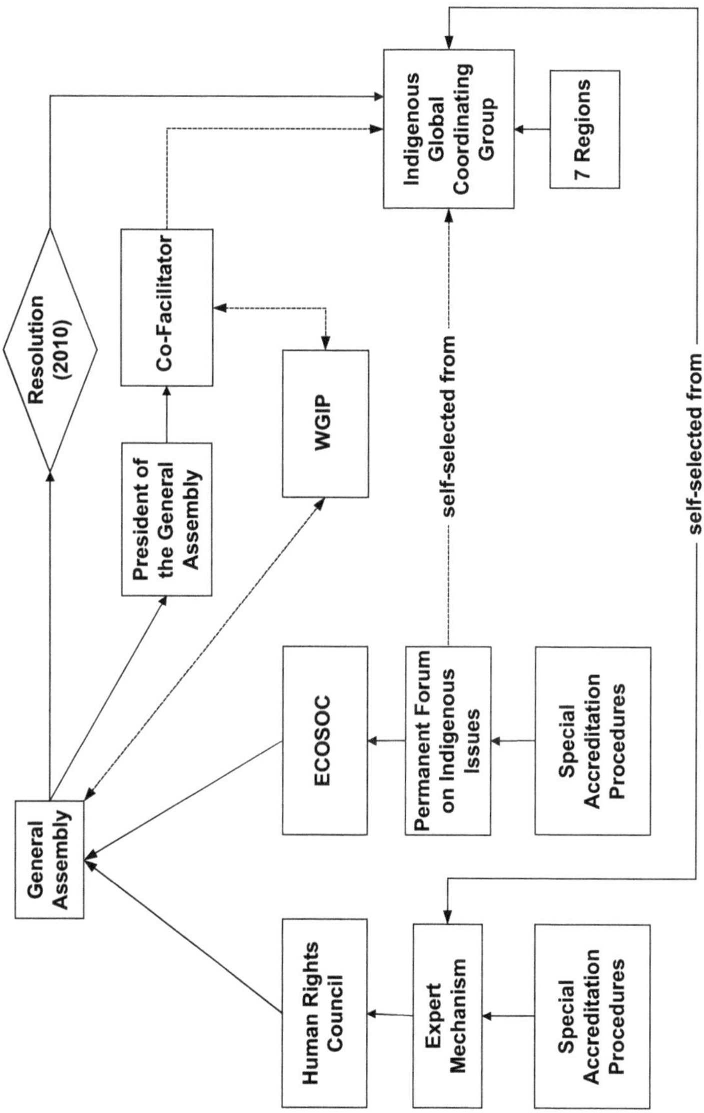

Figure 7.1 How 'consent' was manufactured within the UN system

Appendix C

23 January 2012

TO: Participants
Open-Ended Indigenous Peoples'
Brainstorming Meeting on the
World Conference on Indigenous People

RE: Comments on the Resolution

Aloha kakou,

Mahalo nui loa for including us in the Open-Ended Indigenous Peoples' Brainstorming Meeting on the World Conference on Indigenous Peoples 2014 in Copenhagen, Denmark, 13–14 January 2012.

We have reviewed the Resolution that was adopted and want to clarify our opposition and dissent so that it can be properly registered.

During the closing summary of the Rapporteur for the Copenhagen meeting, we requested that the minutes show that we dissented. Specifically our dissent concerned 1) the inordinate rush to adopt the resolution, allowing no time for consultation with our Elders and people, and 2) the failure to fully discuss and properly reconcile conflicting answers to questions raised pertaining to the powers that this group would vest the 'co-facilitator' and the 'coordinating group'. (The answers went from 'only logistical' to 'everything'.)

While we agree that we must make the best use of this WCIP opportunity to make the urgency of Indigenous Peoples' conditions known to the members of the UN General Assembly, let us have no delusions that this is still the sandbox of the member states. They have the final say as to the rules of engagement. Indigenous Peoples are at a serious disadvantage in having to make all the concessions to conform to the terms dictated by the UN and its member states. Therefore, for us to rush headlong into creating the two critical liaison/modalities positions, the 'co-facilitator' and the 'coordinating group', without careful, prayerful counsel and negotiating strategies from our Elders almost guarantees there will be no provisions for a level playing field at WCIP.

Further comments on item 1. As much as the 'co-facilitator' may demand for Indigenous Peoples to have an equal voice, there is no equal footing when one side completely controls the playing field and the rules. The Indigenous co-facilitator can express our concerns to the UN bureaucracy as loudly, eloquently and passionately as possible, but simply has no authority or mechanism to compel the UN or its Member States to listen to, much less satisfy, any of our requests. Experience has abundantly demonstrated that states will allow certain concessions to Indigenous Peoples only if it suits the interests of the state and only from within the internal mechanisms provided by the state.

Further comments on item 2. The nine members of the coordinating group would be too few to represent the full spectrum of Indigenous Peoples' concerns. A small 'coordinating group' consisting of members picked because they are adept at working the UN and state systems are (like it or not) biased by those systems. Tunnel-vision, grass-roots advocates should be included in order to stay focused on the issues and not be distracted by the mechanics. Also, a small 'coordinating group' will not have what is necessary to represent Indigenous Peoples and their wide range of issues and desired outcomes. For instance, among Hawaiians, there is strong disagreement on what redress and remedies should be sought from the U.S. for violations of the right to self-determination and for the human rights abuses committed against Hawaiians. While many Hawaiians are satisfied with the present political arrangement and are simply seeking better treatment from within the existing system, there are many of us who are advocating for self-determination in the form of full independence so that we, the people, can be the arbiters of our own future.

Even more so, a single regional representative from the Pacific is simply not going to effectively advocate for both ends of the spectrum for Hawaii, not to mention the many diverse areas of the Pacific region. This will be especially problematical if the representative does not personally subscribe to, or is strongly opposed to, or even not well-enough acquainted to the varied positions. In such a situation, there will be some constituencies that will not be fairly and vigorously represented.

Just for the sake of manageability, the regional coordinator will be inevitably put into the position of having to screen the myriad issues and recommendations to determine which ones are more likely to succeed at the WCIP. Thus, many worthy but too controversial or non-viable issues will fall by the wayside during this self-actuating screening process. Will there be another way for those that don't fit the criteria to have access to the WCIP? Or will this 'coordinating group' be the only vehicle to approach the WCIP? Will those with 'dissenting opinions' have to go it alone or form another group to develop access to the WCIP?

With regard to native rights, we are all too familiar with the insincerity and deceptiveness of the states and their mutual admiration clubs. Some of us have been commissioned by our Elders and our people to speak in clear, uncompromising terms to call to task the offending states, the UN and other international bodies. Would our message be deemed too strong or abrasive or controversial and thus fall outside the parameters of what this Copenhagen group may be willing to support?

Regarding item 3. This is a good objective to pursue as over the past few years, member states have used the UN to block access by certain Indigenous Peoples to the Permanent Forum and other UN organs. In fact, perhaps the co-facilitator could start immediately by unblocking the Permanent Forum.

Regarding item 4. This is a good objective to pursue. This would go a long way to showing that the UN is willing to welcome participation by non-UN-member, unrepresented peoples.

Regarding item 5. This is a good objective. Official recognition of preparatory steps and funding would show commitment on the part of the UN to treat the WCIP seriously and not just a token act of good public relations and image enhancement.

I hope you take these comments in the spirit from which they are being offered … with Aloha. And I hope we can dialog to ameliorate these concerns.

Malama pono,

Leon Siu
The Koani Foundation
Ke Aupuni o Hawaii

Chapter 8

'Kill the Indian in the child': genocide in international law

Tamara Starblanket

> The way the Creator put us here on this continent, so that we could live in peace and harmony and be able to raise our children in a good way, and follow our Indian way of life.
>
> (Elder Peter Waskahat, Frog Lake, Treaty Six Territory)[1]

Introduction

This critical and timely compilation aptly affirms that *we were here first*. What does a statement like this convey? Our national identities are integral to our oral histories of Creation on our 'Great Turtle Island'.[2] Our responsibility as the 'Original Nations'[3] and Peoples is to defend and honour the land so that the future generations can benefit from our Mother Earth.[4] The continent now commonly known as North America belongs to the Anishinaabe, Dene, Haida Gwaii, Kanai, Lenape, Nehiyaw, Nuxalk, Oneida and Shawnee among many other Original Nations. Absent from the global dialogue is the acknowledgement of the past and present destruction caused by colonialism. Settler and colonial states claim that we are non-existent as nations in international law.[5] James Crawford in the foreword to Antony Anghie's *Imperialism, Sovereignty and the Making of International Law* writes that the development

1 'Treaty Six First International Meeting, 17–20 July 1989 Onion Lake First Nation, Treaty Six Territory' in Sharon Venne (ed), *Honour Bound: Onion Lake and the Spirit of Treaty Six: The International Validity of Treaties with Indigenous Peoples* (International Working Group for Indigenous Affairs, 1997) 68.
2 Sharon Venne, 'Treaties Made in Good Faith' in Paul W DePasquale (ed), *Natives and Settlers Now and Then: Historical Issues and Current Perspectives on Treaties and Land Claims in Canada* (University of Alberta Press, 2007) 1, 3.
3 Steven Newcomb, *Pagans in the Promised Land: Decoding the Christian Doctrine of Discovery* (Fulcrum Publishing, 2008) 131. Newcomb coined the term 'Original Nations'.
4 Venne, 'Treaties Made in Good Faith', above n 2, 2.
5 See especially Antony Anghie, *Imperialism, Sovereignty and the Making of International Law* (Cambridge University Press, 2005) 32–100. Anghie examines the domination of Indigenous Peoples in international law.

DOI: 10.4324/9781315628318-9

of international law was framed under 'pattern[s] of domination and subordination'.[6] Illusions of 'invisibility'[7] or non-existence are solidified by the myth of the benevolent colonial society. Settler states and scholars invoke the sham that colonialism is 'benevolent'[8] and this dodges the implication that colonialism is a genocidal process. Genocide denial conceals the dark colonial laws and policies of the past and present.[9]

It is an oppressive experience for peoples that have physically survived colonial invasion. 'Domination'[10] and 'dehumanisation'[11] are maintained

6 James Crawford, 'Foreword' in Anghie, above n 5, xi.

7 Sharon Venne, 'Introduction' in Ward Churchill, *Perversions of Justice* (City Lights Books, 2003) xiii.

8 See, eg, Arthur J Ray, Jim Miller and Frank Tough, *Bounty and Benevolence: A History of Saskatchewan Treaties* (McGill Queen's University Press, 2000). See also Helen Gilbert and Chris Tiffins (eds), *Burden or Benefit? Imperialism Benevolence and its Legacies* (Indiana University Press, 2008) for a review of the rhetoric of benevolence.

9 See Ottawa, *Statement of Apology to Former Students of the Indian Residential Schools*, 11 June 2008; see especially Tamara Starblanket, *Suffer the Little Children: Genocide, Indigenous Nations and the Canadian State* (Clarity Press, forthcoming); see also Tamara A Starblanket, *Genocide: Indigenous Nations and the State of Canada* (LLM Thesis, University of Saskatchewan, 2014). This chapter is based on my Master of Laws thesis and forthcoming book, and the legal question of Canadian state culpability for crimes of genocide. In my thesis, I claimed that the government violates customary laws on genocide as well as being criminally culpable for crimes of genocide into present times. It is based on a legal examination of residential schools and the child welfare system.

10 On domination, see especially Newcomb, *Pagans*, above n 3. The analysis of domination and dehumanisation originates from Newcomb's work on deconstructing the domination code in the colonial language. His domination cognitive model (cognitive legal theory) explains that language and law is a system or framework of domination and dehumanisation by analysing the doctrine of discovery. This domination code is embedded into the legal framework of the United States. The same analysis can be applied to Canadian jurisprudence. The case of *St Catherine's Milling and Lumber Co v R* (1886) CanLII 30 (ON CA) cites *Johnson & Graham's Lessee v M'Intosh* 21 US (8 Wheat) 543 (1823) from the United States. The domination is encoded in the language. See also Steven Newcomb and Birgil Kills Straight, *The Doctrine of Discovery and the Protocol of Domination: A Short Essay for the North American Indigenous Caucus Preparatory Meeting for the UN Permanent Forum on Indigenous Issues* (Indigenous Law Institute, 2012). Newcomb and Kills Straight refer to the law and language as a protocol of domination that is maintained by dehumanising descriptors.

11 On dehumanisation, see especially Newcomb, *Pagans*, above n 3, 1–36; Steven Newcomb, 'On Historical Narratives and Dehumanization', *Indian Country Today*, 20 June 2012 <http://indiancountrytodaymedianetwork.com/2012/06/20/historical-narratives-and-dehumanization>. See generally Robert Williams Jr, *Savage Anxieties: The Invention of Western Civilization* (Palgrave Macmillan, 2012); Frantz Fanon, *The Wretched of the Earth* (Grove Press, 1963); Ward Churchill, *A Little Matter of Genocide: Holocaust and Denial in the Americas 1492 to the Present* (Arbiter Ring Publishing, 1998); David Stannard, *American Holocaust* (Oxford University Press, 1992).

through various methods, such as the forced indoctrination of the Original Peoples and Nations' children. Shawnee and Lenape scholar Steven Newcomb in his work on cognitive legal theory refers to the 'paradigm of domination'.[12] He writes:

> The fact remains however, that the ideas used to construct and maintain such patterns of domination are not a physical container, nor a physical object; they are nothing more than mental processes. The paradigm of domination is more and foremost, a product of the mind.[13]

Patterns of forced indoctrination have caused the paradigm of domination. The colonial mission could not have been accomplished without the widespread destruction experienced by Indigenous Peoples' children in government-controlled residential schools and child welfare systems.

The crime of genocide – the forcible transferring of Indigenous Peoples' children into colonial residential institutions – continues unrelenting and without redress in international law. The *Convention on the Prevention and Punishment of the Crime of Genocide* (UNGC) holds the following in art 2:

> In the present Convention, genocide means any of the following acts committed with intent to destroy in whole or in part, a national, ethnical, racial or religious group, as such:
>
> a Killing members of the group;
> b Causing serious or bodily mental harm to members of the group;
> c Deliberately inflicting on the group conditions of life calculated to bring about its physical destruction in whole or in part;
> d Imposing measures intended to prevent births within the group;
> e Forcibly transferring children of the group to another group.[14]

In this chapter, I will review the drafting of the crime of genocide in international law from an Indigenous Peoples standpoint, and reveal the domination of state interests and the exclusion of the Indigenous experience of 'cultural genocide' or 'forced assimilation'. As Cree international lawyer and scholar Sharon Venne writes, 'genocide is genocide no matter what form it

12 Steven Newcomb, 'The UN Declaration on the Rights of Indigenous Peoples and the Paradigm of Domination' (2011) 20(3) *Griffith University Law Review* 578, 580. Newcomb argues that patterns of domination are maintained through a conceptual framework of domination.

13 Ibid.

14 *Convention on the Prevention and Punishment of the Crime of Genocide*, opened for signature 9 December 1948, 78 UNTS 277 (entered into force 12 January 1951, accession by Canada 3 September 1952).

takes and no matter what you call it'.[15] I will show the connection between genocide and colonisation and reveal that the Canadian state violates the UNGC. The forcible removals that began in the residential schools are ongoing as Indigenous children are now removed by the state into child welfare foster homes. Under the guise of the 'best interests of the child' the state justifies the removals by referring to the conditions that were created in the residential school system. The genocide continues unabated.

A note on the language is crucial as it is foundational to the genocidal experience of our Nations. The colonial language requires us to submit to the domination of settler states. Many examples abound such as 'land claims', 'reconciliation' and 'self-government'. An example is the recent change by the former Harper Canadian government of the title of the Department of Indian and Northern Affairs to Aboriginal Affairs and Northern Development. With the recent change in colonial government, it is now termed Indigenous and Northern Affairs. This is in line with Newcomb's contention that the term Indigenous Peoples means dominated peoples.[16] Given this important point, in this chapter I identify the term 'Indigenous Peoples' to mean the Original Nations and Peoples with capital letters from an international legal standpoint.

Peace and friendship in international law

The Elders affirm that our inherent obligations and responsibilities as the Original Nations are granted by the Creation.[17] In *Our Elders Understand Our Rights: Evolving International Law Regarding Indigenous Peoples* Venne contends that Indigenous Peoples and Nations are subjects of international law.[18] The peace and friendship treaties made between Indigenous Nations and the Crown of Great Britain early in the colonial invasion of Great Turtle Island affirm and secure the international legal status of the Original Nations.[19]

15 Sharon H Venne, 'Opening Line' in Ward Churchill, *Kill the Indian Save the Man: The Genocidal Impact of American Indian Residential Schools* (City Lights Books, 2004) xiii, xiii.
16 Newcomb, 'The UN Declaration', above n 12.
17 See especially Venne, *Honour Bound*, above n 1.
18 Sharon H Venne, *Our Elders Understand Our Rights: Evolving International Law Regarding Indigenous Peoples* (Theytus Books, 1998).
19 See especially Miguel Alfonso-Martinez (Special Rapporteur), *Final Report: Human Rights of Indigenous People Study on Treaties, Agreements and Other Constructive Arrangements between States and Indigenous Populations*, UN Commission on Human Rights, E/CN4/Sub 2/1999/20 (1999). For a review of treaties as international, see especially Venne, *Honour Bound*, above n 1; see also Sharon Venne, 'Understanding Treaty Six: An Indigenous Perspective' in Michael Asch (ed), *Aboriginal and Treaty Rights in Canada: Essays on Law, Equality and Respect for Difference* (UBC Press, 1997) 173; Isabelle Schulte-Tenckhoff, 'Reassessing the Paradigm of Domestication: The Problematic of Indigenous Treaties' (1994) 5 *Review of Constitutional Studies* 239.

Miguel Alfonso Martínez, Special Rapporteur on the Study on Treaties, stipulates that Indigenous Peoples are 'subjects'[20] of international law.

Canada as a colony of Great Britain inherited the legal obligation to implement the treaties according to the original spirit and intent.[21] The treaties affirm the inherent authority granted by the Creation to our land, nationalities, laws and governments. Elder Peter Waskahat of Frog Lake stated the case at an international meeting on treaties: 'In the past, before the whiteman came to this continent, this island, the Indian People were able to determine for themselves their daily lives and were also able to govern themselves.'[22] Venne described the laws of the Cree when Treaty Six was negotiated, and concluded:

> When Indigenous Peoples talk about the land and the making of treaty, we are talking about our life and the life of the future generations. Land is central to the process. We have a relationship with our Creation based on a legal system designed to protect and honour the land. These are the laws that guided Cree Peoples when the chiefs negotiated and concluded Treaty Six in 1876.[23]

The authority to protect the land or underlying title and their children was never relinquished or surrendered by Indigenous Nations.[24] Instead, the state has violated the treaties through several means, the most important being the forcible transferring of Indigenous Peoples' children from our Nations to the coloniser's people and society. As Nations we depend on our future generations. The ability to protect our children was terminated by the imposition of colonial laws and policies and the intent to destroy our Peoples was evidenced by the forcible removals.

Colonial framework

Civilising missions

The residential school system was designed by the government of Canada to civilise or 'absorb'[25] Indigenous Peoples' children into Canadian society or the

20 Alfonso Martinez, above n 19, [112], [189]. 'In the case of indigenous peoples who concluded treaties or other legal instruments with the European settlers and/or their continuators in the colonisation process, the Special Rapporteur has not found any sound legal argument to sustain the argument that they have lost their international juridical status as nations/peoples': ibid [265].

21 *The Queen v The Secretary of State for Foreign and Commonwealth Affairs, ex parte The Indian Association of Alberta, Union of New Brunswick Indians, Union of Nova Scotian Indians* [1984] 4 CNLR 86; see Alfonso Martinez, above n 19; Venne, *Honour Bound*, above n 1, 57–119.

22 In Venne, *Honour Bound*, above n 1, 115.

23 Venne, 'Treaties Made in Good Faith', above n 2, 2.

24 See especially Venne, *Honour Bound*, above n 1.

25 E Brian Titley, *A Narrow Vision: Duncan Campbell Scott and the Administration of Indian Affairs in Canada* (University of British Columbia Press, 1986) 50: 'our

colonial 'body politic'.[26] This is genocide, despite attempts to conceal the atrocity of the forced civilisation of our children. International legal scholar Martti Koskenniemi in *The Gentle Civilizer of Nations: The Rise and Fall of International Law* writes, 'No word is more vague and has permitted the commission of more crimes than that of civilization.'[27] Koskenniemi supports the contention that the forced civilisation of Indigenous Peoples is criminal conduct. Koskenniemi, citing Charles Salomon, affirms that 'the history of all colonies begins with violence, injustice and the shedding of blood: the result is everywhere the same; the disappearance of the native races (des races sauvages) coming into a contact with civilized races'.[28] Anghie supports the contention of this chapter by his argument that:

> colonialism was central to the constitution of international law in that many of the basic doctrines of international law – including most importantly the sovereignty doctrine – were forged out of the attempt to create a legal system that could account for relations between the European and non-European worlds in the colonial confrontation.[29]

Anghie's contention is evidenced by the drafting of the prohibition on genocide in international law. He further examines:

> the relationship between international law and colonialism by focusing on the civilizing mission, the grand object that justified colonialism as a means of redeeming the backward, aberrant, violent, oppressed under-developed people of the non-European world by incorporating them into the universal civilization of Europe.[30]

Dehumanisation of Original Peoples and Nations gives the dominating colonial state the licence to destroy with impunity with no qualms or afterthought. The residential school system provides an excellent example that portrays this destructive civilising mission that continued into the 1990s.

objective is to continue until there is not a single Indian in Canada that has not been absorbed into the body politic ...'. See especially Canada, Royal Commission on Aboriginal Peoples, *Report of the Royal Commission on Aboriginal Peoples, Vol 1: Looking Forward, Looking Back* (Canada Communications Group, 1996) ch 10 for a review of the early policy statements made by the government about civilising Indigenous Peoples by force.

26 Titley, above n 25, 50; see especially Newcomb, *Pagans*, above n 4, 15–16. Newcomb refers to the colonial 'body politic' as a predator.

27 Martti Koskenniemi, *The Gentle Civilizer of Nations: The Rise and Fall of International Law 1870–1960* (Cambridge University Press, 2001) 106.

28 Ibid.

29 Anghie, above n 5, 3.

30 Ibid.

Webster's *Third New International Dictionary* provides the following definition under 'civilization': 'the act of civilizing; esp the *forcing* of a particular cultural pattern on a population to whom it is foreign'.[31] From this perspective, forcing a cultural pattern onto an Original Nation is genocide in the context of colonisation. Raphael Lemkin, international lawyer, created the term by combining the 'Greek word *genos* (race, tribe) and the Latin *cide* (killing)'.[32] More importantly, Lemkin's analysis explained that colonial invasion is integral to the crime of genocide.[33] According to Lemkin, genocide means the 'destruction of a nation or of an ethnic group'.[34] Samantha Power in *A Problem From Hell* clearly articulates that Lemkin understood that genocide is directed against national group identities.[35] Power writes, 'In *Axis Rule* he wrote that "genocide" meant a "coordinated plan of different actions aiming at the destruction of essential foundations of the life of national groups, with the aim of annihilating the group themselves".'[36] She continues:

> The perpetrators of genocide would attempt to destroy the political and social institutions, the culture, language, national feelings, religion, and economic existence of national groups. They would hope to eradicate the personal security, liberty, health, dignity, and lives of individual members of the targeted group.[37]

In this regard, the emphasis is on national identities and the attack is against the individuals of those Original Nations in the colonial invasion of Indigenous Peoples and Nations' lands and territories. Lemkin explained that genocide was accomplished when two phases of genocide were implemented by the perpetrator invading state:

> one, the destruction of the national pattern of the oppressed group; the other, the imposition of the national pattern of the oppressor. This imposition, in turn, may be made upon the oppressed population which is allowed to remain, or upon the territory alone, after removal of the population and the colonization of the area by the oppressor's own nationals.[38]

31 *Webster's Third New International Dictionary of the English Language Unabridged, sub verbo* 'civilization'; see Newcomb, 'UN Declaration', above n 12, 581 for the original citation.
32 Raphael Lemkin, *Axis Rule in Occupied Europe: Laws of Occupation, Analysis of Government, Proposals for Redress* (Lawbook Exchange, 2nd edn, 2008) 79.
33 Ibid 79–90.
34 Ibid 79.
35 Samantha Power, '*A Problem from Hell': America and the Age of Genocide* (Harper Perennial, 2002) 43.
36 Ibid.
37 Ibid.
38 Lemkin, above n 32, 79.

Certainly, the forced civilisation of the Indigenous Peoples of Great Turtle Island constitutes genocide by the forced imposition of a cultural pattern over the Original Nations' national identities. So, based on Lemkin's view of genocide, the civilising mission matches the definition of the crime as understood by the man who coined the term.

The destructive and genocidal nature of the civilisation process, or the forcing of a cultural pattern by a dominating colonial state over another national identity, has been concealed by the removal of 'cultural genocide'[39] from the crime of genocide in international law. To be clear, forced civilisation is a process of colonialism. Newcomb is articulate on this point: 'what is referred to as civilization may involve a process of colonization, which is a process by which an empire expands in land, population, wealth and power'.[40] Of course, the removal of cultural genocide as a crime does not lessen its destructive effects on the victims of colonisation.

The civilising process justifies colonial violence and the illegitimate claiming of Indigenous Peoples' lands with the use of descriptors designed to dehumanise. Colonial law and policy is rampant with destructive language. The effect is brutal. Birgil Kills Straight and Steven Newcomb refer to the doctrine of discovery as a 'protocol of domination', as they examine the dehumanisation code embedded in the colonial language: 'wild, barbarous, savage, heathen, pagan, infidel, wandering (around free of domination), roaming (free of domination), uncivilized, domesticated, conquered, uncivilized (not yet dominated), minors, tribes, tribal, aborigines, aboriginal, ethnic groups, rude, primitive, ignorant, dirty and so forth'.[41] This violent categorisation is used to justify the genocide. Newcomb and Kills Straight continue, 'These terms have been used in a subhumanizing and dehumanizing manner in colonizing law and policy to rationalize [and] justify'[42] the theft of the Original Nations and Peoples' lands and territories. These derogatory terms are encoded in the framework of the state to the detriment of the Original Nations. The subhumanising codification into settler-state laws is the cornerstone of colonisation and genocide. Lemkin explains that the 'laws of occupation'[43] are indispensable to colonial invasion.

Laws of occupation

The mandate to civilise is evidenced in colonial laws and policy statements by government officials. John A MacDonald expressed to the Canadian House of

39 See especially Hirad Abtahi and Philippa Webb, *The Genocide Convention: The Travaux Préparatoires* (Martinus Nijhoff Publishers, 2008) vols 1–2.
40 Newcomb, *Pagans*, above n 3, 14.
41 Newcomb and Kills Straight, above n 10, 3; see also Robert Williams Jr, *The American Indian in Western Legal Thought: The Discourses of Conquest* (Oxford University Press, 1990).
42 Newcomb and Kills Straight, above n 10, 3.
43 Lemkin, above n 32, ix.

Commons in 1883 that the government intended to change the 'uncivilised' condition of the 'savage' Indian child to a child who would speak, think and write like a white person. MacDonald openly stated in parliament:

> the first object is to make them better men, and, if possible, good Christian men by applying proper moral restraints, and appealing to the instincts for worship which is to be found in all nations, whether *civilized* or *uncivilized* ... When the school is on the Reserve the child lives with its parents, who are *savages*; he is surrounded by *savages*, and though he may learn to read and write his habits, and training and mode of thought are Indian. He is simply a *savage* who can read and write ... Indian children should be withdrawn as much as possible from the parental influence, and the only way to do that would be to put them in central training industrial schools where they will acquire the habits, modes and thought of white men.[44]

Constitutional scholar Kent McNeil contends that early conceptions of colonial Aboriginal law and policy were based on theories of racial superiority or what he terms 'social Darwinism'.[45] Racist and dehumanising descriptors were encoded into the framework of the oppressor state. McNeil finds that the case of *St Catherine's Milling and Lumber Co v The Queen*[46] of the 1880s reveals the racist attitudes that guided the judiciary in its determination of Aboriginal title. The Ontario Court of Appeal in 1886 in the *St Catharine's Milling* case cited the Marshall Trilogy of the United States and invoked the discovery doctrine and dehumanising descriptors to claim Indigenous Peoples' lands and territories.[47] McNeil writes:

44 Canada, *Parliamentary Debates*, House of Commons, 9 May 1883, 14: 1107–8 (MacDonald) (emphasis added); see also Canada, Royal Commission on Aboriginal Peoples, above n 25; Titley, above n 25.

45 Kent McNeil, 'Social Darwinism and Judicial Conceptions of Indian Title in Canada in the 1880s' (1999) 38 *Journal of the West* 68.

46 (1885) 10 OR 196 (Chancery). The court determined that 'Indian Peoples were found scattered wide cast over the continent having as a characteristic, no fixed abodes, but moving as the exigencies of living demanded. As heathens and barbarians it was not thought that they had any proprietary title to the soil': [206].

47 *St Catherine's Milling and Lumber Co v R* (1886) CanLII 30 (ON CA) <http://canlii.ca/t/1vpsp>. 'The whole discussion and judgment in that case are very interesting and instructive. Counsel referred to the practice of all civilized nations to deny the right of the Indians to be considered as independent communities having a permanent property in the soil. And it was said in argument that the North American Indians could have acquired no proprietary interest in the vast tract of territory which they wandered over, and their right to the lands on which they hunted, could not be considered as superior to that which is acquired to the sea by fishing in it; the use in the one case as in the other, is not exclusive. According to every theory of property the Indians had no individual right to the land; nor had they any collectively, or in their national capacity, for

> There can be no doubt that the evolutionary theories of human societies prevalent in the latter half of the 19th century influenced government policy toward Indians in the United States and Canada. For example, allotment of tribal lands to individuals in the United States, and the residential school system in both countries, which were actively pursued in the 1880s, were primarily designed to bridge the supposed gap between Indian savagery or barbarism and Euro-based civilization, so that Indians could be raised to the level of Whites through a process of education and assimilation.[48]

The basis of the forcible removal of children to the residential school system in Canada was theories of racial superiority and the civilisation framework. The intent of the colonial framework for the forcible transferral of children was to 'kill the Indian in the child'.[49] In this regard, genocide is integral to colonialism. The Canadian government legislated the forcible transferral through its *Indian Act*.[50]

Drafting of the crime of genocide

Colonial clause and cultural genocide

The Genocide Convention: The Travaux Préparatoires[51] details the discussions and debates among states at the United Nations. The 'colonial clause' was a significant discussion during the drafting of the crime.[52] The colonial clause gives a contracting state the freedom of designating to which 'colonial territories' the *Genocide Convention* will apply.[53] The colonial clause sheds light on

the lands used by each tribe were not used by them in such manner as to prevent their being appropriated by settlers': [50].

48 McNeil, above n 45, 70.

49 See Ottawa, *Statement of Apology*, above n 9.

50 See *An Act to Amend and Consolidate the Laws Respecting Indians*, SC 1880, c 28; ss 137(2) and 138 of the *Indian Advancement Act*, RSC 1886, c 44; s 11 of *An Act Further to Amend the Indian Act*, 1894, c 32, 57–58 Victoria; ss 9 and 10 of *An Act to Amend the Indian Act*, SC 1920, c 50.

51 Abtahi and Webb, above n 39.

52 United Nations General Assembly, 6th Comm, 93rd mtg, UN Doc A/C6/SR93 (6 November 1948), cited in Abtahi and Webb, ibid 1609. The issue came up in the discussion on state responsibility and the amendment was raised again in the context of the 'colonial clause in the following discussion': United Nations General Assembly, 6th Comm, 107th mtg, UN Doc A/C6/SR107 (15 November 1948), cited in Abtahi and Webb, ibid 1812. The colonial clause concerned issues of protection under the *Genocide Convention* being extended to non-self-governing territories.

53 See Marko Milanović, 'Territorial Application of the Convention and State Succession' in Paola Gaeta (ed), *The UN Genocide Convention: A Commentary* (Oxford University Press, 2009) 473, 473: 'In essence, these clauses give the contracting

the connection between colonialism and genocide. The USSR's push to have cultural genocide retained in the convention directly related to its concern that '[c]olonial policy had been a dark page in history'.[54] In fact, there was contention between the USSR and the United Kingdom on this 'dark history', as the United Kingdom delegation 'denied the moral authority of the Soviet Union Government to make any such statement, or to set itself up as a model of conduct before the world'.[55] The USSR's strong opposition to the deletion of cultural genocide reflected its position that 'fascism, Nazism and doctrines of racial superiority'[56] were at the root of genocide.

On the concept of cultural genocide, the Ukraine stated:

> It was generally recognized that genocide is aimed at the extermination of a group of people. That aim could be attained by exterminating all the members of the group or by destroying its characteristics. In the opinion of the Ukrainian delegation, no country which was genuinely anxious to combat the crime of genocide and to prevent it as well as punish it, could oppose the inclusion of cultural genocide among the acts to which the convention applied.[57]

The USSR's arguments against the deletion of cultural genocide during the Sixth Committee debates show that genocide is an end product of colonialism.[58] The issue came to a head in the debate on the USSR's proposed amendment.[59] The USSR was concerned about loopholes which 'might prevent the punishment of those who perpetrated the crime of genocide or

states the freedom of designating those parts of their territories to which the treaty will apply, thereby avoiding the customary the customary presumption in favour of territorial application to all of the territories of a state party, now codified in Article 29 of the 1969 *Vienna Convention on the Law of Treaties*'.

54 UN Doc A/C6/SR107, cited in Abtahi and Webb, above n 39, 1817. The committee did not wish to see those dark pages prolonged by a failure to extend the provisions of the convention on genocide to the colonial territories. See Jean-Paul Sartre and Arlette El Kaim-Sartre, *On Genocide and the Summary of the Evidence and Judgments of the International War Crimes Tribunal* (Beacon Press, 1968) 63: colonialism 'is by its very nature an act of cultural genocide. Colonization cannot take place without systematically liquidating all the characteristics of the native society.'

55 UN Doc A/C6/SR107, cited in Abtahi and Webb, ibid 1822. The United Kingdom denied many of the assertions made by the USSR and the denial is important to the overall question of its colonial history globally.

56 United Nations General Assembly, 6th Comm, 179th mtg, UN Doc A/PV179 (9 December 1948), cited in Abtahi and Webb, ibid 2082–3.

57 United Nations General Assembly, 6th Comm, 65th mtg, UN Doc A/C6/SR65 (2 October 1948), cited in Abtahi and Webb, ibid 1319.

58 United Nations General Assembly, 6th Comm, 82nd mtg, UN Doc A/C6/SR83 (25 October 1948), cited in Abtahi and Webb, ibid 1501–19.

59 A/766, cited in Abtahi and Webb, ibid 2039.

incited others to do so'.[60] The USSR was concerned that Nazism and theories of racial superiority were not included in the preamble of the UNGC and '[t]o say that the crime had no connexion with racial theories amounted, in fact, to a re-instatement of such theories'.[61] It was also concerned that cultural genocide had been removed and the delegation 'of the USSR could not agree with that view, for it regarded cultural genocide as an aspect of genocide'.[62] The USSR further argued that:

> Article XII gave the colonial Powers discretion to extend or not to extend the provisions of the convention to their colonies. The rejection of the USSR amendment providing for the extension of the convention to all Non-Self-Governing Territories diminished the value of the present text.[63]

Yugoslavia and Poland supported the position taken by the USSR because of the genocidal experience they encountered at the hands of the Nazi state.

The significance to Indigenous Peoples under domination is that the doctrine of discovery is founded on western ideals of civilisation and theories of racial superiority. Doctrines of racial superiority are what led to the demonisation, isolation and destruction of Original Nations on Great Turtle Island and the world over. Genocide followed:

> racial theories intended to develop racial and national hatreds, the domination of the so-called 'higher races' and the extermination of the so-called 'lower races.' The crime of genocide formed an integral part of the plan for world domination of the supporters of racial ideologies.[64]

The destruction of Indigenous Peoples and Nations is guided by dehumanising terminology that is deeply imbedded into the framework of the colonial settler-state systems. The discussion raised by the USSR and the rebuttal by the United Kingdom over the colonial clause and the dark history of colonisation is instructive. The Polish delegate stated, 'Genocide had often been committed in the colonies; the colonial peoples were always in danger from the metropolitan States in that respect, whether in the direct physical form or in the form of cultural genocide.'[65] The amendment by the USSR was rejected by the United Nations General Assembly; however, it supports my contention that genocide is linked to theories of the so-called higher races and

60 UN Doc A/PV179, cited in Abtahi and Webb, ibid 2082.
61 United Nations General Assembly, 6th Comm, 178th mtg, UN Doc A/PV178 (9 December 1948), cited in Abtahi and Webb, ibid 2044.
62 Ibid 2045, citing UN Doc A/PV178.
63 Ibid 2083, citing UN Doc A/PV179.
64 Ibid 2044, citing UN Doc A/PV178.
65 Ibid 2076, citing UN Doc A/PV179.

the lower races. The USSR's comment is informative, 'unless some provision regarding cultural genocide is included in the convention'[66] states may use this to 'justify crimes of genocide'.[67] From the USSR's position, the colonial powers 'intended to have a free hand to ensure that colonial territories were maintained in a position of inferiority'.[68]

Canada is a settler[69] state comprised of many different immigrants that have come here from abroad. The French and English are two of the many immigrant cultures. The French are from France and the English are from the United Kingdom. Is it any wonder that Canada vociferously opposed cultural genocide? In fact, it was the only point they objected to:

> His delegation was not, therefore, opposed to the idea of cultural genocide, but only to the inclusion in the convention of measures to suppress it. His delegation did not wish to limit the scope of the convention in any way, as was shown by the fact that it had voted in favour of the inclusion of the protection of the political group, but it felt that the idea of genocide should be limited to the mass physical destruction of human groups.[70]

Instead, the solution Canada proposed was to recommend the 'protection of language, religion and culture within the framework of the international declaration on human rights'.[71] The effect of considering issues of colonialism under a human rights framework was to conceal the destruction caused by settler-state laws, policies and programmes. State concerns centred on whether the treatment of Indigenous Peoples would be construed as genocide. According to Mathew Lippman, 'The United States did not want to risk international recrimination for the country's continued practice of racial segregation and mistreatment of Native Americans.'[72] The standard argument against including cultural genocide was that the protections in the convention 'went too far'.[73] The Travaux Préparatoires provides compelling evidence that

66 Ibid 2045, citing UN Doc A/PV178.
67 Ibid, citing UN Doc A/PV178.
68 Ibid 2046, citing UN Doc A/PV178.
69 See, eg, Grenfell Price, *White Settlers and Native Peoples: An Historical Study of Racial Contacts between English-Speaking Whites and Aboriginal Peoples in the United States, Canada, Australia, and New Zealand* (Cambridge University Press, 1950) for a review of the term 'settler'.
70 UN Doc A/C6/SR83, cited in Abtahi and Webb, above n 39, 1510.
71 Ibid.
72 Matthew Lippman, 'The Drafting and Development of the 1948 Convention on Genocide and the Politics of International Law' in H G van der Wilt, J Vervliet, G K Sluiter and J T M Houwink ten Cate (eds) *The Genocide Convention: The Legacy of 60 Years* (Martinus Nijhoff, 2012) 15, 19.
73 United Nations General Assembly, 6th Comm, 64th mtg, UN Doc A/C6/SR64 (1 October 1948), cited in Abtahi and Webb, above n 39, 1301.

the United Kingdom resisted the implication that its colonial policy globally was genocidal. This is supported by the Canadian delegate's vehement opposition to the inclusion of cultural genocide and its threatened 'reservation'.[74] Removing cultural genocide from the convention maintains ongoing destruction by preventing Original Nations and Peoples making claims in international law for crimes of genocide in the colonisation of their lands and territories.

The deletion of cultural genocide gives the colonial settler state the licence to destroy with impunity. It allows genocide to go unchecked and is a continuation of the colonial objective. The discussion of the colonial clause affirms that Indigenous Peoples have not entered into a 'post-colonial era'.[75] The removal of cultural genocide as a legal concept in international law renders the Original Nations invisible.[76] It masks the destruction caused by colonialism. According to the USSR, the removal:

> might be utilized by those who wished to carry out [genocide] against national, cultural and racial [human groups/nations]. Such [destruction] did exist at the present time and prevailed in certain territories and colonies administered by countries who prided themselves on their civilization.[77]

The USSR's point is instructive in that cultural genocide is linked to the civilisation process. The 'civilising missions'[78] with the use of dehumanising inferior classifications such as 'pagans' or 'savages' and the use of those descriptors as a basis for claiming Indigenous Peoples and Nations were not sovereign[79] were the justifications for the legislated state removal of Indigenous Peoples' children away from loving families and, ultimately, their Nations.

Forcible transferral of children

The Travaux Préparatoires provides clarity about the forcible transferral of children. It was acknowledged during the drafting of the convention that

74 Ibid 1510, citing UN Doc A/C6/SR83.
75 Venne, 'Introduction', above n 7, xiii.
76 Ibid.
77 UN Doc A/PV179, cited in Abtahi and Webb, above n 39, 2083.
78 Anghie, above n 5, inside cover (The project of governing non-European peoples).
79 Ibid 29: 'the one distinction which Vitoria insists upon and which he elaborates in considerable detail is the distinction between the sovereign Spanish and the non-sovereign Indians. Vitoria bases his conclusion that the Indians are not sovereign on the simple assertion that they are pagans. In doing so he resorts to exactly the same crude reasoning which he had previously refuted when denying the validity of the Church's claim that the Indians lack right under divine law because they are heathens'.

human groups depend on their children for the continuance of their distinct national identities. The French delegate acknowledged, 'The forced transfer of children had not only cultural, but also physical and biological effects since it imposed on young persons conditions of life likely to cause them serious harm or even death.'[80] The forcible removal would lead to the eventual disappearance of the targeted nationality because as nations they depend on their children.[81] The Greek delegate Mr Vallindas held:

> There could be no doubt that a forced transfer of children, committed with the intention of destroying a human group, in whole, or at least in part, constituted genocide. The forced transfer of children could be as effective a means of destroying a group as that of imposing measures intended to prevent births, or inflicting conditions of life likely to cause death.[82]

Greece emphasised the importance of including the '"forced transfer of children", a means of committing genocide, which had not only been used in the past but was still being used'.[83] The representative from Uruguay, Mr Maniniy Rios, held that 'there was reason also to condemn measures intended to destroy a new generation through abducting infants, forcing them to change their religion and educating them to become enemies of their own people'.[84] More importantly, the Greek delegate determined that the forcible removal of children was not 'primarily an act of cultural genocide. Although it could in certain cases be considered as such, it could be perpetrated rather with the intent to destroy or to cause serious physical harm to members of a group.'[85] According to Art 32 of the *Vienna Convention on the Law of Treaties* the Travaux Préparatoires may be used as a 'supplementary means of interpretation':

> Recourse may be had to supplementary means of interpretation, including the preparatory work of the treaty and the circumstances of its conclusion, in order to confirm the meaning resulting from the application of article 31, or to determine the meaning when the interpretation according to article 31:
>
> a leaves the meaning ambiguous or obscure; or
> b leads to a result which is manifestly absurd or unreasonable.[86]

80 United Nations General Assembly, 6th Comm, 83rd mtg, UN Doc A/C6/SR82 (23 October 1948), cited in Abtahi and Webb, above n 39, 1492.
81 Ibid 1492–5, 1504.
82 Ibid 1493.
83 Ibid.
84 Ibid 1494.
85 Ibid 1495.
86 *Vienna Convention on the Law of Treaties*, opened for signature May 23 1969, 1155 UNTS 331 (entered into force 27 January 1980).

Given this important point, the Travaux Préparatoires is utilised as a source of clarity with respect to the crime of forcibly transferring children away from Indigenous Peoples and Nations to the colonial society. The deliberate removal by colonial member states of the legal concept of 'cultural genocide' and the 'loopholes'[87] put in place to avoid international recrimination in international law can be challenged by reframing the legal issue another way. Despite the attempted block by colonial governments and the 'greatly truncated'[88] version of genocide adopted by the United Nations General Assembly, there is enough latitude to determine when a crime occurs.

Genocide Convention

Model of domination and dehumanisation

In my Master of Laws thesis entitled *Genocide: Indigenous Nations and the State of Canada*[89] and my book entitled *Suffer the Little Children: Genocide, Indigenous Nations and the Canadian State*,[90] the tables are turned on the colonial state or western reader. Newcomb's groundbreaking work in *Pagans in the Promised Land: Decoding the Christian Doctrine of Discovery* provided the cognition that I had developed a metaphor to explain our collective experience of colonial invasion and genocide. It is an alternative way of viewing the forcible transferring of Indigenous Peoples' children. In the study of law, I learned colonial language is paramount to the entrapment that Indigenous Peoples and Nations encounter when bringing their issues before colonial courts or processes. An example is the 'land claims' policy in Canada. The term is a contradiction to our existence on Great Turtle Island since the beginning of time. Why do we 'claim' the land that has been gifted to our Original Peoples and Nations by Creation? Given this line of reasoning, a challenge from the outset is the language. Newcomb articulates, 'Words have a history. Words from the past have the ability to colonize the present. Words shape and create reality.'[91] From an Indigenous legal standpoint, 'language' is foundational to the rhetorical manoeuvres that entrench state domination. An example is the apology by the Canadian government in which Prime Minister Harper invoked words such as 'abuse', 'neglect' and 'mistreatment' to explain the harm experienced by Indigenous children in state-controlled residential

87 UN Doc E/794, E/794/Corr 1 and E/AC 27/1, cited in Abtahi and Webb, above n 39. The diminishment of the crime has allowed for what Poland referred to as 'loopholes of escape for perpetrators of the crime': 710.
88 Ward Churchill, *Perversions of Justice* (City Lights Books, 2003) 250.
89 See Starblanket, *Genocide*, above n 9.
90 Starblanket, *Suffer the Little Children*, above n 9.
91 Steven Newcomb, 'A Critique of a Doctrine of Reconciliation', *Indian Country Today*, 15 June 2011 <http://indiancountrytodaymedianetwork.com/2011/06/15/critique-doctrine-reconciliation>.

institutions.[92] It is difficult to convey a genocidal experience with euphemistic words.[93]

In the practice of law, attorneys invoke the use of models and metaphors to prove a case. Metaphorical explanation can be a useful tool to deconstruct colonialism, as is clearly demonstrated by Newcomb's cognitive legal theory on decoding the domination and dehumanisation in international and domestic law. In this regard, the model explains the process and the result. The process is colonialism and the result is genocide. The model challenges the state government, scholarly and societal denial about the crime of genocide that ensues from colonial invasion. The colonial state and society demonises, isolates and destroys Indigenous Peoples and Nations in the colonisation process.[94] The model entitled 'the domination and dehumanization of Original Nations and Peoples'[95] unpacks the colonial experience, namely the forcible transferral of Indigenous Peoples' children into the colonial body politic. Newcomb describes this colonising 'body politic':[96]

> [a] collective body (composed of individual humans interacting in their social and cultural lives) arrives to a 'new' continent with a colonizing, ravenous 'hunger' (desire) for land. From an indigenous perspective, this collective colonizing body can be metaphorically thought of as predator that pursues its indigenous spoil and prey; it sets out to catch, devour, and consume everything in sight (this correlates with the common expressions 'this is a consumer society' and 'we're in the belly of the beast').[97]

Duncan Campbell Scott (Superintendent of Indian Affairs) also referred to this colonial body politic in 1920 in his statement that 'our objective is to continue until there is not a single Indian in Canada that has not been absorbed into the body politic, and there is no Indian question, and no Indian department and that is the whole object of the Bill'.[98] The model invokes the metaphor of the machine or engine that is the tool of the colonial body that prepares its prey for consumption into the predatory colonial 'body politic' or

92 Ottawa, *Statement of Apology*, above n 9. For a review of the euphemisms, see John S Milloy, *A National Crime: The Canadian Government and the Residential School System, 1879 to 1986* (University of Manitoba Press, 1999).

93 See especially Roland Chrisjohn, Sherri Young and Michael Maruan, *The Circle Game: Shadows and Substance in the Indian Residential School Experience in Canada* (Theytus Books, 2006) for a review of the rhetoric concerning residential schools.

94 See especially Starblanket, *Suffer the Little Children*, above n 9; Starblanket, *Genocide*, above n 9.

95 See especially Newcomb, *Pagans*, above n 3; Starblanket, *Suffer the Little Children*, above n 9.

96 Newcomb, *Pagans*, above n 3, 15.

97 Ibid 16.

98 Canada, Royal Commission on Aboriginal Peoples, above n 25, 577.

Canadian state and society. From an Indigenous standpoint, the metaphor of the machine compels the western reader to view the reality that is concealed in present-day discussions about residential schools and the child welfare system. Consider the definition in the *Canadian Oxford Dictionary* that an engine is 'a thing that is an agent or instrument of a desired end or achievement (drive the engine of progress faster)'.[99] This same colonising body (from the US side) in the words of Theodore Roosevelt said that state law and policy was to be a 'mighty pulverizing engine to break up the tribal mass'.[100] The metaphor of the 'pulverizing engine' conveys that the prey are being prepared for consumption into the colonial body.

The metaphor of the machine is supported by the classification of the harm experienced in Roland Chrisjohn, Sherry Young and Michael Maraun's book *The Circle Game* in their analysis of the residential school as a 'total institution'.[101] The total institution 'unmakes[s]'[102] and then remakes Indigenous Peoples' children into the government's intended 'vision'[103] of a civilised person with the 'modes and thoughts of white men'.[104] The *Oxford Dictionary* defines 'dehumanise' as 'deprive of human characteristics [or] make impersonal or machine-like'.[105] 'Indoctrination' is defined as 'to teach (a person or a group of people) to systematically accept doctrines, esp. uncritically'.[106] The synonym for indoctrination is 'brainwashing'.[107] Total institutions serve as modes of forced indoctrination or brainwashing. Brainwashing is defined as 'to effect a radical change in the ideas and beliefs (of a person) esp. by methods based on isolation, sleeplessness, hunger, extreme discomfort, pain, and the alternation of kindness and cruelty'.[108] Ward Churchill in his compelling analysis in *Kill the Indian Save the Man* describes the children's experiences of torture, sexually predatory acts, forced starvation, forced labour,

99 *The Canadian Oxford Dictionary*, 2nd edn, *sub verbo* 'engine'.
100 Theodore Roosevelt, 'The Struggle for Self-Determination' (1901), in *Digital History*, <http://www.digitalhistory.uh.edu/disp_textbook.cfm?smtid=3&psid=720>.
101 Chrisjohn, Young and Maruan, above n 93; see also Erving Goffman, *Asylums: Essays on the Social Situation of Mental Patients and Other Inmates* (Anchor Books, 1961) for a review of the total institution as a process that unmakes human beings.
102 Chrisjohn, Young and Maruan, ibid 91.
103 Canada, Royal Commission on Aboriginal Peoples, above n 25, 313: 'The government looked to the young for a complete change of condition.'
104 Canada, *Parliamentary Debates*, above n 44.
105 *The Concise Oxford Dictionary*, 9th edn, *sub verbo* 'dehumanise'
106 *Collins English Dictionary*, 2nd edn, *sub verbo* 'indoctrination'.
107 *Webster's New Dictionary and Thesaurus, sub verbo* 'brainwashing'.
108 *Collins English Dictionary*, 2nd edn, *sub verbo*, 'brainwashing'; see also Naomi Klein, *The Shock Doctrine: The Rise of Disaster Capitalism* (Knopf, 2007) 25–48. Klein quotes George Orwell's book *Nineteen Eighty-Four*: 'We shall squeeze you empty, and then we shall fill you with ourselves.'

and death by disease and dilapidated living conditions.[109] Viewed from this reality, the metaphor of the brainwashing machine matches the violent and brutal colonial destruction experienced by the young ones.

For clarification, the use of the terms 'machine' or 'engine' metaphorically explains the process of forced indoctrination or the serious bodily and mental harm that occurred as a result of the forcible transfer. Clarification is necessary because genocide is a human decision. The model explains the process Indigenous Nations collectively have undergone by the forcible transferral of their children from one group (family, community and nations) to another group (residential institutions and ultimately Canadian society).[110] The use of the word 'machine' is by no means an attempt to downgrade the human decision of genocide. Human beings plan, create and drive the machines and tools they construct. The model explains not just the act but the colonising 'state of mind' behind the act. Most importantly, the description of the brainwashing machine is not meant to dehumanise the experience of Indigenous Peoples' children's collective terror and violence. The term conveys the reality of the forced indoctrination by colonial violence through imposition of the dominant cultural pattern onto the children and the methods used to dehumanise the innocent. The forced indoctrination process brutally conditioned children to think, speak and write like the so-called civilised society they were being forcibly transferred to away from their loving families and Nations. The model explains the sadistic process of conditioning innocent children into a Christian western world view.

The forced imposition of the colonial English language dehumanises Indigenous Peoples and Nations' world view. The forcible transferral severs the child's relationship with her land and territory and ultimately her identity as a 'Nehiyaw' because she has been trained to become an 'enemy' of her own people.[111] The child views her people as inferior. Churchill recounts one student's experience at Oblate's St Phillips School in Ontario: 'Long before she completed her schooling, she learned to hate, not simply the people who oppressed her, but herself and her race as well.'[112] This process turns the child against her national identity, spirituality, culture, language, original laws and instructions, parents and families. The worst effect is the disconnection of her identity from the land or Mother Earth and from her responsibility to 'protect and honour the land'.[113]

The spiritual relationship embodied in Creation's laws with Mother Earth (Great Turtle Island) becomes severed in the residential school.[114] An example

109 Ward Churchill, *Kill the Indian Save the Man: The Genocidal Impact of American Indian Residential Schools* (City Lights Books, 2004).
110 Article 2(b) and (e) of the *Genocide Convention*.
111 UN Doc A/C6/SR82, cited in Abtahi and Webb, above n 39, 1494.
112 Churchill, *Kill the Indian*, above n 109, 24.
113 Venne, 'Treaties Made in Good Faith', above n 2, 2.
114 Sharon Venne, interview, 4 January 2013.

is the Indigenous language (name) designated to identify a territory.[115] The Nehiyaw language exemplifies spiritual laws that embody how people are to relate in a beneficial way to that land or territory. Spiritual laws are encoded into Indigenous Peoples' languages.[116] The dominating society forces another language (for example, English) onto scores of children, and the result is those children were never taught or do not remember why they have a relationship with their land (Mother Earth).[117] It becomes a deliberate process to isolate children from their land. Newcomb writes:

> From a cognitive science perspective [the dominating conceptual system has] become part of the neural circuitry and structuring of our brains. As a result, non-Indian strands of meaning have become interwoven into our social and cultural lives as Indian people, thereby making the constraints of [the dominating system] an integral part of the fabric of our own imaginations and an integral part of the daily interactions of Indian people in Indian communities.[118]

As a result, Indigenous children who have undergone forcible indoctrination will not have been raised Nehiyaw and so in what way can the children claim to be reared by their families, communities and Nations? The spiritual laws embedded in the language become severed by not being passed on to new generations.[119] The young ones are now a product of the dominating society's language and culture and not their own. The fall-out for successive generations of Indigenous children is catastrophic.[120] Indigenous children become dominated and dehumanised through the methods employed in the total institutions. The isolation from loving families, communities and Nations renders children vulnerable to the forced indoctrination. The end product is destruction in the name of 'civilisation'.[121]

In other words, the forcible transferral of Indigenous Peoples' children causes serious bodily or mental harm. Dehumanising denigrations against a child's spirituality, nationality, history, people, culture and way of life cause great destruction. Tell a child his or her people are worthless and savages

115 Ibid.
116 Ibid.
117 Ibid; see also Venne, *Honour Bound*, above n 1, 90–4. Elder Alex Twinn of Louis Bull First Nation explains that a residential school severed the teachings that should have been passed onto him. Elder Alex Bonais of Little Pine First Nation refers to the white man 'destroy[ing] us tak[ing] away our children'.
118 Newcomb, *Pagans*, above n 3, 19.
119 Sharon Venne, interview, 4 January 2013.
120 Churchill, *Kill the Indian*, above n 109, 68–76; see also Chrisjohn, Young and Maruan, above n 93.
121 See Aimé Césaire, *Discourse on Colonialism* (Monthly Review Press, 1972). Césaire explains that the civilisation process is a disease. See also Starblanket, *Genocide*, above n 9; Starblanket, *Suffer the Little Children*, above n 9.

and it is likely that the child will come to see herself or himself through the eyes of the coloniser.[122] The situation is exacerbated by torture such as poking needles through tongues, whippings and beating children into submission.[123] As an example, the 'insertion of a needle'[124] into or 'dry ice'[125] on the tongue to force an Indigenous child not to speak her own language, but to speak the coloniser's language instead, will cause serious bodily and mental harm and compel that child to speak and think in the language being forcibly imposed on him or her. Add the experiences of starvation, forced labour and death by disease and other methods, and the oppressor society creates a child that has been conditioned and unmade into something that is 'unrecognizable'[126] or severely traumatised. Take the situation further and sexually prey upon a child and that child becomes utterly destroyed in the process. The effect is catastrophic as collectively the trauma and dysfunction is transmitted from generation to generation.[127] Collective trauma and dysfunction brought about by the residential school phase is then used by the very dominating society that created it to justify the child welfare system phase of the process.[128] The state uses its imposed standards of judgement to create the institutions that create the destructive conditions, and then uses its standards of judgement to take away another generation of children by force. It is well acknowledged in scholarship and government reports that the child welfare system is a direct

122 See Agnes Grant, *No End of Grief: Indian Residential Schools in Canada* (Pemmican Publications, 1996) 225–7; Churchill, *Kill the Indian*, above n 109, 19–24.

123 See Churchill, *Kill the Indian*, above n 109, 51–60; Chrisjohn, Young and Maruan, above n 93, 49–51.

124 Chrisjohn, Young and Maruan, above n 93, 49, 255.

125 Steven Newcomb, interview, 2 December 2012.

126 Chrisjohn, Young and Maruan, above n 93, 91.

127 See Ernie Crey and Suzanne Fournier, *Stolen From Our Embrace: The Abduction of First Nations Children and the Restoration of Aboriginal Communities* (Douglas and McIntyre, 1997); Churchill, *Kill the Indian*, above n 109, 68–76; Chrisjohn, Young and Maruan, above n 93.

128 See Leroy Little Bear, 'Section 88 of the Indian Act and the Application of Provincial Laws to Indians' in Anthony Long and Menno Boldt (eds), *Governments in Conflict? Provinces and Indian Nations in Canada* (University of Toronto Press, 1992) 175. With the amendments to the *Indian Act*, s 88 authorises the removal of Indigenous children by the provinces. See Marilyn Bennett, *First Nations Fact Sheet: A General Profile on First Nations Child Welfare in Canada First Nations Child and Family Caring Society* <http://www.fncfcs.com/docs/FirstNationsFS1.pdf>. Bennett writes: 'As there is no explicit reference to child welfare in either the *Indian Act* or the *Constitutional Act, 1867, 1982*, it has subsequently been deemed to be the responsibility of the provinces' at 2. Bennett refers to the Supreme Court of Canada case in which it was 'confirmed in 1976 that the legal jurisdiction of the Provinces' ability to extend child welfare services onto reserve, regardless of the provincial incursion into a federal sphere of responsibility (*Natural Parents v Superintendent of Child Welfare,* (1976) 60 D.L.R. 3rd 148 S.C.C.)' at 2.

effect of the residential school system.[129] The rates of removal are catastrophic in the child welfare system.[130] It is reported that in some provinces 80 per cent of children in care are Aboriginal, yet they make up only 5 per cent of the total population of Canada.[131] The massive and widespread trauma and dysfunction destroys entire Original Peoples and Nations on Great Turtle Island because Indigenous Peoples depend on their children to transmit healthy identities to future generations.

Turning the tables

Indigenous Nations' ability to protect the rights of our children are limited under current international and national laws. It is a challenge to protect our children from forcible state removals when the framework under which this occurs is oppressive. Given the deliberate exclusion from international law of cultural genocide and forced assimilation measures by colonial settler states, it is nearly impossible to articulate a claim of this nature in international law. Anghie supports this contention through his analysis of the development of colonialism in international law to the detriment of the Original Peoples and Nations of the world.[132]

The domination of settler-state interests is evidenced by the limited definition of the crime of genocide in the Canadian *Criminal Code*. Upon accession to the UNGC, state governments have an obligation to ratify the convention into domestic laws. Canada implemented a hate propaganda law that gutted out critical components of the UNGC.[133] The omission of the international

129 See Aboriginal Justice Implementation Commission, *Report of the Aboriginal Justice Inquiry of Manitoba* (1999) vol 1, ch 14 <http://www.ajic.mb.ca/volume.html>; Andrew Armitage, *Comparing the Policy of Aboriginal Assimilation: Australia, Canada and New Zealand* (University of British Columbia Press, 1995); Jacqueline Marie Maurice, *Despiriting Aboriginal Children: Aboriginal Children During the 1960s and 1970s Child Welfare Era* (PhD Thesis, University of Toronto, 2003).

130 See National Collaborating Centre for Aboriginal Health, *Aboriginal and Non-Aboriginal Children in Child Protection Services* (National Collaborating Centre for Aboriginal Health, 2009–2010) <http://nccah.netedit.info/docs/fact%20sheets/child%20and%20youth/NCCAH_fs_childhealth_EN.pdf>.

131 See Cindy Blackstock et al, 'Pathways to the Overrepresentation of Aboriginal Children in Canada's Child Welfare System' (2004) 78 *Social Service Review* 577.

132 Anghie, above n 5, 1–12.

133 Section 318 of the *Criminal Code, An Act Respecting the Criminal Law*, RS 1985, c C-46; 2004, c 14, s 1. Section 318 is as follows:

> (1) Everyone who advocates or promotes genocide is guilty of an indictable offence and liable to imprisonment for a term not exceeding five years.
> (2) In this section, 'genocide' means any of the following acts committed with intent to destroy in whole or in part any identifiable group, namely,
> (*a*) killing members of the group; or
> (*b*) deliberately inflicting on the group conditions of life calculated to bring about its physical destruction.

definition of genocide in the penal code has 'had important ramifications for what {Indigenous} peoples can claim as genocide in Canadian courts'.[134] Responsibility under customary international law creates an obligation on states to refrain from acts of genocide.[135] The significance is that a state cannot pardon itself of criminal conduct by creating loopholes, internationally and domestically. The state of Canada does not include Arts 2(b), (d) and (e) of the UNGC in its *Criminal Code*.[136] The fact that its penal laws exclude crimes it is actively engaged in calls into question the ability of the UNGC to protect Indigenous Peoples and Nations from genocide.

The model of domination and dehumanisation turns the actions of the Canadian state on their face by compelling the western reader to view the destructive colonial framework under which the removals occurred into present times. After the euphemistic language is revealed to the reader, the sources that exist, including the government apology, support the contention that the government is criminally culpable for genocide. The genocidal experience is evidenced in many reports, books and academic articles in Canada.[137] Despite the challenges, there is enough leeway to demonstrate genocide in the colonisation of our lands and territories. Articles 2(b) and (e) of the *Genocide Convention* stipulate it is genocide to forcibly transfer children

(3) No proceeding for an offence under this section shall be instituted without the consent of the Attorney General.
(4) In this section, 'identifiable group' means any section of the public distinguished by colour, race, religion, ethnic origin or sexual orientation.

See Churchill, *Perversions of Justice*, above n 88, 249–51.

134 David B MacDonald and Graham Hudson, 'The Genocide Question and Indian Residential Schools in Canada' (2012) 45 *Canadian Journal of Political Science* 427, 435.

135 John Quigley, *The Genocide Convention: An International Law Analysis* (Ashgate, 2006) 80.

136 See Starblanket, *Suffer the Little Children*, above n 9 for further in-depth analysis.

137 On the transfer of children causing serious bodily and mental harm, see Chrisjohn, Young and Maruan, above n 93; Canada, Royal Commission on Aboriginal Peoples, above n 25; Ottawa, *Statement of Apology*, above n 9; Grant, above n 122; Crey and Fournier, above n 127; Milloy, above n 92; Elizabeth Furniss, *Victims of Benevolence: The Dark Legacy of the Williams Lake Residential School* (Arsenal Pulp Press, 1995); Constance Deiter, *From Our Mother's Arms: The Intergenerational Impact of the Residential Schools in Saskatchewan* (United Church Publishing House, 1999); P H Bryce, *The Story of a National Crime Being an Appeal for Justice to the Indians of Canada* (James Hope and Sons, 1922); Agnes Jack (ed), *Behind Closed Doors: Stories from the Kamloops Indian Residential School* (Theytus Books, 2006); Carl Urion, 'Introduction: The Experience of Indian Residential Schooling' (1991) 18S *Canadian Journal of Native Education* i; Celia Haig-Brown, *Resistance and Renewal: Surviving the Indian Residential School* (Tillacum Library, 1988); Isabelle Knockwood, *Out of the Depths: The Experiences of Mi'kmaw Children at the Indian Residential School at Shubenacadie, Nova Scotia* (Roseway Publishing, 1992); JR Miller, *Shingwauk's Vision: A History of the Native Residential Schools* (University of Toronto Press, 1996). This list of sources is not exhaustive.

from one group to another group and to cause serious bodily or mental harm to members of the group. William Schabas in *Genocide in International Law* explains that to demonstrate genocide material facts along with intent or 'guilty mind' must be proven.[138] The chapeau in Art 2 establishes the *mens rea*, which is the 'intent to destroy, in whole or in part, a national, ethnical, racial or religious group'. Article 2 establishes the *actus reus* or the criminal acts of the offence in Arts 2(a)–(e). The legal application of the convention is outside the scope of this chapter; however, I will briefly summarise it. International jurisprudence supports the claim that the Canadian state is guilty of genocide.[139]

The apology by the Canadian government expresses the requisite standard required to show the specific intent to destroy a group. The phrase 'kill the Indian in the child' conveys the intent to destroy the national identity of Indigenous children. The specific intent to destroy the national identity is satisfied by the admission of the intent to destroy that which is distinctly 'Indian'. The policy objectives and the legislation that forced the transfer of Indigenous Peoples' children conveys specific intent because of the effort the government undertook in designing colonial laws that compelled the massive forced transfer of children.[140] The International Criminal Tribunal for the Former Yugoslavia in *Karadzić* determined that intent can be satisfied by the general political doctrine and patterns of conduct.[141] The massive and widespread collective serious bodily and mental harm also supports the intention of destroying a group in whole or in part.[142] Children were subjected to wide-scale torture, sexual abuse, starvation and forced labour.[143] At a basic standard, specific intent is satisfied to show a case of genocide.

138 William A Schabas, *Genocide in International Law: The Crime of Crimes* (Cambridge University Press, 2nd edn, 2009) 172: 'Criminal law analysis of an offence proceeds from a basic distinction between the physical element (*actus reus*) and the mental element (*mens rea*). The prosecution must prove specific material facts, but must also establish the accused's criminal intent or guilty mind.'

139 See especially Starblanket, *Suffer the Little Children*, above n 9 for an explanation of the jurisprudence that supports Canada's culpability; see also Starblanket, *Genocide*, above n 9.

140 See *An Act to Amend and Consolidate the Laws Respecting Indians*, SC 1880, c 28; s 137(2) and 138 of the *Indian Advancement Act*, RSC 1886, c 44; s 11 of *An Act Further to Amend the Indian Act*, 1894, c 32, 57–58 Victoria; ss 9 and 10 of *An Act to Amend the Indian Act*, SC 1920, c 50. For a review of the legislation, see especially Canada, Royal Commission on Aboriginal Peoples, above n 25. For a review of the policy objectives, see Titley, above n 25.

141 International Criminal Tribunal for the Former Yugoslavia, Decision of Trial Chamber 1, *Radovan Karadzic, Ratko Mladic* case (Case Nos IT-95-5-R61 and IT-95-18-R61), Consideration of the Indictment within the Framework of Rule 61 of the Rules of Procedure and Evidence, [94].

142 See *Prosecutor v Akayesu* (Case No ICTR-96-4-T), Judgment, 2 September 1998.

143 See above n 137.

Forcibly transferring Indigenous children and causing serious bodily and mental harm will affect the ability of Indigenous Peoples and Nations to survive because of their dependence on their future generations.[144] The system-wide serious bodily and mental harm shows patterns of conduct and this combined with the massive nature of the harm suffices to show specific intent. The colonial brutality and horror has certainly impeded the ability of Indigenous Peoples to transmit their national identities onto further generations. The forcible removal to residential institutions has contributed to the destruction of the national group identity.

The Venezuelan delegate to the *Genocide Convention* discussions articulated that:

> the forced transfer of children to a group where they would be given an education different from that of their own group, and would have new customs, a new religion and probably a new language, was in practice tantamount to the destruction of their group, whose future depended on that generation of children.[145]

The children were not just assimilated; they were forcibly indoctrinated or brainwashed by the massive and widespread colonial abominations.

The success of the colonial enterprise depends on the degree of brainwashing or indoctrination of oppressed peoples.[146] As a result of the widespread forced indoctrination, Indigenous children have come to self-loath their identity and their Peoples and Nations. It has been demonstrated that forcibly removing children can make them enemies of their own people.[147] The children do not remember why they should have a mutual beneficial relationship with Mother Earth. Indigenous Peoples' original languages are fundamental to the national identities on Great Turtle Island. The young ones are forcibly 'civilised' and consumed into the 'predatory colonial body politic' and come to identify with the colonising language rather than their own languages. An effect is that Indigenous Peoples enter into colonial processes that terminate their national identity.

The large-scale termination of land claims processes requires Original Nations and Peoples to submit to a destructive framework that cedes and surrenders the land to the settler state. Indigenous Peoples depend on our Mother Earth and protect and honour our lands and territories for our future

144 Abtahi and Webb, above n 39, 235, 1493, 1494, 1504; see also Shauna Troniak, 'Addressing the Legacy of Residential Schools' (Background Paper No 2011-76-E, Library of Parliament, 2011) 2 <http://publications.gc.ca/collections/collection_2011/bdp-lop/bp/2011-76-eng.pdf>.

145 UN Doc A/6/SR83, cited in Abtahi and Webb, ibid 1504.

146 Rarihowkwats, speech delivered at the Sixth Annual National Treaties 1–11 Gathering, Regina, Saskatchewan, 12–15 October 2010.

147 UN Doc A/C6/SR82, cited in Abtahi and Webb, above n 39, 1494.

generations. It is difficult to accomplish this spiritual law when children are collectively indoctrinated in the language that dominates and dehumanises their very existence. The severing of the child's relationship with the land by wiping out the language and 'spiritual laws encoded in the language'[148] contributes to the destruction of the group as a whole or in part. Indigenous children were targeted for forced removal because they are the children of Indigenous Peoples and Nations. According to the chamber in *Krstić*, intent means that 'the perpetrators of genocide need not seek to destroy the entire group protected by the Convention, they must view the part of the group they wish to destroy as a distinct identity which must be eliminated as such'.[149]

A potential criticism is that the colonial government did not intend to harm the children; however, the government was aware of the harms and never corrected the large-scale atrocities and the revolting acts of violence against the young ones. Many autobiographical stories, books and government reports support this contention.[150] One example is the report made by the chief physician of the Department of Indian Affairs in 1907. Dr P H Bryce publicly criticised the atrocious and dilapidated living conditions that children were forced to live under in the residential institutions.[151] Milloy writes that Dr Bryce condemned the '[d]epartment for its failure to act in the face of the white plague, tuberculosis'.[152] The disease and death created by unsanitary living conditions were well known to staff and officials in the schools and the government apparatus.[153] Duncan Campbell Scott asserted that, system wide, 'fifty percent of children who passed through these schools did not live to benefit from the education which they received therein'.[154] Did the government stop the system in its tracks and return the children to their parents and nations? Did the government rectify the harm that had already taken place up to that point in the early 1900s? The inaction by the government aggravated, and did not mitigate, its conduct. The enrolment rates went up with the 1920 amendment to the *Indian Act*[155] and this legislated action exacerbated the government's conduct and supports the specific intent required under international law. Given these were children who endured years of inhumane suffering and dehumanisation from an early age of human development, there

148 Sharon Venne, interview, 4 January 2013.
149 *Prosecutor v Krstić* (Case No IT-98-33-T), Judgment, 2 August 2001, [590].
150 See especially all references cited above n 137; see also P H Bryce, *Report on the Indian Schools of Manitoba and the Northwest Territories* (Government Printing Bureau, 1907); Canada, Royal Commission on Aboriginal Peoples, above n 25, 349–59.
151 Bryce, ibid.
152 Milloy, above n 92, 51.
153 See Canada, Royal Commission on Aboriginal Peoples, above n 25, 353–65; Milloy, above n 92, 51–107.
154 Canada, Royal Commission on Aboriginal Peoples, above n 25, 330–1.
155 Sections 9 and 10 of *An Act to Amend the Indian Act*, SC 1920, c 50.

is no doubt that these children were traumatised and forcibly conditioned. Chrisjohn, Young and Maruan write:

> If inmates become available at a young enough age, the tactics of total institutions won't merely 'disrupt or defile' selves, but hinder their development in the first place. By not allowing the formation of 'adult executive competency,' the inmates are prevented from being or becoming persons *at all*.[156]

Given that these forcible removals occurred over several generations, the effects would be catastrophic. The international jurisprudence supports the contention that there are long-term effects of genocide.[157]

Shauna Troniak, researcher for the Canadian Parliament, writes:

> The traumas of physical and sexual abuse, social and emotional dislocation, and cultural loss have manifested, for many survivors and their communities, in after effects such as substance abuse, violence, and family breakdown. Many survivors' descendants have experienced and continue to experience inter-generational traumas as a result of this unresolved trauma.[158]

The result is the possible disappearance of our distinct national identities as each generation passes off the massive patterns of trauma and dysfunction. The greatest effect is the dislocation from our territories. Collectively, as a result, Indigenous Peoples do not understand that we have a relationship of protection and care for our Mother Earth. Children indoctrinated in the English language through acts of colonial violence will not remember that Indigenous laws are codified into the languages of our Original Nations. The long-term impacts exhibited by Indigenous Peoples and Nations today are the extensive and immense social issues that are rampant. Suicides, drug and alcohol addictions, poverty (to name a few) are the direct result of the residential school era. The result is that, over time, Indigenous Peoples are collectively and forcibly indoctrinated (assimilated) into Canadian society. The worst effect is the dysfunctional parenting patterns exhibited by the survivors.[159] In this regard, the genocide has not ceased and continues into the present day.

156 Chrisjohn, Young and Maruan, above n 93, 91 (emphasis in original).
157 *Prosecutor v Krajisnik* (Case No IT-9-3-T), Judgment, 27 September 2006, [862]
158 Troniak, above n 144, 2–3.
159 See Patrick J Morrissette, 'The Holocaust of First Nations People: Residual Effects on Parenting and Treatment Implications' (1994) 16 *Contemporary Family Therapy* 381; Rosalind Ing, 'The Effects of Residential Schooling on Native Child-Rearing Practices' (1991) 18 *Canadian Journal of Native Education* 65; Linda Bull, 'Indian Residential Schooling: A Native Perspective' (1991) 18S *Canadian Journal of Native Education* 1.

Child welfare system

The 'sixties scoop'[160] as coined by Patrick Johnston is the mass removal of Indigenous children into the 2000s.[161] Provincial legislation compels the forcible transferral of Indigenous Peoples' children at appalling rates.[162] This is genocide and it is ongoing. This is the face of colonisation that continues to this day. Venne states:

> The child welfare system is worse than the residential school system because unlike the children who had each other to comfort one another in the boarding schools, a child in the child welfare system is isolated and alone from his or her people and Nation.[163]

Ernie Crey of the Sto'lo Nation writes:

> children stayed in an aboriginal peer group; they always knew their First Nation of origin and who their parents were, and they knew that eventually they were going home. In the foster and adoptive care system, aboriginal children typically vanished with scarcely a trace, the vast majority placed until they were adults in non-aboriginal homes where their cultural identity, their legal Indian status, their knowledge of their own First Nation and even their birth names were erased, often forever.[164]

The collective trauma and dysfunction brought about by the residential school phase is then used by the very dominating society that created that trauma to justify the child welfare system phase of the process.[165]

The government invokes the traumatic parenting patterns it created that lead to the massive and widespread removals in the child welfare system. The concept of the 'best interests of the child' is a coloniser value-based judgement. It is a concept that was created to continue the domination and dehumanisation of our nations. The violence that children endured in the residential

160 Patrick Johnston, *Native Children and the Child Welfare System* (James Lorimer and the Canadian Council on Social Development, 1983).
161 See Crey and Fournier, above n 127; Erin Hanson, 'Sixties Scoop: The Sixties Scoop and Aboriginal Child Welfare', *Indigenous Foundations* <http://indigenousfoundations.arts.ubc.ca/home/government-policy/sixties-scoop.html>.
162 See all references above n 128; Emily Alston-O'Connor, 'The Sixties Scoop: Implications for Social Workers and Social Work Education' (2010) 11 *Critical Social Work* 1.
163 Sharon Venne, interview, 4 January 2013; see also Andrew Armitage, 'Family and Child Welfare in First Nations Communities' in B Wharf (ed), *Rethinking Child Welfare in Canada* (Oxford University Press, 1993) 131.
164 Crey and Fournier, above n 127, 81.
165 See Aboriginal Justice Implementation Commission, above n 129.

school system is experienced by our children in the system today.[166] The collective serious bodily and mental harm has not ceased. The death rates of children in the system are evidenced by recent media reports.[167] In the worst-case scenario, the forcible removals in the residential school system and their effects in the child welfare system destroy our nations as our children do not relate to our original laws and instructions, languages, spirituality, cultures, families, and most importantly an identity that embodies a healthy relationship with Mother Earth.

Children have been forcibly transferred and deprived of the socialisation and enculturation process within their own nations that enable them to become an integral part of their nation or people's distinct national identity. This is a genocidal process. In other words, children have not been raised Anishnaabe or Nehiyaw or Lil'wat or Nuxalk and so in what way can the children claim to be socialised or raised within their families, communities and Nations? They cannot because they are now a product of the dominating society's language, culture and society and not their own. This time around, the Canadian state cannot claim they do not know that this is the end result because the government has already apologised for having done this with residential schools. Now the target destination is the non-Indigenous residence, or child welfare home.

Moving beyond colonialism

Perhaps the most vital aspect of this chapter is the solution offered as a way to move out of the domination of colonial state oppression. Decolonised critical analysis is necessary to enable a true movement towards healing on a global level. Self-determination is the road home and the way we re-centre our Nations as subjects in international law. It is the way we re-humanise ourselves as Original Nations and begin to heal from the dehumanising experience of colonial domination. It is time for the settler state of Canada and other settler states such as Australia and the United States to acknowledge the atrocities they have engaged in and to be accountable and responsible for their crimes of genocide in the colonisation of our Great Turtle Island and other parts of the world.

Our Nations on Great Turtle Island and the globe were given 'laws set by the Creator'[168] to live according to in our relationship with all of Creation (Mother Earth). Those laws were severed with the forcible transferral of

166 See especially Crey and Fournier, above n 127.

167 Jason Proctor, 'Death of BC Aboriginal Teen Paige under RCMP Investigation', *CBC News British Columbia*, 18 September 2015 <http://www.cbc.ca/news/canada/british-columbia/death-of-b-c-aboriginal-teen-paige-under-rcmp-investigation-1.3234158>; 'Paige's story: Death of troubled teen prompts action from BC government', *CBC News British Columbia*, 20 October 2015 <http://www.cbc.ca/news/canada/british-columbia/paige-death-government-release-report-1.3280603>.

168 Venne, *Honour Bound*, above n 1, 9.

Indigenous Peoples' children into residential institutions. Our Peoples are forced to enter into destructive processes from a perspective or reality that denigrates our Nations and future generations. We depend on our Mother Earth for life and the life of our future generations. Indigenous Peoples and Nations are collectively forced to:

> utilize the language and conceptual system of the dominating society as a means of thinking, speaking, and writing about our own existence while challenging certain negative, oppressive and dominating concepts that have been mentally and, from an indigenous perspective, illegitimately imposed on our existence.[169]

Churchill writes:

> We shoulder the burden, whatever it may entail, of ensuring that the order of colonialism at last is shattered, never to be restored. Most importantly, we owe it, all of us, to our coming generations ... to bequeath unto them lives free of the nightmarish reality in which ourselves remain so mired.[170]

So for the survivors of genocide, the road home is the international right of self-determination and our status as 'subjects' in international law. The colonisers must come to grips with the destruction they have engaged in to dominate our lands and territories the world over. They must acknowledge the genocide and admit their crimes in the colonisation of our lands, and cease and desist the genocidal practices. It is our inalienable right and responsibility to live according to Creation's laws. It is a most fundamental aspect of the healing that is necessary for our Original Nations and Peoples. In fact, it is the only solution for true justice. This is integral for world peace and the good health of our Mother Earth and ultimately humankind because we depend on the earth for our very survival. Most importantly, it is necessary that Original Nations and Peoples understand the genocidal effects so that we can protect our Mother Earth for our future generations of Creation.

169 Newcomb, *Pagans*, above n 3, 18.
170 Churchill, *Kill the Indian*, above n 109, 82.

Bibliography

Articles/books/reports

Aboriginal Justice Implementation Commission, *Report of the Aboriginal Justice Inquiry of Manitoba* (1999)

Acuña, Rodolfo, *Occupied America* (Canfield Press, 1972)

Agamben, Giorgio, *Homo Sacer* (Stanford University Press, 1998)

Agamben, Giorgio, *State of Exception* (University of Chicago Press, 2005)

Alston-O'Connor, Emily, 'The Sixties Scoop: Implications for Social Workers and Social Work Education' (2010) 11 *Critical Social Work: An Interdisciplinary Journal Dedicated to Social Justice* 1

Aly, Götz, *Hitler's Beneficiaries* (Metropolitan Books, 2007)

Ambos, Kai, 'What Does "Intent to Destroy" in Genocide Mean?' (2009) 91 *International Review of the Red Cross* 833

Anaya, James, *International Law and Indigenous Peoples* (Oxford, 2nd edn, 2004)

Anaya, James, 'Derecho de los Pueblos Indígenas a la Libre Determinación tras la Adopción de la Declaración' in Claire Charters and Rodolfo Stavenhagen (eds), *El desafío de la declaración: Historia y Futuro de la Declaración de la ONU sobre Pueblos Indígenas* (IWGIA, 2009) 194

Anderson, Gary Clayton, *The Conquest of Texas* (University of Oklahoma Press, 2005)

Anderson, Gary Clayton, *Ethnic Cleansing and the American Indian* (University of Oklahoma Press, 2014)

Andreopoulos, George (ed), *Genocide* (University of Pennsylvania Press, 1994)

Anghie, Antony, *Imperialism, Sovereignty and the Making of International Law* (Cambridge University Press, 2008)

Anghie, Antony, 'Western Discourses of Sovereignty' in Julie Evans, Ann Genovese, Alexander Reilly and Patrick Wolfe (eds), *Sovereignty: Frontiers of Possibility* (University of Hawai'i Press, 2013) 19

Arbon, Veronica, *Arlathirnda Ngurkarnda Ityirnda: Being – Knowing – Doing: De-colonising Indigenous Tertiary Education* (Post Pressed, 2008)

Arendt, Hannah, *Eichmann in Jerusalem* (Viking Press, 1963)

Armitage, Andrew, 'Family and Child Welfare in First Nations Communities' in B Wharf (ed), *Rethinking Child Welfare in Canada* (Oxford University Press, 1993) 131

Armitage, Andrew, *Comparing the Policy of Aboriginal Assimilation: Australia, Canada and New Zealand* (University of British Columbia Press, 1995)

Arocena, F, 'Multiculturalism in Brazil, Bolivia and Peru' (2008) 49 *Race & Class* 21

Asante-Muhammed, Dedrick, Chuck Collins, Josh Hoxie and Emanuel Nieves, *The Ever-Growing Gap: Without Change, African-American and Latino Families Won't Match White Wealth for Centuries* (Institute for Policy Studies, 2016)

Atkinson, Judy, *Trauma Trails, Recreating Song Lines: The Transgenerational Effects of Trauma in Indigenous Australia* (Spinifex Press, 2002)

Australian Law Reform Commission, *Connection to Country: Review of the Native Title Act 1993 (Cth)*, Report No 126 (2015)

Baptiste, Edward E, *The Half Has Never Been Told* (Basic Books, 2014)

Barr, Daniel P, *Boundaries between Us* (Kent State University Press, 2006)

Barsh, Russel Lawrence, 'Indian Land Claims Policy in the United States' (1982) 58 *North Dakota Law Review* 7

Bartlett, Richard, *Native Title in Australia* (Lexis Nexis, 3rd edn, 2014)

Behrendt, Larissa, 'Back to the Future for Indigenous Australia' in Nick Dyrenfurth and Tim Soutphommasane (eds), *All That's Left: What Labor Should Stand For* (University of New South Wales Press, 2010) 113

Benjamin, Walter, *Reflections* (Schocken Books, 1986)

Berger, Peter and Thomas Luckmann, *The Social Construction of Reality: A Treatise on the Sociology of Knowledge* (Anchor Books, 1996)

Berger, Thomas, *A Long and Terrible Shadow: White Values, Native Rights in the Americas since 1492* (University of Washington Press, 1999)

Bergoffen, Debra B, '9/11: America and the Politics of Innocence' in Dennis J Schmidt (ed), *Difficulties of an Ethical Life* (Fordham University Press, 2012) 72

Bey, Hakim, *TAZ: The Temporary Autonomous Zone, Ontological Anarchy, Poetic Terrorism* (Autonomedia, 1991)

Bey, Hakim, *Immediatism* (AK Press, 1994)

Bird, Deborah Rose, Nancy Daiyi, Kathy Deveraux, Margaret Daiyi, Linda Ford and April Bright, *Country of the Heart: An Indigenous Australian Homeland* (Aboriginal Studies Press, 2002)

Bird, George Grinnell, *The Fighting Cheyennes* (University of Oklahoma Press, 1955)

Black, C, 'Maturing Australia through Australian Aboriginal Narrative Law' (2011) 110 *South Atlantic Quarterly* 347

Black, Edwin, *War Against the Weak* (Four Walls Eight Windows, 2003)

Blackmon, Douglas A, *Slavery by Another Name* (Doubleday, 2008)

Blackstock, Cindy et al, 'Pathways to the Overrepresentation of Aboriginal Children in Canada's Child Welfare System' (2004) 78 *Social Service Review* 577

Blum, Rony et al, '"Ethnic Cleansing" Bleaches the Atrocities of Genocide' (2007) 18 *European Journal of Public Health* 204

Boggs, Carl, 'Marxism, Prefigurative Communism, and the Problem of Workers' Control' (1977) 11 *Radical America* 100

Borrows, John, 'Wampum at Niagara: The Royal Proclamation, Canadian Legal History, and Self-Government' in Michael Asch (ed), *Aboriginal and Treaty Rights in Canada* (University of British Columbia Press, 2011) 169

Brack, Gene M, *Mexico Views Manifest Destiny, 1821–1846* (University of New Mexico Press, 1975)

Brodeur, Paul, *Restitution: The Land Claims of the Mashpee, Passamaquoddy, and Penobscot Indians of New England* (Northeastern University Press, 1985)

Brooks, Roy L, *When Sorry Isn't Enough* (New York University Press, 1999)

Browning, Christopher R, *Nazi Policy, Jewish Workers, German Killers* (Cambridge University Press, 2000)
Bryce, P H, *Report on the Indian Schools of Manitoba and the Northwest Territories* (Government Printing Bureau, 1907)
Bryce, P H, *The Story of a National Crime Being an Appeal for Justice to the Indians of Canada* (James Hope and Sons, 1922)
Bull, Hedley, Benedict Kingsbury and Adam Roberts (eds), *Hugo Grotius and International Relations* (Clarendon Press, 1992)
Bull, Linda, 'Indian Residential Schooling: A Native Perspective' (1991) 18 Supp *Canadian Journal of Native Education* 1
Burgoyne, Iris, *The Mirning: We are the Whales* (Magabala Books, 1989)
Carter, Sarah, *Lost Harvests* (University of McGill Press, 1993)
Cave, Alfred A, *Lethal Encounters* (Praeger, 2011)
Césaire, Aimé, *Discourse on Colonialism* (Joan Pinkham trans, Monthly Review Press, 2000) [trans of Discours sur le colonialism (first published 1950)].
Chávez, Ernesto, *The US War with Mexico* (Bedford/St Martin's Press, 2007)
Churchill, Ward, *A Little Matter of Genocide: Holocaust and Denial in the Americas 1492 to the Present* (Arbiter Ring Publishing, 1998)
Churchill, Ward, *Struggle for the Land: Native North American Resistance to Genocide, Ecocide, and Colonization* (City Lights Books, 2002)
Churchill, Ward, *Acts of Rebellion: The Ward Churchill Reader* (Routledge, 2003)
Churchill, Ward, *Perversions of Justice* (City Lights Books, 2003)
Churchill, Ward, *Kill the Indian Save the Man: The Genocidal Impact of American Indian Residential Schools* (City Lights Books, 2004)
Churchill, Ward, 'The Law Stood Squarely on Its Head: U.S. Legal Doctrine, Indigenous Self-Determination and the Question of World Order' (2002) 81 *Oregon Law Review* 663
Churchill, Ward, 'Indigenous Peoples and Imperialism' in Immanuel Ness and Zak Cope (eds), *The Palgrave Encyclopedia of Imperialism and Anti-Imperialism* (Palgrave Macmillan, 2016) vol 2
Churchill, Ward, 'Unthinking Eurocentrism: The Indigenist Alternative to Marxian "Anti-Imperialism"' in Deepa Naik and Trenton Oldfield (eds), *Critical Cities: Ideas* (Middlecourt Press, forthcoming)
Churchill, Winston, *The Gathering Storm* (Cassell, 1948)
Cienciala, Anna M, 'The Foreign Policy of Józef Piłsudski and Józef Beck, 1926–1939: Misconceptions and Interpretations' (2011) 56 *Polish Review* 111
Cigar, Norman, *Genocide in Bosnia* (Texas A&M University Press, 1995)
Clark, Blue, *Lone Wolf v Hitchcock: Treaty Rights and Indian Law at the End of the Nineteenth Century* (University of Nebraska Press, 1994)
Clark, Bruce, *Native Liberty, Crown Sovereignty* (McGill-Queens University Press, 1991)
Cohen, Felix S, 'Indian Claims' in Lucy Kramer Cohen (ed), *The Legal Conscience: Selected Papers of Felix S Cohen* (Yale University Press, 1960) 264
Collard, Len, 'Wangkiny Ngulluck Nyungar Nyittiny, Boodjar, Moort and Katitjin: Talking About Creations, Country, Family and Knowledge of the Nyungar of South Western Australia' in Sally Morgan, Tjalaminu Mia and Blaze Kwaymullina (eds), *Speaking from the Heart* (Fremantle Press, 2007) 262
Collard, Len, 'Djidi Djidi, Wardong, Kulbardi, Walitj and Weitj: Nyungar Dream Time Messengers' (2009) 54 *Westerly* 7

Collier, John, *From Every Zenith: A Memoir* (Sage Books, 1963)
Cornewall, George, *Government of Dependencies: An Essay* (Universal Classics, 1901)
Corntassel, J and T Hopkins, 'Indigenous "Sovereignty" and International Law: Revised Strategies for Pursuing "Self-Determination"' (1995) 17 *Human Rights Quarterly* 343
Correlli, Barnett, *The Collapse of British Power* (Pan, 2002)
Craven, M, 'Statehood, Self-Determination and Recognition' in Malcolm Evans (ed), *International Law* (Oxford University Press, 3rd edn, 2010) 203
Creighton Miller, Stuart, *'Benevolent Assimilation': The American Conquest of the Philippines, 1899–1903* (Yale University Press, 1982)
Crey, Ernie and Suzanne Fournier, *Stolen from Our Embrace: The Abduction of First Nations Children and the Restoration of Aboriginal Communities* (Douglas and McIntyre, 1997)
Chrisjohn, Roland, Sherri Young and Michael Maruan, *The Circle Game: Shadows and Substance in the Indian Residential School Experience in Canada* (Theytus Books, 2006)
Crosby, Alfred, *The Columbian Exchange* (Greenwood Press, 1972)
Crosby, Alfred, *Ecological Imperialism* (Cambridge University Press, 1986)
Daes, E, 'An Overview of the History of Indigenous Peoples: Self-Determination and the United Nations' (2008) 21 *Cambridge Review of International Affairs* 7
Dallin, Alexander, *German Rule in Russia, 1941–1945* (Macmillan, 1957)
Damonte, G, *Construyendo Territorios: Narrativas Territoriales Aymaras Contemporáneas* (CLACSO, 2011)
Dando-Collins, Stephen, *Standing Bear is a Person* (Da Capo Press, 2005)
Davis, S and A Wali, 'Indigenous Land Tenure and Tropical Forest Management in Latin America' (1994) 23 *Journal of the Royal Swedish Academy of Sciences* 485
Dawson, Bruce, *Better than a Few Squirrels: The Greater Productions Campaign on the First Nations Reserves of the Canadian Prairies* (Master's Thesis, University of Saskatchewan, 2002)
Debo, Angie, *And Still the Waters Run: The Betrayal of the Five Civilized Tribes* (Princeton University Press, 1940)
Degregori, C and P Sandoval, 'Dilemas y Tendencias en la Antropología Peruana: del Paradigma Indigenista al Paradigma Intercultural' in C Degregori and P Sandoval (eds), *Saberes Periféricos: Ensayos Sobre la Antropología en América Latina* (Instituto Francés de Estudios Andinos, Instituto de Estudios Peruanos, 2007) 15
Deiter, Constance, *From Our Mother's Arms: The Intergenerational Impact of the Residential Schools in Saskatchewan* (United Church Publishing House, 1999)
de la Cadena, M and O Starn, 'Introduction' in M De la Cadena and O Starn (eds), *Indigenous Experience Today* (Berg, 2007) 1
Del Castillo, L, '¿Tienen Futuro las Comunidades Campesinas?' (1992) 14 *Debate Agrario* 39
Deloria, Vine Jr, *Behind the Trail of Broken Treaties* (Delacourt Press, 1974)
Deloria, Vine Jr, and Clifford M Lytle, *The Nations Within* (University of Texas Press, 1984)
Deloria, Vine Jr, and Raymond J DeMallie, *Documents of American Indian Diplomacy* (University of Oklahoma Press, 1999)
de Soto, H, *The Peruvian Amazon is Not Avatar* (Institute of Liberty and Democracy, 2010)
de Sousa Santos, Boaventura, *Epistemologies of the South: Justice Against Epistemicide* (Paradigm Publishers, 2014)

de Vitoria, Francisco, 'On Civil Power' in Anthony Pagden and Jeremy Lawrance (eds), *Vitoria: Political Writings* (Cambridge University Press, 1991) 1

de Vitoria, Francisco, 'On the American Indians' in Anthony Pagden and Jeremy Lawrance (eds), *Vitoria: Political Writings* (Cambridge University Press, 1991) 231

de Vitoria, Francisco, 'On the Law of War' in Anthony Pagden and Jeremy Lawrance (eds), *Vitoria: Political Writings* (Cambridge University Press, 1991) 293

Diamond, Jared, *Guns, Germs, and Steel* (W W Norton, 1997)

Dietze, Gottfried, *In Defense of Property* (John Hopkins University Press, 1971)

Dowd, Gregory Evans, *A Spirited Resistance* (Johns Hopkins University Press, 1992)

Dumbauld, Edward, *Thomas Jefferson and the Law* (University of Oklahoma Press, 1978)

Duran, Eduardo, Bonnie Duran, Maria Yellow Horse Brave Heart and Susan Yellow Horse-Davis, 'Healing the American Indian Soul Wound' in Yael Danieli (ed) *International Handbook of Multigenerational Legacies of Trauma* (Plenum Press, 1998) 341

Durham, Jimmie, 'Against Internationalism' (2013) 27 *Third Text* 29

Dussel, E, *1942 El Encubrimiento del Otro: Hacia el Origen del Mito de la Modernidad* (UMSA, 1994)

Dutschke, Rudi, 'On Anti-Authoritarianism' in Carl Oglesby (ed), *The New Left Reader* (Grove Press, 1969) 243

Eagleton, Terry, *The Illusions of Postmodernism* (Blackwell, 1996)

Echo-Hawk, Walter, *In the Courts of the Conqueror: The 10 Worst Indian Law Cases Ever Decided* (Fulcrum, 2010)

Eckert, Allan W, *That Dark and Bloody River* (Bantam Books, 1995)

Engle, Karen, *The Elusive Promise of Indigenous Development: Culture, Rights, Strategy* (Duke University Press, 2010)

Engle, Karen, 'On Fragile Architecture: The UN Declaration on the Rights of Indigenous Peoples in the Context of Human Rights' (2011) 22 *European Journal of International Law* 141

Erazo, J, *Governing Indigenous Territories: Enacting Sovereignty in the Ecuadorian Amazon* (Duke University Press, 2013)

Ericson, Edward E, *Feeding the German Eagle: Soviet Economic Aid to Nazi Germany, 1933–1941* (Greenwood Press, 1999)

Eron, Don, Suzanne Hudson and Myron Hulen, 'Colorado Conference of the Association of American University Professors Report on the Termination of Ward Churchill' (2012) 3 *Journal of Academic Freedom* <https://www.aaup.org/sites/default/files/ConferenceReport.pdf>

Errico, S, 'The Draft UN Declaration on the Rights of Indigenous Peoples: An Overview' (2007) 7 *Human Rights Law Review* 741

Estin, Ann Laquer, 'Lone Wolf v. Hitchcock: The Long Shadow' in Sandra L Cadwalader and Vine Deloria Jr (eds), *The Aggressions of Civilization* (Temple University Press, 1984) 215

Eubank, Keith, *Munich* (University of Oklahoma Press, 1963)

Expert Panel on Constitutional Recognition of Aboriginal and Torres Strait Islander Peoples, *Recognising Aboriginal and Torres Strait Islander Peoples in the Constitution: Report of the Expert Panel* (2012)

Faber, David, *Munich* (Simon & Schuster, 2008)

Falk, Richard, *Predatory Globalization* (Polity, 1999)

Fanon, Frantz, *The Wretched of the Earth* (Grove Press, 1963)

Ferguson, Niall, *Empire: The Rise and Fall of the British World Order and the Lessons for Global Power* (Basic Books, 2003)

Ferguson, Niall, *Civilization: The West and the Rest* (Allen Lane, 2011)

Fischer, Klaus P, *Hitler and America* (University of Pennsylvania Press, 2011)

Fitzpatrick, John C (ed), *The Writings of George Washington from the Original Manuscript Sources, 1745–1799* (US Government Printing Office, 1931–1944)

Fitzpatrick, Peter, *Modernism and the Grounds of Law* (Cambridge University Press, 2001)

Fitzpatrick, Peter, 'Surpassing Sovereignty' in Julie Evans, Ann Genovese, Alexander Reilly and Patrick Wolfe (eds), *Sovereignty: Frontiers of Possibility* (University of Hawai'i Press, 2013) 181

Fraser, Steven, *The Age of Acquiescence* (Little, Brown, 2015)

Friedberg, Lilian, 'Dare to Compare: Americanizing the Holocaust' (2000) 24 *American Indian Quarterly* 353

Friedman, Howard, 'Interest on Indian Land Claims: Judicial Protection of the Fisc' (1970) 5 *Valparaiso University Law Review* 26

Fritz, Stephen G, *Ostkrieg* (University Press of Kentucky, 2011)

Fromherz, C, 'Indigenous Peoples' Courts: Egalitarian Juridical Pluralism, Self-Determination, and the United Nations Declaration on the Rights of Indigenous Peoples' (2008) 156 *University of Pennsylvania Law Review* 1341

Funk-Unrau, Neil and Anna Snyder, 'Indian Residential School Survivors and State-Designed ADR: A Strategy for Co-optation?' (2007) 24 *Conflict Resolution Quarterly* 285

Furniss, Elizabeth, *Victims of Benevolence: The Dark Legacy of the Williams Lake Residential School* (Arsenal Pulp Press, 1995)

Galindo, J, 'Cultural Diversity in Bolivia: From Liberal Interculturalism to Indigenous Modernity' in M Janssens (ed), *The Sustainability of Cultural Diversity: Nations, Cities and Organizations* (Edward Elgar Publishing, 2010) 80

Gallay, Alan, *The Indian Slave Trade* (Yale University Press, 2002)

Galloway, Colin, *The Victory with No Name* (Oxford University Press, 2015)

Gammage, Bill, *The Biggest Estate on Earth* (Allen and Unwin, 2011)

García, P and A Surrallés, *Tierra Adentro: Territorio Indígena y Percepción del Entorno* (A Surrallés and García Hierro eds, IWGIA, 2004)

Garner, Van Hastings, 'The Treaty of Guadalupe Hidalgo and the California Indians' (1976) 9 *The Indian Historian* 10

Gehl, Jürgen, *Austria, Germany, and the Anschluss, 1931–1938* (Oxford University Press, 1963)

Gelderloos, Peter, *How Nonviolence Protects the State* (South End Press, 2007)

Gerth, Hans and C Wright Mills, *From Max Weber: Essays in Sociology* (Oxford University Press, 1946)

Gilbert, G M, *Nuremberg Diary* (Da Capo Press, 1995)

Gilbert, Helen and Chris Tiffins (eds), *Burden or Benefit? Imperial Benevolence and Its Legacies* (Indiana University Press, 2008)

Gilbert, J, 'Indigenous Rights in the Making: The United Nations Declaration on the Rights of Indigenous Peoples' (2007) 14 *International Journal on Minority and Group Rights* 207

Gilbert, Martin, *The Roots of Appeasement* (Weidenfeld & Nicolson, 1966)

Giroux, Henry, *Neoliberalism's War on Higher Education* (Haymarket Books, 2014)

Goebbels, Joseph, *Die Zeit ohne Beispiel* (Zentralverlag der NSDAP, 1941)

Goffman, Erving, *Asylums: Essays on the Social Situation of Mental Patients and Other Inmates* (Anchor Books, 1961)

Gollancz, Victor et al, *Guilty Men* (Faber & Faber, 1940)

Gordon, Seth, 'Indigenous Rights in Modern International Law from a Critical Third World Perspective' (2006–07) 31 *American Indian Law Review* 401

Graham, Mary, 'Some Thoughts about the Philosophical Underpinnings of Aboriginal Worldviews' (2008) 45 *Australian Humanities Review* 181

Greene, S, *Customizing Indigeneity: Paths to a Visionary Politics in Peru* (Stanford University Press, 2009)

Grenier, John, *The First Way of War* (Cambridge University Press, 2005)

Grijalva, J, 'Paradoxes of the Inka Utopianism of José Carlos Mariátegui's Seven Interpretative Essays on Peruvian Reality' (2010) 19 *Journal of Latin American Cultural Studies: Travesia* 317

Grotius, Hugo, *The Law of War and Peace* (Francis W Kelsey trans, Bobbs-Merrill Co, 1925)

Grotius, Hugo, *The Rights of War and Peace* (Richard Tuck ed, Jean Barbeyec trans, Liberty Fund, 2005)

Guruma Elders Group, *The Guruma Story* (IAD Press, 2001)

Gutman, Roy, *A Witness to Genocide* (Macmillan, 1993)

Haar, Charles and Lance Liebman, *Property and Law* (Little, Brown, 2008)

Haggenmacher, Peter, 'On Assessing the Grotian Heritage' in TMC Asser Instituut, *International Law and the Grotian Heritage* (TMC Asser Instituut, 1985) 150

Haig-Brown, Celia, *Resistance and Renewal: Surviving the Indian Residential School* (Tillacum Library, 1988)

Halaas, David Fridtjof and Andrew E Masich, *Halfbreed: The Remarkable True Story of George Bent* (Da Capo Press, 2004)

Hale, C, 'Neoliberal Multiculturalism: The Remaking of Cultural Rights and Racial Dominance in Central America' (2005) 28 *Political and Legal Anthropology Review* 10

Hanieh, Adam, 'Praising Empire: Neoliberalism under Pax Americana' in Colin Mooers (ed), *The New Imperialists* (Oneworld, 2006) 167

Harry, Debra and Sharon Venne, 'The Road to the United Nations and Rights of Indigenous Peoples' (2011) 20 *Griffith Law Review* 557

Havercroft, Jonathon, *Captives of Sovereignty* (Cambridge University Press, 2011)

Hehn, Paul N, *A Low, Dishonest Decade* (A&C Black, 2005)

Hildebrand, Klaus, *The Foreign Policy of the Third Reich* (B T Batsford, 1973)

Hildebrand, Klaus, *The Nazi Dictatorship* (Arnold, 2000)

Hillgruber, Andreas, *Germany and the Two World Wars* (Harvard University Press, 1981)

Hinton, Alexander Laban (ed), *Hidden Genocides* (Rutgers University Press, 2014)

Hitler, Adolf, *Mein Kampf* (Houghton-Mifflin, Sentry Editions, 1962)

Hoig, Stan, *The Sand Creek Massacre* (University of Oklahoma Press, 1961)

Horsman, Reginald, *Race and Manifest Destiny* (Harvard University Press, 1981)

Horsman, Reginald, 'American Indian Policy and the Old Northwest, 1783–1812' in Roger L Nichols (ed), *The American Indian* (Alfred A Knopf, 3rd edn, 1986) 137

Horton, L, 'Contesting State Multiculturalisms: Indigenous Land Struggles in Eastern Panama' (2006) 38 *Journal of Latin American Studies* 829

Hughes, N, 'Indigenous Protest in Peru: The "Orchard Dog" Bites Back' (2010) 9 *Social Movement Studies* 85

Hughes, R Gerald, 'The Ghosts of Appeasement: Britain and the Legacy of the Munich Agreement' (2013) 48 *Journal of Contemporary History* 688

Indigenous Bar Association of Canada, 'Strengthening Partnerships between States and Indigenous Peoples: Treaties, Agreements, and Other Constructive Arrangements' (16–17 July 2012)

Ing, Rosalind, 'The Effects of Residential Schooling on Native Child-Rearing Practices' (1991) 18 *Canadian Journal of Native Education* 65

Irabinna Rigney, Lester, 'Internationalization of an Indigenous Anticolonial Cultural Critique of Research Methodologies: A Guide to Indigenist Research Methodology and Its Principles' (1999) 14 *Wicazo Sa Review* 109

Jack, Agnes (ed), *Behind Closed Doors: Stories from the Kamloops Indian Residential School* (Theytus Books, 2006)

Jaffe, Sarah, 'Trickle-Down Feminism', *Dissent*, Winter 2013 2013 <https://www.dissentmagazine.org/article/trickle-down-feminism>

Jahoda, Gloria, *The Trail of Tears* (Holt, Rinehart and Winston, 1975)

Jochmann, Werner (ed), *Adolf Hitler* (Knaus, 1980)

Jones, David S, *Rationalizing Epidemics* (Harvard University Press, 2004)

Jones, Dorothy V, *License for Empire* (University of Chicago Press, 1982)

Johnston, Patrick, *Native Children and the Child Welfare System* (James Lorimer and the Canadian Council on Social Development, 1983)

Josephson, Harold, 'Outlawing War: Internationalism and the Pact of Paris' (1979) 3 *Diplomatic History* 377

Kakel, Caroll P III, *The American West and the Nazi East* (Palgrave, 2011)

Kakel, Carroll P III, *The Holocaust as Colonial Genocide* (Palgrave Macmillan, 2013)

Kaplan, Amy and Donald L Pease (eds), *Cultures of United States Imperialism* (Duke University Press, 1993)

Kappler, Charles J, *Indian Treaties, 1778–1883* (Interland, first published 1904, 1972 edn)

Keal, P, *European Conquest and the Rights of Indigenous Peoples: The Moral Backwardness of International Society* (Cambridge University of Press, 2003)

Kershaw, Ian, *Hitler, 1889–1936: Hubris* (W W Norton, 1998)

Kershaw, Ian, *Hitler, 1936–1945: Nemesis* (W W Norton, 2000)

Kershaw, Ian, *Fateful Choices* (Penguin Press, 2007)

Klein, Christine A, 'Treaties of Conquest: Property Rights, Indian Treaties, and the Treaty of Guadalupe Hidalgo' (1996) 26 *University of New Mexico Law Review* 201

Klein, Naomi, *The Shock Doctrine: The Rise of Disaster Capitalism* (Knopf, 2007)

Knockwood, Isabelle, *Out of the Depths: The Experiences of Mi'kmaw Children at the Indian Residential School at Shubenacadie, Nova Scotia* (Roseway Publishing, 1992)

Kopp, Kristin, *Germany's Wild East* (University of Michigan Press, 2012)

Korman, Sharon, *The Right of Conquest: The Acquisition of Territory by Force in International Law* (Clarendon Press, 1996)

Koskenniemi, Martti, *The Gentle Civilizer of Nations: The Rise and Fall of International Law 1870–1960* (Cambridge University Press, 2001)

Kühl, Stefan, *The Nazi Connection* (Oxford University Press, 2002)

Kwaymullina, Ambelin, 'Seeing the Light: Aboriginal Law, Learning and Sustainable Living in Country' (2005) 6 *Indigenous Law Bulletin* 12

Kwaymullina, Ambelin and Blaze Kwaymullina, 'Learning to Read the Signs: Law in an Indigenous Reality' (2010) 34 *Journal of Australian Studies* 195

Laplante, L and S Spears, 'Out of the Conflict Zone: The Case for Community Consent Processes in the Extractive Sector' (2008) 11 *Yale Human Rights & Development Law Journal* 69
Lemkin, Raphaël, *Axis Rule in Occupied Europe* (Carnegie Endowment for World Peace, 1944)
Lens, Sidney, *The Forging of the American Empire* (Thomas Y Crowell, 1971)
Leupp, Francis, *The Indian and His Problem* (Scribner's, 1910)
Li Xiu Woo, Grace, *Ghost Dancing with Colonialism* (University of British Columbia Press, 2011)
Lindsay, Brendan C, *Murder State* (University of Nebraska Press, 2012)
Linenthal, Edward T and Tom Engelhardt (eds), *History Wars* (Henry Holt, 1996)
Lippman, Matthew, 'The Drafting and Development of the 1948 Convention on Genocide and the Politics of International Law' in H G van der Wilt, J Vervliet, G K Sluiter and J T M Houwink ten Cate (eds) *The Genocide Convention: The Legacy of 60 Years* (Martinus Nijhoff, 2012) 15
Lipscomb, Andrew A (ed), *The Writings of Thomas Jefferson Vol 1* (Thomas Jefferson Memorial Association, 1903–1904)
Little Bear, Leroy, 'Section 88 of the Indian Act and the Application of Provincial Laws to Indians' in Anthony Long and Menno Boldt (eds), *Governments in Conflict? Provinces and Indian Nations in Canada* (University of Toronto Press, 1992) 175
Little Bear, Leroy, 'Jagged Worldviews Colliding' in Marie Battiste (ed) *Reclaiming Indigenous Voice and Vision* (UBC Press, 2000) 77
Lochner, Louis P (ed), *The Goebbels Diaries* (Charter, 1948)
Lorde, Audre, 'There is No Hierarchy of Oppression' (1983) 14 *Homophobia and Education* 9
Lowe, Lisa, *The Intimacies of Four Continents* (Duke University Press, 2015)
MacDonald, David B and Graham Hudson, 'The Genocide Question and Indian Residential Schools in Canada' (2012) 45 *Canadian Journal of Political Science* 427
Madley, Benjamin, *An American Genocide: The United States and the California Indian Catastrophe* (Yale University Press, 2016)
Mann, Barbara Alice, *George Washington's War on Native America* (Praeger, 2005)
Mann, Barbara Alice, *The Tainted Gift* (Praeger, 2009)
Marable, Manning, *Race, Reform, and Rebellion* (University of Mississippi Press, 1984)
Marcuse, Herbert, 'Repressive Tolerance' in Robert Paul Wolff, Barrington Moore Jr and Herbert Marcuse, *A Critique of Pure Tolerance* (Beacon Press, 1965) 95
Marcuse, Herbert, *An Essay on Liberation* (Beacon Press, 1971)
Martin, Karen, 'Ways of Knowing, Ways of Being and Ways of Doing: A Theoretical Framework and Methods for Indigenous Re-search and Indigenist Research' (2003) 76 *Journal of Australian Studies* 203
Martin, Karen, *Please Knock Before You Enter: Aboriginal Regulation of Outsiders and the Implications for Researchers* (Post Pressed, 2008)
Matos, J, 'Comunidades Indígenas del área Andina' in J Matos (ed), *Hacienda, Comunidad y Campesinado en el Perú* (Instituto de Estudios Peruanos, 1976) 179
Maurice, Jacqueline Marie, *Despiriting Aboriginal Children: Aboriginal Children During the 1960s and 1970s Child Welfare Era* (PhD Thesis, University of Toronto, 2003)
Mazower, Mark, *Hitler's Empire* (Penguin Press, 2008)
McDonough, Frank, *Neville Chamberlain, Appeasement and the British Road to War* (Manchester University Press, 1998)

McNeil, Kent, 'Social Darwinism and Judicial Conceptions of Indian Title in Canada in the 1880s' (1999) 38 *Journal of the West* 68
Means, Russell and Bayard Johnson, *If You've Forgotten the Names of the Clouds, You've Lost Your Way* (Treaty Publications, 2012)
Meiksins Wood, Ellen, 'Democracy as Ideology of Empire' in Colin Mooers (ed), *The New Imperialists: Ideologies of Empire* (Oneworld, 2006) 9
Meriam, Lewis, *The Problem of Indian Administration* (Johns Hopkins University Press, 1928)
Merino, R, 'Critical Human Rights and Liberal Legality: Struggling for "The Right to Have Communal Rights"' (2013) 3 *Philosophy Study* 246
Miéville, China, 'Anxiety and the Sidekick State: British International Law After Iraq' (2005) 46 *Harvard International Law Journal* 441
Miéville, China, *Between Equal Rights: A Marxist Theory of International Law* (Haymarket Books, 2005)
Mignolo, W, *The Darker Side of Western Modernity: Global Futures, Decolonial Options* (Duke University Press, 2011)
Milanović, Mark, 'Territorial Application of the Convention and State Succession' in Paola Gaeta (ed), *UN Genocide Convention: A Commentary* (Oxford University Press, 2009) 473
Miller, J R, *Shingwauk's Vision: A History of the Native Residential Schools* (University of Toronto Press, 1996)
Miller, Robert, Jacinta Ruru, Larissa Behrendt and Tracey Lindberg (eds), *Discovering Indigenous Lands: The Doctrine of Discovery in the English Colonies* (Oxford University Press, 2010)
Milloy, John S, *A National Crime: The Canadian Government and the Residential School System, 1879 to 1986* (University of Manitoba Press, 1999)
Mittleman, James H (ed), *Globalization: Critical Reflections* (Lynne Rienner, 1997)
Moiseyevich Nekrich, Aleksandr, Adam Bruno Ulam and Gregory L Freeze, *Pariahs, Partners, Predators* (Columbia University Press, 1997)
Moorhouse, Roger, *The Devil's Alliance* (Bodley Head, 2014)
Moreton-Robinson, Aileen, 'Virtuous Racial States' (2011) 20 *Griffith Law Review* 641
Moreton-Robinson, Aileen and Maggie Walter, 'Indigenous Methodologies in Social Research' in Maggie Walter (ed), *Social Research Methods: An Australian Perspective* (Oxford University Press, 2nd edn, 2009) 1
Morgan, Sally, 'The Balance for the World' in Sally Morgan, Tjalaminu Mia and Blaze Kwaymullina (eds), *Heartsick for Country: Stories of Love, Spirit and Creation* (Fremantle Press, 2008) 265
Morison, Samuel, *The Oxford History of the American People* (Oxford University Press, 1965)
Morris, Glenn, 'International Law and Politics: Toward a Right of Self-Determination for Indigenous Peoples' in Annette Jaimes (ed), *The State of Native America: Genocide, Colonization and Resistance* (South End Press, 1992) 55
Morrissette, Patrick J, 'The Holocaust of First Nations People: Residual Effects on Parenting and Treatment Implications' (1994) 16 *Contemporary Family Therapy* 381
Muehlebach, A, 'What Self in Self-Determination? Notes from the Frontiers of Transnational Indigenous Activism' (2003) 10 *Identities: Global Studies in Culture and Power* 241
Mueller, Claus, *Politics of Communication: A Study in the Political Sociology of Language, Socialization and Legitimation* (Oxford University Press, 1977)

Murray, Daniel, 'Prefiguration or Actualization? Radical Democracy and Counter-Institution in the Occupy Movement', *Berkeley Journal of Sociology*, 3 November 2014 <http://berkeleyjournal.org/2014/11/prefiguration-or-actualization-radical-democracy-and-counter-institution-in-the-occupy-movement/>

Naimark, Norman M, *Fires of Hatred* (Harvard University Press, 2002)

Nakata, Martin, *Disciplining the Savages, Savaging the Disciplines* (Aboriginal Studies Press, 2007)

Napoleon, V, 'Aboriginal Self Determination: Individual Self and Collective Selves' (2005) 29 *Atlantis* 1

Nash, Gary B, Charlotte Crabtree and Ross E Dunn, *History on Trial* (Alfred A Knopf, 1997)

National Collaborating Centre for Aboriginal Health, *Aboriginal and Non-Aboriginal Children in Child Protection Services* (NCAH, 2009–2010)

Neu, Dean and Richard Therrien, *Accounting for Genocide: Canada's Bureaucratic Assault on Aboriginal Peoples* (Fernwood Publishing, 2003)

Newcomb, Steven, 'The Evidence of Christian Nationalism in Federal Indian Law: The Doctrine of Discovery, Johnson v M'Intosh and Plenary Power' (1993) 20 *New York University Review of Law and Social Change* 303

Newcomb, Steven, *Pagans in the Promised Land: Decoding the Doctrine of Christian Discovery* (Fulcrum, 2008)

Newcomb, Steven, 'The UN Declaration on the Rights of Indigenous Peoples and the Paradigm of Domination' (2011) 20(3) *Griffith University Law Review* 578

Newcomb, Steven and Birgil Kills Straight, *The Doctrine of Discovery and the Protocol of Domination: A Short Essay for the North American Indigenous Caucus Preparatory Meeting for the UN Permanent Forum on Indigenous Issues* (Indigenous Law Institute, 2012)

Nielson, Richard A, 'American Indian Land Claims: Land versus Money as a Remedy' (1972) 25 *University of Florida Law Review* 308

Nock, Albert, *Our Enemy the State* (William Morrow & Company, 1935)

Norgren, Jill, *The Cherokee Cases* (McGraw-Hill, 1996)

Nussbaum, Arthur, *A Concise History of the Law of Nations* (Macmillan, 5th edn, 1964)

Onuma, Yasuaki, *A Normative Approach to War: Peace, War and Justice in Hugo Grotius* (Clarendon Press, 1993)

Onuma, Yasuaki, 'When was the Law of International Society Born? An Inquiry of the History of International Law from an Intercivilizational Perspective' (2000) 2 *Journal of the History of International Law* 1

Onuma, Yasuaki, 'Multi-civilizational International Law in the Multi-centric 21st Century World: Transformation of West-centric to Global International Law as Seen from a Trans-civilizational Perspective' in Peter Haggenmacher, Pierre-Marie Dupay and Vincent Chetail (eds), *The Roots of International Law* (Martinus Nijhoff Publishers, 2014) 599

Orihuela, J C, 'The Making of Conflict-Prone Development: Trade and Horizontal Inequalities in Peru' (2012) 24 *European Journal of Development Research* 688

Owens, Robert M, *Mr Jefferson's Hammer* (University of Oklahoma Press, 2007)

Pagden, Anthony and Jeremy Lawrance (eds), *Vitoria: Political Writings* (Cambridge University Press, 1991)

Pasqualucci, J, 'International Indigenous Land Rights: A Critique of the Jurisprudence of the Interamerican Court of Human Rights in Light of the United Nations

Declaration on the Rights of Indigenous Peoples' (2009) 27 *Wisconsin International Law Journal* 51
Payne, Leigh A, *Unsettling Accounts* (Duke University Press, 2008)
Peang-meth, A, 'The Rights of Indigenous Peoples and Their Fight for Self-Determination' (2002) 174 *World Affairs* 101
Peat, David, *Blackfoot Physics* (Fourth Estate, 1995)
Perkins Abernathy, Thomas, *Western Lands and the American Revolution* (Russell and Russell, 2nd edn, 1959)
Petras, James and Henry Veltmeyer, *Globalization Unmasked* (Zed Books, 2001)
Philpott, D, 'In Defense of Self-Determination' (1995) 105 *Ethics* 352
Pilon, Lori, 'Introduction' in Agnes Jack (ed), *Behind Closed Doors: Stories from the Kamloops Indian Residential School* (Theytus Books, 2006) 1
Pollefeyt, Didier, 'The Significance of Nazi Eugenics for Medical Ethics Today' in Michael Alan Signer (ed), *Humanity at the Limit* (Indiana University Press, 2000) 250
Potter, Pamela M, *Art of Suppression* (University of California Press, 2016)
Power, Samantha, *'A Problem from Hell': America and the Age of Genocide* (Harper Perennial, 2002)
Prazmowska, Anita J, *Britain, Poland and the Eastern Front, 1939* (Cambridge University Press, 2004)
Price, Grenfell, *White Settlers and Native Peoples: An Historical Study of Racial Contacts between English-Speaking Whites and Aboriginal Peoples in the United States, Canada, Australia, and New Zealand* (Cambridge University Press, 1950)
Quigley, John, *The Genocide Convention: An International Law Analysis* (Ashgate, 2006)
Quijano, A, 'Coloniality of Power, Eurocentrism, and Latin America' (2000) 1 *Nepantla: Views from the South* 533
Rauschning, Hermann, *The Voice of Destruction: Conversations with Hitler* (GP Putnam's Sons, 1940)
Ray, Arthur J, Jim Miller and Frank Tough, *Bounty and Benevolence: A History of Saskatchewan Treaties* (McGill Queen's University Press, 2000)
Rice, William, '25 USC § 71: The End of Indian Sovereignty or a Self-Limitation of Contractual Ability?' (1977) 5 *American Indian Law Review* 239
Rich, Norman, *Hitler's War Aims* (W W Norton, 1973)
Rifkin, Mark, 'Indigenizing Agamben: Rethinking Sovereignty in Light of the "Peculiar" Status of Native Peoples' in Marcelo Svirsky and Simone Bignall (eds), *Agamben and Colonialism* (Edinburgh University Press, 2012) 77
Rivera Cusicanqui, S, 'The Notion of "Rights" and the Paradoxes of Postcolonial Modernity: Indigenous Peoples and Women in Bolivia' (2010) 18 *Qui Parle: Critical Humanities and Social Sciences* 29
Rivera Cusicanqui, S, *Oprimidos pero no Vencidos: Luchas del campesinado Aymara y Qhechwa 1900–1980* (WA-GUI, 4th edn, 2010)
Roberts, Geoffrey, 'The Soviet Decision for a Pact with Nazi Germany' (1992) 44 *Soviet Studies* 57
Rodríguez-Garavito, C, 'Ethnicity.gov: Global Governance, Indigenous Peoples, and the Right to Prior Consultation in Social Minefields' (2011) 18 *Indiana Journal of Global Legal Studies* 263
Roldán, R, 'Models for Recognizing Indigenous Land Rights in Latin America' (Biodiversity Series, Paper No 99, World Bank Environment Department, 2004)

Romeyn-Sanabria, Marjorie, 'Feminism Is for White Women', *Arts.Mic*, 12 August 2013 <https://mic.com/articles/60319/feminism-is-for-white-women#.Yy5FOwQTG>

Rosenthal, Harvey D, *Their Day in Court* (Garland, 1990)

Rossi, Christopher R, *Broken Chain of Being: James Brown Scott and the Origins of Modern International Law* (Kluwer Law International, 1998)

Royal Commission on Aboriginal Peoples, *Looking Forward, Looking Back* (Canada Communications Group, 1996)

Ruiz, J, *La Implementación del Derecho a la Consulta Previa de los Pueblos Indígenas: Una Mirada Constitucional* (IDL, 2011)

Ruiz, J, 'Problemas Jurídicos en la Implementación de la Consulta Previa en el Perú' (2014) 42 *Derecho & Sociedad* 79

Russell, Peter H, *Recognizing Aboriginal Title: The Mabo Case and Indigenous Resistance to Settler Colonialism* (University of Toronto Press, 2005)

Ryback, Timothy W, *Hitler's Private Library* (Alfred A Knopf, 2008)

Sagan, Eli, *The Honey and the Hemlock: Democracy and Paranoia in Ancient Athens and Modern America* (Basic Books, 1991)

Saito, Natsu Taylor, *From Chinese Exclusion to Guantánamo Bay* (University Press of Colorado, 2006)

Saito, Natsu Taylor, *Meeting the Enemy* (New York University Press, 2012)

Sakai, J, *Settlers* (Morningstar Press, 1989)

Salmón, E, 'The Struggle for Laws of Free, Prior, and Informed Consultation in Peru: Lessons and Ambiguities in the Recognition of Indigenous Peoples' (2013) 22(2) *Pacific Rim Law & Policy Journal* 353

Sartre, Jean-Paul and Arlette El Kaim-Sartre, *On Genocide and the Summary of the Evidence and Judgments of the International War Crimes Tribunal* (Beacon Press, 1968)

Satterthwaite, M and D Hurwitz, 'The Right of Indigenous Peoples to Meaningful Consent in Extractive Industry Projects' (2005) 22 *Arizona Journal of International & Comparative Law* 1

Scalamburio-D'Annibale, Valerie, *Cold Breezes and Idiot Winds* (Sense, 2011)

Schabas, William A, *Genocide in International Law: The Crime of Crimes* (Cambridge University Press, 2nd edn, 2009)

Schilling-Vacaflor, Almut, 'Rethinking the Link between Consultation and Conflict: Lessons from Bolivia's Gas Sector' (2014) 35 *Canadian Journal of Development Studies / Revue Canadienne d'études du Développement* 503

Schmitt, Carl, *Political Theology* (MIT Press, 1988)

Schmitt, Carl, *The Nomos of the Earth in the International Law of Jus Publicum Europaeum* (Telos Press, 2003)

Schmitt, Carl, *Dictatorship* (Polity, 2014)

Schrecker, Ellen (ed), *Cold War Triumphalism* (New Press, 2004)

Schuker, Stephen, 'End of Versailles' in Gordon Martel (ed), *Origins of the Second World War Reconsidered* (Routledge, 1999) 38

Schulte-Tenckhoff, Isabelle, 'Reassessing the Paradigm of Domestication: The Problematic of Indigenous Treaties' (1994) 5 *Review of Constitutional Studies* 239

Seed, Patricia, *Ceremonies of Possession in Europe's Domination of the New World 1492–1640* (Cambridge University Press, 1995)

Senate Select Committee on Regional and Remote Indigenous Communities, *Third Report* (2009) <http://www.aph.gov.au/binaries/senate/committee/indig_ctte/reports/2009/report3/a01.pdf>

Sharp, Alan, *The Versailles Settlement* (Palgrave Macmillan, 2nd edn, 2008)
Shaw, Martin, *What Is Genocide?* (Polity Press, 2nd edn, 2015)
Shirer, William, *The Rise and Fall of the Third Reich* (Simon & Schuster, 1960)
Short, Damien, *Redefining Genocide* (Zed Books, 2016)
Sieder, R, '"Emancipation" or "Regulation"? Law, Globalization and Indigenous Peoples' Rights in Post-war Guatemala' (2011) 40 *Economy and Society* 239
Sinclair, Ian, *The Vienna Convention on the Law of Treaties* (Manchester University Press, 2nd edn, 1984)
Smith, E B, *Indian Tribal Claims Decided in the US Court of Claims* (University Publications of America, 1976)
Smith, Linda, *Decolonizing Methodologies: Research and Indigenous Peoples* (Zed Books, 2nd edn, 2012)
Smith, R C, 'Lo Transnacional, Instrumento y Desafío para los Pueblos Indígenas' in F Morin, and R Santana (eds), *Los Indígenas Amazónicos suben al Escenario Internacional: Reflexiones sobre el Accidentado Camino Recorrido* (Abya-Yala, 2003) 203
Spector, Barry, *Madness at the Gates of the City* (Regent Press, 2010)
Spirling, Arthur, 'US Treaty-Making with American Indians: Institutional Change and Relative Power, 1784–1911' (2012) 56 *American Journal of Political Science* 84
Spivak, G, *A Critique of Postcolonial Reason* (Harvard University Press, 1999)
Stamatopoulou, E, 'Indigenous Peoples and the United Nations: Human Rights as a Developing Dynamic' (1994) 16 *Human Rights Quarterly* 58
Stannard, David E, *American Holocaust* (Oxford University Press, 1992)
Stannard, David E, 'Uniqueness as Denial: The Politics of Genocide Scholarship' in Alan S Rosenbaum (ed), *Is the Holocaust Unique?* (Westview Press, 1996) 163
Starblanket, Tamara, *Genocide: Indigenous Nations and the State of Canada* (PhD Thesis, University of Saskatchewan, 2014)
Starblanket, Tamara, *Suffer the Little Children: Genocide, Indigenous Nations and the Canadian State* (Clarity Press, forthcoming)
Stavelsberg, Joachim J and Ryan D King, *American Memories* (Russell Sage Foundation, 2013)
Stetson, G, 'Oil Politics and Indigenous Resistance in the Peruvian Amazon: The Rhetoric of Modernity Against the Reality of Coloniality' (2012) 21 *Journal of Environment and Development* 76
Story, Joseph, *Commentary on the Constitution of the United States Vol III* (Hilliard, Gray and Company, 1833)
Sublette, Ned and Constance Sublette, *The American Slave Coast* (Lawrence Hill Books, 2016)
Sweptson, L and R Plant, 'International Standards and the Protection of the Land Rights of Indigenous and Tribal Populations' (1985) 124 *International Labor Review* 91
Sword, Wiley, *President Washington's Indian War* (University of Oklahoma Press, 1985)
Szablowski, D, 'Re-empaquetando el CLPI: las conexiones globales y el debate sobre el consentimiento indígena para la extracción industrial de recursos' (2010) 28 *Anthopologica* 217
Taylor, A J P, *The Origins of the Second World War* (Hamish Hamilton, 1961)
Thompson, Richard S, *Great Britain: A Reference Guide from the Renaissance to the Present* (Infobase, 2014)
Tibebu, Teshale, *Hegel and the Third World* (Syracuse University Press, 2011)

Titley, E Brian, *A Narrow Vision: Duncan Campbell Scott and the Administration of Indian Affairs in Canada* (University of British Columbia Press, 1986)

Toland, John, *Adolf Hitler* (Doubleday, 1976)

Tooley, T Hunt, *National Identity and Weimar Germany* (University of Nebraska Press, 1997)

Tooze, Adam, *Wages of Destruction* (Viking Press, 2006)

Trerise, Vicki, *Aboriginal Children and the Dishonour of the Crown: Human Rights Best Interests and Customary Adoption* (LLM Thesis, University of British Columbia, 2011)

Trevor-Roper, H R (ed), *Hitler's Table Talk, 1941–1944* (Weidenfeld & Nicolson, 1953)

Troniak, Shauna, 'Addressing the Legacy of the Residential Schools' (Background Paper No 2011-76-E, Library of Parliament, 2011) <http://publications.gc.ca/collections/collection_2011/bdp-lop/bp/2011-76-eng.pdf>

Truth and Reconciliation Commission Canada, *Honoring the Truth, Reconciling the Future* (Truth and Reconciliation Commission Canada, 2015)

Tully, J, 'Aboriginal Property and Western Theory: Recovering a Middle Ground' (1994) 11 *Social Philosophy and Policy* 153

Tully, J, *Strange Multiplicity: Constitutionalism in an Age of Diversity* (Cambridge University Press, 1995)

Tzu, Sun, *The Art of War* (Filaquarian, 2007)

Urion, Carl, 'Introduction: The Experience of Indian Residential Schooling' (1991) 18 Supp *Canadian Journal of Native Education* i

Van Cott, D, *The Friendly Liquidation of the Past: The Politics of Diversity in Latin America* (University of Pittsburgh Press, 2000)

Van Gelder, Sarah and the Staff of YES! Magazine (eds), *This Changes Everything: Occupy Wall Street and the 99% Movement* (Berrett-Koehler, 2011)

Van Gestel, Allan, 'When Fictions Take Hostages' in James A Clifton (ed), *The Invented Indian* (Transaction, 1990) 291

Venne, Sharon, *Indian Acts and Amendments 1868–1975: An Indexed Collection* (University of Saskatchewan Press, 1981)

Venne, Sharon (ed), *Honour Bound: Onion Lake and the Spirit of Treaty Six: The International Validity of Treaties with Indigenous Peoples* (International Working Group for Indigenous Affairs, 1997)

Venne, Sharon, 'Understanding Treaty Six: An Indigenous Perspective' in Michael Asch (ed), *Aboriginal and Treaty Rights in Canada: Essays on Law, Equality and Respect for Difference* (UBC Press, 1997) 173

Venne, Sharon, *Our Elders Understand Our Rights* (Theytus Books, 1998)

Venne, Sharon, 'Introduction' in Ward Churchill (ed), *Perversions of Justice* (City Lights Books, 2003) xiii

Venne, Sharon H, 'Opening Line' in Ward Churchill (ed), *Kill the Indian Save the Man: The Genocidal Impact of American Indian Residential Schools* (City Lights Books, 2004) xiii

Venne, Sharon, 'Treaties Made in Good Faith' in Paul W DePasquale (ed), *Natives and Settlers Now and Then: Historical Issues and Current Perspectives on Treaties and Land Claims in Canada* (University of Alberta Press, 2007) 1

Venne, Sharon, 'NGOs, Indigenous Peoples and the United Nations' in Aziz Choudry and Dip Kapoor (eds), *NGOization, Complicity, Contradictions and Prospects* (Zed Books, 2013) 75

Veracini, Lorenzo, *Settler Colonialism: A Theoretical Overview* (Palgrave Macmillan, 2010)
Wainwright, J and J Bryan, 'Cartography, Territory, Property: Postcolonial Reflections on Indigenous Counter-Mapping in Nicaragua and Belize' (2009) 16 *Cultural Geographies* 178
Wallerstein, I, *World System Analysis: An Introduction* (Duke University Press, 2004)
Wallis, Jim, *America's Original Sin* (Brazos Press, 2016)
Watson, Blake A, 'The Impact of the American Doctrine of Discovery on Native Land Rights in Australia, Canada, and New Zealand' (2011) 34 *Seattle University Law Review* 507
Watson, Irene, 'In the Northern Territory Intervention, What is Saved or Rescued and at What Cost?' (2009) 15 *Cultural Studies Review* 45
Watson, Irene, 'Aboriginal(ising) International Law and Other Centres of Power' (2011) 20 *Griffith Law Review* 631
Watson, Irene, *Aboriginal Peoples, Colonialism and International Law: Raw Law* (Routledge, 2014)
Watson, Irene, 'Genocide, the State, and Original First Nations' in Vincent Negri and Isabelle Schulte-Tenckoff (eds), *Towards International Normativity: Between Mimetism and Dissemination* (A Pedone, 2016) 171
Watson, Nicole, 'The Northern Territory Emergency Response: Has It Really Improved the Lives of Aboriginal Women and Children?' (2011) 35 *Australian Feminist Law Journal* 147
Watt, Cameron, *How War Came* (Pantheon, 1989)
Wehberg, Hans, 'Pacta Sunt Servanda' (1959) 53 *American Journal of International Law* 775
Weinberg, Gerhart, *Hitler's Foreign Policy* (Enigma Books, 2013)
Wheaton, Henry, *Elements of International Law* (B Fellowes, 1836)
White, John R, 'Barmecide Revisited: The Gratuitous Offset in Indian Land Claims Cases' (1978) 25 *Ethnohistory* 179
White Face, Charmaine, *Indigenous Nations' Rights in the Balance: An Analysis of the Declaration on the Rights of Indigenous Peoples* (Living Justice Press, 2013)
Wild, Rex and Pat Anderson, *Ampe Akelyernemane Meke Mekarle 'Little Children are Sacred': Report of the Northern Territory Board of Inquiry into the Protection of Aboriginal Children from Sexual Abuse* (Northern Territory Government, 2007)
Wilkinson, Charles F and John M Volkman, 'Judicial Review of Indian Treaty Abrogation: As Long as the Water Flows, or Grass Grows Upon the Earth – How Long a Time is That?' (1975) 63 *California Law Review* 610
Williams, Robert, *The American Indian in Western Legal Thought: The Discourses of Conquest* (Oxford University Press, 1990)
Williams, Robert, *Savage Anxieties: The Invention of Western Civilization* (Palgrave Macmillan, 2012)
Wilson, Ronald, *Bringing Them Home: Report on the National Inquiry into the Separation of Aboriginal and Torres Strait Islander Children from Their Families* (HREOC, 1997)
Winter, Steven, *A Clearing in the Forest: Law, Life and Mind* (University of Chicago Press, 2001)
Woolford, Andrew, Jeff Benvento and Alexander Laban Hinton (eds), *Colonial Genocide in Indigenous North America* (Duke University Press, 2014)
Worthington, C Fred et al (eds), *Journals of the Continental Congress, 1774–1789* (US Government Printing Office, 1904)

Yarrcali Barlow, Maisie (author) and Michael Boiyool Anning (illustrator), *Jirrbal: Rainforest Dreamtime Stories* (Magabala Books, 2001)
Young, Simon, *The Trouble with Tradition* (Federation Press, 2008)
Youngblood Henderson, James (Sakej), 'Ayukpachi: Empowering Indigenous Thought' in Marie Battiste (ed) *Reclaiming Indigenous Voice and Vision* (University of British Colombia Press, 2000) 248
Youngblood Henderson, James (Sakej), 'The Context of the State of Nature' in Marie Battiste (ed), *Reclaiming Indigenous Voice and Vision* (University of British Colombia Press, 2000) 11

Cases

A-G Israel v Eichmann (1968) 36 ILR 5 (District Court, Jerusalem)
Calder v British Columbia (AG) (1973) SCR 313
Case Concerning the Application of the Convention on the Prevention and Punishment of the Crime of Genocide (Bosnia and Herzegovina v Serbia and Montenegro), 26 February 2007
Cherokee Nation v Georgia 30 US (5 Pet) 1 (1831)
Choctaw Nation v Oklahoma 397 US 620 (1970)
Coe v Commonwealth (1979) 53 ALJR 403
Coe v Commonwealth (No 2) (1993) 68 ALRJ 110
Connelly v Woolrich (1867) 11 LCJ 197
Hul'qumi'num Treaty Group v Canada, Inter-American Commission on Human Rights, Case No 12.374, accepted on 30 October 2009
In Re Southern Rhodesia (1919) AC 211
Johnson & Graham's Lessee v M'Intosh 21 US (8 Wheat) 543 (1823)
Lone Wolf v Hitchcock 187 US 553 (1903)
Mabo v Queensland (No 2) (1992) 175 CLR 1
Mark Lane Jangala v Commonwealth, Northern Land Council and Others [2014] FC (unreported)
Montana Band of Indians v Canada (Minister of Indian and Northern Affairs) [1989] 1 SC 143 (TD)
Natural Parents v Superintendent of Child Welfare (1976) 60 DLR 3rd 148 SCC
Northwest Band of Shoshone Indians v US 324 US 335 (1945)
Oyekan v Adele (1957) 2 All ER 788
Prosecutor v Akayesu (Case No ICTR-96-94-T), 2 September 1998
Prosecutor v Blagojević (Case No IT-02-60-T), 17 January 2005
Prosecutor v Krajisnik (Case No IT-9-3-T), 27 September 2006
Prosecutor v Krstić (Case No IT-98-33-T), 2 August 2001
Prosecutor v Popović et al (Case No IT-05-88-T), 10 June 2010
Prosecutor v Stakić (Case No IT-97-24-T), 31 July 2003
Prosecutor v Tolimir (Case No IT-05-88/2T), 12 December 2012
Queen, The v Symonds (1847) NZPCC 387
Queen, The v The Secretary of State for Foreign and Commonwealth Affairs, ex parte The Indian Association of Alberta, Union of New Brunswick Indians, Union of Nova Scotian Indians [1984] 4 CNLR 86
R v Badger (1996) 1 SCR 771
R v Murrell (1836) 1 Legge 72
R v Sioui (1990) 1 SCR 1025

R v Sundown (1999) 1 SCR 393
R v The Secretary of State for Foreign and Commonwealth Affairs, ex parte The Indian Association of Alberta, Union of New Brunswick Indians, Union of Nova Scotian Indians [1982] QB 892 (CA)
Simon v The Queen (1985) 2 SCR 387
St Catherine's Milling and Lumber Co v The Queen (1885) 10 OR 196 (Ch D)
St Catherine's Milling and Lumber Co v R (1886) CanLII 30 (ON CA)
Tijani v Sec, Southern Nigeria (1921) 2 AC 399
United States v Sioux Nation of Indians 448 US 371 (1980)
US ex rel Standing Bear v George Crook 25 Fed Cas 695 (CCD, Nebraska, 1879)
Western Sahara (Advisory Opinion) [1975] ICJ 12
Worcester v Georgia 31 US (6 Pet) 515 (1832)
Yorta Yorta Aboriginal Community v Victoria (2002) 214 CLR 422

Legislation

Aboriginals Protection and Restriction of the Sale of Opium Act 1897 (Qld)
Aborigines Act 1890 (Vic)
Aborigines Act 1911 (SA)
Aborigines Protection Act 1886 (Vic)
Aborigines Protection Act 1890 (WA)
Aborigines Protection Act 1909 (NSW)
An Act to Amend the Indian Act, SC (1920)
Appropriation (Northern Territory National Emergency Response) Act (No 1) 2007 (Cth)
Appropriation (Northern Territory National Emergency Response) Act (No 2) 2007 (Cth)
Burke Act, 34 Stat 182 (1906)
Curtis Act, 30 Stat 495 (1898)
Family, Community Services, Indigenous Affairs and Other Legislation Amendment (Northern Territory National Emergency Response and Other Measures) Act 2007 (Cth)
Five Civilized Tribes Act, 34 Stat 325 (1906)
Indian Advancement Act, RSC (1886)
Native Title Act 1993 (Cth)
Northern Territory Aboriginals Act 1910 (SA)
Northern Territory National Emergency Response Act 2007 (Cth)
Oklahoma Organic Act, 26 Stat 81 (1890)
Social Security and Other Legislation Amendment (Welfare Payment Reform) Act 2007 (Cth)
Social Security Legislation Amendment Act 2012 (Cth)
Stronger Futures in the Northern Territory Act 2012 (Cth)
Stronger Futures in the Northern Territory Act 2013 (Cth)

Treaties and United Nations Documents

Anaya, James, *Observations on the Northern Territory Emergency Response in Australia*, UN Doc A/HRC/15/13/Add4 (4 March 2010)
Cobo, Jose Martinez, *Study of the Problem of Discrimination against Indigenous Populations*, UN Doc E/CN4/Sub2/1986/7/Add 4 (1 March 1987)
Committee on Economic, Social and Cultural Rights, *Concluding Observations: Australia*, UN Doc E/C12/AUS/CO/4 (12 June 2009)

Committee on the Elimination of Racial Discrimination, *Concluding Observations: Australia*, UN Doc CERD/C/AUS/CO/15-17 (27 August 2010)
Convention on the Prevention and Punishment of the Crime of Genocide, opened for signature 9 December 1948, 78 UNTS 277 (entered into force 12 January 1951)
Declaration on the Rights of Indigenous Peoples, adopted by the General Assembly 2 October 2007, UN Doc A/RES/61/295
Department of Economic and Social Affairs, UN Secretariat, *State of the World's Indigenous Peoples*, UN Doc ST/ESA/328 (2009)
Final Report of the Commission of Experts Established Pursuant to Security Council Resolution 780 (1992), UN Doc S/1994/674 (1994)
General Treaty for Renunciation of War as an Instrument of National Policy, 94 LNTS (entered into force 24 July 1929)
International Covenant on Civil and Political Rights, adopted by the General Assembly 19 December 1966, UN Doc A/6316 (entered into force 23 March 1976)
International Covenant on Economic, Social and Cultural Rights, opened for signature 16 December 1966, 993 UNTS 3 (entered into force 3 January 1976)
United Nations Economic and Social Council, *Study on Treaties, Agreements and Other Constructive Arrangements between States and Indigenous Populations: Final Report by Miguel Alfonso Martinez, Special Rapporteur*, UN Doc E/CN.4/Sub.2/1999/20 (22 June 1999)
United Nations General Assembly, *The Situation in Bosnia and Herzegovina*, UN Doc A/RES/47/121 (18 December 1992)
United Nations Permanent Forum on Indigenous Issues, *State of the World's Indigenous Peoples*, UN Doc ST/ESA/328 (2009)
United Nations Permanent Forum on Indigenous Peoples, *Report on the Eleventh Session*, E/2012/43-E/C 19/2012/13 (7–18 May 2012)
US Statement to UN ECOSOC (1987), E/CN4/Gr1987/7/Add12 (30 September 1987)
Vienna Convention on the Law of Treaties, opened for signature 23 May 1969, 1155 UNTS 331 (entered into force 27 January 1980)

Other

Agorist, Matt, 'Police are Killing Native Americans at a Higher Rate than Any Race, and Nobody Is Talking About It', *Free Thought*, 2 August 2015
Coe, Paul, 'Mabo: Confirming Dispossession', *Broadside*, 10 February 1993
Cohen, Roger, 'Beyond America's Original Sin', *New York Times*, 20 March 2008
Committee on the Elimination of Racial Discrimination, *Urgent Action Letters to the Australian Government* (13 March 2009 and 28 September 2009)
Davis O'Brien, Rebecca, Christopher M Matthews and Farnaz Fassihi, 'Former United Nations General Assembly President Charged in Bribery Scheme', *The Wall Street Journal*, 6 October 2015
Fitzsimmons, Hamish, 'The Victorian Government Will Enter Talks to Draft Australia's First Treaty with Aboriginal People', *ABC Lateline*, 26 February 2016
Hetland, Cara, 'South Dakota Has Country's Poorest County', *Minnesota Public Radio*, 1 October 2002
Kobler, John, 'These Indians Struck It Rich: The Utes' Treaty Land', *Saturday Evening Post*, 6 September 1972
Morris, Glenn, 'Invader-States Hijacked UN World Conference on Indigenous Peoples', *Indian Country Today*, 16 October 2014

Newcomb, Steven, 'A Critique of a Doctrine of Reconciliation', *Indian Country Today*, 15 June 2011 <http://indiancountrytodaymedianetwork.com/2011/06/15/critique-doctrine-reconciliation>

Newcomb, Steven, 'On Narratives and Dehumanization', *Indian Country Today*, 20 June 2012

Newcomb, Steven, 'The U.S.'s Interpretation of the UN High-Level Outcome Document', *Indian Country Today*, 12 October 2014

Newcomb, Steven, 'The Alta Outcome Document and the Issue of Interpretation', *Indian Country Today*, 8 July 2013

Ojibwa, 'Indians 101: Reservation Poverty', *Daily Kos*, 6 December 2012

'Paige's Story: Death of Troubled Teen Prompts Action from BC Government', *CBC News British Columbia*, 20 October 2015 <http://www.cbc.ca/news/canada/british-columbia/paige-death-government-release-report-1.3280603>

Proctor, Jason, 'Death of BC Aboriginal Teen Paige under RCMP Investigation', *CBC News British Columbia*, 18 September 2015 <http://www.cbc.ca/news/canada/british-columbia/death-of-b-c-aboriginal-teen-paige-under-rcmp-investigation-1.3234158>

Safire, William, 'On Language', *New York Times Magazine*, 14 March 1993

Schwartz, Daniel, 'Inside Attawapiskat's Financial Troubles', *CBC News*, 9 January 2013

Sevillano, M, *El Derecho a la Consulta de los Pueblos Indígenas en el Perú: Últimos Avances* (Programa Social Indígena, Lima, Derecho, Ambiente y Recursos Naturales, 2010)

Toohey, Paul, 'Scheming Blacks behind Fires: Farmers', *The Australian/Weekend Australian Magazine*, 22 September 2001

Index

For Product Safety Concerns and Information please contact our EU representative GPSR@taylorandfrancis.com
Taylor & Francis Verlag GmbH, Kaufingerstraße 24, 80331 München, Germany

www.ingramcontent.com/pod-product-compliance
Ingram Content Group UK Ltd.
Pitfield, Milton Keynes, MK11 3LW, UK
UKHW021721240926
475702UK00029BA/1747
9780367180775